Tales from the Trails
of a Rock 'n' Roll Bus Driver

By Jerry Fitzpatrick
Contributed and edited by
Jillian McGehee, Marcia Camp and Richard Duke

ISBN 978-0-9856076-0-9

Photo credits:
Cover Photo by Taylor Raine Fitzpatrick
Back Cover Photo by Jerry B. Fitzpatrick

Cover Design by Michael Bragg
Book Layout by Tim Hose and Aaron Malyk
Publishing Logo by Ted Nichols

May 2012

Cowboy Buddha Publishing, LLC
Benton, Arkansas

PUBLISHING

CONTENTS

ABOUT THE AUTHOR

Jerry Fitzpatrick has compiled a valuable social history. He pulls no punches in telling his readers details about the music and musicians who changed our country—of what goes on behind the scenes and of the sounds and behavior that altered a culture ready and eager for that change.

Fitzpatrick shares his observations in a conversational style laced with humor. Situations range from shocking to heart-warming, from Milli Vanilli to Barbara Mandrell. Through it all, Fitzpatrick shares his personal spiritual journey of redemption, forgiveness and grace. This journey is revealed through his stories of a life that led him from a troubled beginning, to his own experiences as a musician, and later his successful career on the road.

He has dared to capture the entertainment touring reality of the 20th century before it becomes a myth.

AUTHOR'S NOTE

Bus drivers "entertain the entertainers." Marc Silag, an admirable friend, made that remark to me one day as we sat in a Long Island, New York diner, discussing tales from the trails we had traveled, or "road stories," as most bus drivers call them.

Bus drivers, specifically ones who specialize in driving the custom coaches that you see parked backstage at entertainment events, "entertain the entertainers," he said, as we laughed about the approach of the one we were chatting about that day. It struck me the moment he said it, knowing of the many experiences I've lived and the many shared stories I've heard from entertainer drivers through the years. Marc owns Right Side Management/Left Side Productions, an artist management and music production company. A well-traveled person like myself, Marc has traveled with entertainment entourages in America and around the world for years. Marc worked in the Paul Simon camp, among others, so among tons of other things, Marc knows bus drivers.

Depending on the level of expertise and experience of the bus driver and the group traveling behind them, just about anything can happen and does. That doesn't matter! Everything MUST look normal to the fans. Well, normal in relation to the genre of entertainment you're working, of course. Through it all, you must have a smile on your face when you turn around to face the masses.

This book is not a tell-all book. You won't find any specifics here about briefs, boxers or bras. Nothing about who's kissing who and what they were wearing when they did it. It's a partial story of my life as an entertainment bus driver, the things I've experienced and how I ended up in this adventurous career that is as unique as it is misunderstood. Those who know me, truly know me, know I have made an interesting life for myself. Many have questioned why I have continued to do it. For me, it's always just been about living day to day.

Since becoming aware of the world around me as a child, I have nearly always looked forward to the next day, the next adventure, the next mile, just wanting to know what is there and what it has to offer. I try to learn something from each journey and each adventure. Many times, I smile and feel good about the joys of living a life lived well. Sometimes not, and I shake my head, reflecting on and wondering where all of the rude, crude and socially unacceptable behavior comes from.

My pattern of writing explains the work of an entertainment bus driver, the job and the craziness of day to day. It then explains why I do what I do, how my path led me here and the confusing, lost beginnings of my life. If I was wide awake and sober or drunk, stoned, or inebriated in some weird fashion, it was a sign of the times and how I saw it. If you were wide awake and sober or drunk, stoned and inebriated in some weird fashion, then that's how you saw it. Nothing can be changed now. These stories are just giggles left from a time, when retold, that always begin with "remember when?" No malice is intended toward anyone or anything. The language and the details may be offensive to some. The truth sometimes is.

A bit of a loner who likes to work on "the team," this project wouldn't have been possible without the help of others, "our team." A great singer/songwriter, Kim Richardson, explained how to do it. Thank you, Kim. Without the time spent with Richard Duke recording and translating the stories to paper, I would have never gotten out of the gate with this project. Without the support from Jillian McGehee and her constant improving of my literary skills, no one would even be able to understand this book. Marcia Camp, a wonderful knowledgeable person of all things Arkansan, sent us all in the right direction and helped give me my voice in the project. I want to thank Katie Cooper and Michael Bragg for their creative ideas that brought us to the final cover of the book and Aaron Malyk and Tim Hose for establishing the book's final form with layout and design. Ted Nichols' incredible art talent gave insight to my publishing logo. I owe a special thanks to Mark Whitworth for printing test editions, so we could get some invaluable critiques from trusted folks.

The many friends along the way, some who read as I developed, some who encouraged and those who cheered me on, were all team players on a team they never realized they were on. Margaret Murray and Zach Peters at Red Light Management, how you must have giggled, but your professional input was greatly appreciated. A BIG, BIG THANK YOU TO THOSE WHO BELIEVED IN ME AND THE MEANING OF THIS PROJECT TO ME.

This book is dedicated to the memory of my mother and father and to my children, who grew up wondering where their dad was on any given day and why I am who I am. Now they know.

p.s. August 8, 2004, Chicago, Illinois

"I DID NOT DO THAT."

~ Jerry Fitzpatrick

FOREWORD | JOHN DAVID NIXON

When I first met Jerry Fitzpatrick, I felt an unspoken kindred sprit between us that was more than the "Brothers of the Road" bond. I was aware that he was a top notch entertainer coach driver. He had been Dave Matthews' personal coach driver for more than 10 years, which pretty much told me he was a driver of the first water. But, there was something else, something more. I soon discovered that he was an Air Force brat like me. Well, that explains everything. There is a certain vibe that military dependents give off. We brats have lived out of foot lockers and hand-me-down B-4 bags from the day we were born. We grow up looking at America from the back of the family station wagon, or staring at the white caps of an ocean from a military air transport, to spending weeks at sea on WW II era Liberty ships. You can be stationed on a beautiful exotic island or a barren frozen prairie. It doesn't matter. You make the most of it because either way, the family will be transferred. Before the age of 12, most Air Force brats have seen the world, and it is not flat.

Jerry rebelled as a teenager, and did a stint in the Marines, when he realized that he was not going to inherit the family business of war. So, it was only natural to run off with the circus and tour the world with rock bands. After nearly 30 years, he remains a nomad, as one of the best entertainer coach drivers in the concert touring industry. Jerry became as proficient as a Marine One pilot. His meticulous preparation in equipment maintenance and his "safety first" attitude, have earned him the respect of many in the touring industry. But what really separates Jerry, and others like him, is his ability to be accommodating and malleable to the whims of the famous entertainers in his charge. That is to say that safety should be a forgone conclusion, and confidence in the driver's ability is confirmed in the first 100 miles of a new tour. However, being a member of the family can be dicey. It's as if someone is sitting in their home, at the kitchen table for weeks at a time and is privy to everything in their daily life. This can be a tipping point when it comes to being in their space, and breathing their air. Trust is paramount, and this is where Jerry excels. On the other hand, not all tourists have been house trained. Some artists do not touch all the bases on their way to becoming a star.

And the entourage with empowered minions classified as tour managers is prevalent. This is a business that has no basic training, and many sneak by. It is also a brutal business, and you can be kicked to the curb so quickly that you may never fully recover.

Jerry Fitzpatrick has written a wonderful story about how the combination of life's tumblers click, and all of a sudden, there you are! It's full of delightful tales of historic concerts, amazing characters and a tragic front row seat to death. Jerry brings together his passion for music and storytelling that includes how to navigate the dynamics of touring. While this is not a handbook for touring etiquette or protocol, you will come away with a few important rules of the road.

So, toss your bag in the junk bunk. Go up front and hop in the buddy seat where so many legends have spent hours across from Jerry. Kick back, light up, and take a sip. Burn through the pages as fast as Jerry's wheels leave the concrete behind. Let Jerry take you down the highway toward the sunrise, as he beams on the next horizon and yet another show beyond the curvature of the earth.

John David Nixon is a veteran in the touring industry with more than 30 years of experience. As a tour manager, his clients have included Big & Rich, Hank Williams Jr., Lynyrd Skynyrd, Patty Loveless, Jo Dee Messina, Gov't Mule, George Thorogood, Travis Tritt, Tracy Byrd, Diamond Rio and many others.

PROLOGUE | STEALING THE MAGIC

I'm a thief.

Not literally … although I'm sure I've grabbed a free meal from time to time, and I "borrowed" a motorcycle every morning while the rest of the world slept during my reckless youth.

No, what I take is what other people are glad to share. They may not realize they're giving it, but I take it anyway. When a show is about to start, I steal some of the love and joy that is meant for others. At any concert where I'm working and not one of the huddled masses yearning to break free, I have stolen a little something from the entertainer, and they never even realize it.

There is a moment when the lights go down, just before that rock star and his merry band of music makers walk out on stage, when everyone's expectations and anticipations meet in the dark. There is an explosion of energy that is nearly indescribable, that moment when thousands erupt in a roar that is almost as much about relief as excitement. The roar of the crowd is deafening, and no matter where I go, it always sounds and feels the same.

That moment is entrenched in everyone's mind, especially the first time they are part of it. It will stay with them the rest of their lives. They are pouring out so much love for whoever is on stage, and taking a bit of it isn't really stealing. I just can't help myself.

People have told me I have the coolest job in the world. Some days I agree. I have been places and seen things that few others have – amazing moments that have burned in my brain for decades. From where I sit, both figuratively and literally, it's an observation post to this crazy world I've learned to live in. The gamut of human behavior is on full display during an entertainment tour, and there are so many different forms that it would take Wikipedia to absorb it.

I know one thing: I couldn't imagine doing anything else. Even the way I fell into this line of work felt almost like fate. There had to be one strange path dotted with so many wrong turns that still led me to this exact spot. What I always remember is that this is still a job. My responsibilities and schedules have to be followed just like anyone else's in the world, and you still have overtime and meetings and taxes and FICA … pretty much the working stiff shebang.

But with the workaday hassle, I get benefits. I get to hear some of the greatest music around, and many times, I have a front row seat. I can go back in my mind and remember musical moments that are special personal memories to me as well as others. As a kid, I saw Boston play the opening spot for Blue Oyster Cult in Little Rock, Arkansas. That was as powerful as seeing U2 at the Pavilion in

Chicago decades later. I shared time with a few thousand people watching George Shearing and Joe Williams at Pabst Hall in Milwaukee. Those performances, like so many others, go on and on in my mind.

I've taken something from each event – something that sticks in my mind and in my heart and most definitely in my soul. The roadies, techs and assorted characters I've met throughout the years and had the undeniable pleasure of working with have left imprints on my mind that will never be erased. I've been involved in one way or another with more than 5,000 events, gatherings and conventions throughout North America. And that's far from any record. I've stacked speakers, pulled cables, adjusted par cans and run spotlights. I've driven trucks that hauled the gear from one event to another, and I've made a career behind the wheel of custom coaches, some of the finest moving houses you'll ever see, hauling the entertainment, the talent, the stars, the rock stars. Driving those coaches has been the most satisfying work to me. There are fans of every single entertainer on the planet, and when they buy those tickets, go to a show and wait in the dark for their star to walk out on stage, for that brief moment, their troubles are gone. Relationships, work, money, you name it. They are set aside when the music starts. For most fans, escaping in the moment is something every one of them will remember for the rest of their lives. It's great to be a small part of that experience.

It doesn't have to be the iconic stars to leave a mark, especially with me. The time I spent with My Life With The Thrill Kill Kult – that's a band by the way – was just as energetic as the time I spent with Barbara Mandrell. Fans are the same, even if they look completely different. All crowds cheer and love the same no matter who is on stage. That first roar is soothing to me. All that love being tossed out in the air ... there's nothing like it.

The Thrill Kill Kult, or TKK, was out there, even for me. The show was devilish, even by Satan's standards. It was the Sexplosion! Tour of 1991, and it had a sort of notorious reputation. In addition to having an actual bar and bartender on stage, the show featured a couple known as Ten and Avaluscious White. Before we get into their guises, let's remember that this was not a show for the kiddies. At one point, Ten dressed as Jesus on the cross with a large black dildo while Avaluscious simulated oral sex on him. Anything for a shock, right? And they were shocking, but I also noticed that behind the controversy laid one of the most musically gifted and tight bands I had ever seen. Even their production crew was top notch. We did shows along the route from Austin, Texas, down to Florida and back up to Dayton, Ohio.

Barbara Mandrell's crowds loved her, and they filled the air with every bit of that energy and love. Barbara was a torchbearer for country music, and after every show, she would sit late into the night signing autographs for everyone who wanted one. I saw the glow that radiated off her every time, and she would smile, and she would hug, and it was genuine. I saw grandmothers cry or even pass out after touching her. There are kings and queens in Nashville, and she was most definitely a queen of country music.

So I steal some of that love. When those lights dim and the energy swells, the crowd escapes their troubles, but I escape mine as well. I squeeze out whatever dose I can, and then it's back out the door, back on the bus and back to wherever we have to go next, searching for that moment again.

My life as a child was not that great. There was a lot of bad parenting and a lot of bad decisions on my part. It led me to be a very depressed and lost person. In my desire to grow out of that situation and find a life with some sort of meaning, I discovered getting on the road was a way to keep moving away from my past so that it didn't affect my future. Most importantly, I think I discovered that by traveling with the show maybe I wasn't such a lost freak after all. The whole world is going to hell, and I'm driving the bus. This is my story.

PART I

SEEING IT ALL

As a bus driver for entertainment stars and their crews, people often tell me, "You must have seen it all." I wouldn't go that far, but I've seen my share of things not everyone is privy to, and a few things I honestly wish I hadn't.

I'm grateful for the gigs I've worked, the entertainers I've driven and the music I've experienced. It's so gratifying to be able to travel throughout the United States and across the border to Canada, seeing North America in a fashion few have the privilege of experiencing. I've learned lessons I wouldn't trade for anything. As with any traveling job, memories are created, and there are stories to be told.

The reality is, though, that being an entertainment bus driver is a real job. I'm a small part of a system that helps the entertainers do their jobs entertaining the masses. It's a lot of work and responsibility. I'm not saying my job is more important than anyone else's. Things I've seen on various music tours just might be more colorful than things seen in your average job.

The road is my office. Unlike ordinary, fluorescent lit offices, the scenery outside my office window changes daily. The commotion outside my door is never the same. I've witnessed and experienced some one-of-a-kind scenarios; things you probably imagine, and some things you can't imagine, when you think of someone working in live entertainment. I'll let you be the judge as you read a handful of some of my favorite tales from the trails. I haven't seen it all, that's for sure.

A CROWDED MENTALITY

But before I delve into some rock 'n' roll stories, I want to offer a glimpse into the nuts and bolts of my industry, all from my perspective, of course. First, I need to note that I never cared for the custom coaches I drive to be referred to as a "bus." It's like comparing night and day. Buses, like the Greyhound ones you see traveling along the highway, are completely different. I drive custom coaches, vehicles that cost more than half of a million dollars to build. Land yachts, if you will, complete with satellite TVs and upholstered couches to relax on while watching your favorite sport or show as we travel around North America. Bus is too simple a term for these rides, but that's its common name, so be it. I tend to follow the crowd, so we'll call the half a million-dollar ride a bus.

The first rule of being a star is you have to look like one to pull it off. A clean shiny bus, one that glitters in the sun and glows in the dark, is a good start.

Ask any entertainer. Ask any tour or production manager. Ask a tour accountant or band manager, and any one of those people will tell you that a tour bus and a driver are necessary evils. A good one is worthy to have around. Buses are the most cost effective way to transport and house traveling working people.

An entertainment bus transports the life of a tour. It helps keep the energy and people behind the music safe and sound. The driver behind the wheel helps it roll so musicians can rock the crowds from city to city. The bus is where the tour starts and stops. The bus is home when you're away from home. You eat, sleep and do everyday things on it. It's where you rest, unwind, laugh, cry, be yourself – it's a touring home, a land yacht moving from destination to destination, and the driver is the captain. It's a big job, many drivers don't make it more than a few years, but somebody has to do it.

Drivers come in all different shapes, sizes and mental capacities. Some wear their emotions on their sleeves, others keep to themselves. Doing a good job is top priority no matter what, at least to the drivers who last a significant amount of time. My mindset is what I like to call a crowded mentality. I didn't have the ideal upbringing and didn't gain a traditional mindset from my parents like many kids I knew. I somehow managed to develop a strong work ethic from my parents and adopted basic moral values … you know, the all-American, do-good, neighborly type of stuff. As I entered adulthood, my frame of mind became shaped by the crowds around me, some good, some bad, it doesn't matter now. Their influences and energy tapped into me and helped shape the person I am today. That energy still shapes and changes me every day, while I still try to keep my values steady and at my core. No matter how many lewd, crude and socially unacceptable things I have seen, smelled, heard and tasted, I try to be an informed, caring citizen, father and friend.

Many drivers have nicknames like Gator, Turbo, Spider, English, Hollywood, Heavy Duty, Shaggy, Casper, Mickey Moe the Social Director and the list goes on. They come from all over the country and world with different upbringings, values, educations and personalities. Those who are good at it desire to be the best, or at least better than the other driver. There's always a competition among drivers. It's common for drivers to be assigned to work on a tour together. We typically work well as a team, but there always seems to be an element of bumping chests and "I'm better at this than you are" attitude. Less than a 100 men and women over the years have made it a long-term career choice. Many try it for a few years and move on to something else. Few stay around for 20 years or more. There are no retirement plans in this business. The hours can be long and the time away from home can devastate and rip apart a relationship or a family. Then there are the passengers. Their attitudes can be overbearing at times. Add the frustration of mechanical problems, red tape with management, daily issues of the "rules of the road" and any number of other matters thrown in, and the job can take its toll.

I've been around it more than 25 years. I've met thousands of people of all races and beliefs along the way, even lived in close quarters with many of them for months at a time. It's an interesting thing to meet and live with celebrities who share thought control over a portion of the masses.

I've worked on more than 100 tours through the years. I won't tell you I'm the best there is, but I know a few who will. Me, I do a good job at it, and it has kept me working. Bus driver personalities can go from one extreme to another and yet good ones — the professional ones, if there is such a thing — share a common knowledge: early is on time and on time is late.

Personnel who work the daily grind of a tour, be it crew or talent, must be transported from city to city. Expense and logistics make it very hard to fly, although there are a few stars who use airplanes from time to time. Roadies, as tour employees are called, are all hard working technicians. I admire most of them and taking good care of them has always been a priority for me. Eighteen to 20-hour workdays for roadies are not uncommon. The least I can do is give them a comfortable ride for the few hours they get to sleep.

In the entertainment touring business, everything works in a military type fashion. Can you imagine the organization it takes to move the stage and production equipment to mid-field for the Super Bowl halftime show, do a short set and get it off the field in time for the second half? That happens every day in a different town in the touring business. With a chain of command, there are generals, captains, sergeants and privates. It's just like a military operation. Although, a lot more hair is involved.

A large tour with shows in arenas, stadiums and amphitheaters has, just like any corporation, many departments of men and women. It's like a 24-hour factory. You have the rigging department, lighting department, sound, security, personnel, and transportation of equipment departments, among others. I work in the personnel relocation department. That's what bus drivers do: relocate people to the next destination.

When an entertainment group plans a tour, coaches are secured with drivers from one or several of the coach companies providing coach-leasing services. Most coaches are chosen based on the tour budget and the amount of people who have to be transported. Generally, the newer the coach, the more expensive the coach, which also means higher wages for the driver. Groups may request a certain driver if schedules work for both parties, but that is never guaranteed. When the touring season is in full swing, a specific driver is not always an option for the group if they have not taken care of coach leasing well ahead of when the tour is scheduled to start.

Tour managers and production managers usually make the last call as to whether a driver is right for their particular tour. Of course the passengers riding in the coach, which may or may not be the coach that one of the managers is riding in, have the final say as to whether a particular driver makes them feel safe or if personalities conflict.

As the "designated driver," I get to see the world in a different way than most. It's a crazy world and it's even crazier when you travel with the circus. At a younger age, I participated in a lot of it – sex, drugs and rock 'n' roll – just amazed by it all. Having survived my expeditions and now being an adult with bills, mortgage payments and family issues, I can still be a part of the party, just not the life of it. I can still find those happy moments that only this business could provide. Driving the bus is a front-row seat where I can see others and all the wild things that pass by. It's a pretty amusing seat to have.

I, and drivers like me, get to see human nature at its best ... and sometimes at its worst. Strange behavior has played out right before my eyes by the entertainers themselves, the behind-the-scenes crews, and of course, the fans. Fans can and will do just about anything to get attention from their favorite entertainers, and I've seen some very obnoxious things, from careless driving to flashing boobs (and other body parts). Well, that's not all bad, but it can be distracting, and distractions can slow down the operation, something you don't want in show business.

Following the show-must-go-on mission, being on time is number one. A day or night's work is an endless competition against the clock, which can be just as exhausting as running a marathon. Many days average 12- to 24-hour work shifts, and it can be a mental nightmare. It's an awesome way to live and work if you can understand it. The joy comes in working with people you admire and entertaining the masses.

Working with people in an atmosphere of mutual respect and support is what keeps me coming back. I haven't found such an atmosphere in any other line of work I've experienced. No one gives up, and no one is trying to stab a co-worker in the back just to get that quarter-an-hour raise. Everyone works as a team to get the show up and running and putting it back into the truck for tomorrow. I wouldn't consider working in any other atmosphere. Being part of a touring crew that clicks and does it every day no matter the conditions is where I have found many days of satisfying work.

It's not all work. After all, you have to eat. Sometimes there is time for play. And when you're on the road, you tend to gravitate toward others working just like you. We work odd hours, run into strange scenes – some good, some bad. It's only natural to share "war" stories with fellow roadies. Barney's Beanery in Hollywood is a good place to do just that.

When in the celebrity-infused city, many roadies hit Barney's just to see who they might run into. The who's who of roadies can be found there on any given day or night. Many roadies live in the L.A. area and many more stay in the Hollywood area when their respective groups are performing nearby. Barney's is just down the hill from high-dollar hotels on Sunset Boulevard, where travel agents put their touring roadies and smaller up-and-coming bands. It's an easy walk down the hill on La Cienega Boulevard to Santa Monica where Barney's is located. It's a very bad trip back up the hill when you're drunk and full of a Barney's burger.

Speaking of food, it can be an adventure to find sustenance on the road. Many times on long rides, passengers have to be fed. Usually a chain restaurant is the most convenient to feed a bus full of people. When I travel with an empty coach, I can put a little more thought into feeding my hunger. Denton's Trotline, just off I-30 in my hometown, feeds my catfish cravings. Like Denton's, local eateries can be found and become regular dining stops along the road. For me, an important factor is easy access from the interstates and routes I'm traveling. Real Italian food can be found at many locations in the Northeast. Just about any "mom and pop" Mexican restaurant in Arizona or New Mexico can fulfill cravings for spicy and savory. Get sushi when in San Francisco's Japan town. L.A. has a few good sushi places, too. Clam chowder in Boston and lobster in Portland, Maine shouldn't be missed. Pork chops with white beans and red cabbage in Iowa is the best around. Barbecue in Memphis is like no other anywhere in the country. There's great food everywhere in this country, and finding it is one accident I am always glad to encounter.

A LITTLE HISTORY, NUTS AND BOLTS

I, and others in the entertainment touring industry, wouldn't be enjoying the efficient, comfortable touring ways of today if it weren't for our pioneers.

By driving some of the older eccentric entertainers, entourages and old roadies, I have learned plenty about the touring history. The touring standards have changed and improved much over the years. The mentality of the people who entertain and work behind the scenes seems to remain the same, however: hard work and "balls to the walls" party till you pee-uuke self-indulgence.

I've driven folks who worked for musicians of the 1960s like Janis Joplin, Jimi Hendrix and The Band, with tales of partying on trains as they road cross-country from coast to coast before buses were the norm. In the '60s, those bands only played the big cities on the train routes and only transported band gear and luggage. Many of the gospel groups traveling the back roads of the U.S. traveled in very large automobiles pulling trailers and with luggage tied to the roof of the vehicles.

As modern entertainment expanded throughout America, buses became more and more a part of the equation. The tour bus industry in the late '40s and '50s didn't have the luxury liners or land yachts of today. Instead they were seated buses with a few seats removed here and there for room. Curtains hung from the ceilings to give the feeling of some privacy, but there were no bunks, beds, couches or TVs.

Gospel groups were using buses long before the rock 'n' roll touring world came to be. Country acts started catching on in the '40s and '50s, but coaches back then were basically used Greyhound and Trailways line-haul buses. First-class amenities were not really an option. According to rumor, plumbing and piping in the "old days" were taken out of the old Greyhounds and the shit would literally hit the ground.

It's hard to establish who came up with the idea of making a bus into a comfortable home away from home and renting it to an entertainer. J.D. Sumner has been listed in the *Guinness Book of World Records* as the World's Lowest Bass Singer. J.D.'s many other contributions mentioned in the record book include the introduction of the tour bus to the music industry in 1955. Lots of folks point their fingers at Milo Ligett of Nashville, Tennessee, who put beds into his gospel group's bus. Norm Basden in Besemer, Alabama did the same with his group's bus, and The Thrasher Brothers Gospel Group was doing the same with their buses. I'm not sure who exactly did it first, but I sure am grateful for them.

In modern day, the coach leasing business is unique in that several entities all depend on the other to function profitably and properly. Each entity has to interact to keep everything moving along. The drivers are the glue and sweat equity that make it all work. The driver represents himself, his company/owner, the builder and the maintenance crew that maintains it. The driver, who many times is the only person seen by the customer, presents the culmination of all the entities to the people leasing the coach.

There are the coach owners who own the coaches and lease them, running small fleets of one to 20 buses, to the large corporations whose fleets have 50 or more coaches available for lease. In some ways, it's much like the trucking business, where there are fleet owners and owner operators servicing company accounts. In many other ways, it's completely different. There are less than 1,000 coaches for lease in North America with more than 50 coach leasing companies competing for the business. The business is seasonal with most coaches leased April through November. The competition is tough. Every coach owner will tell you that their coaches are the best on the road. I got my start in the business in the '80s, the same time the live entertainment touring business really rocketed. Having driven more than 35-plus different coaches over the years, I have my own opinions about who builds and maintains the best.

Senators Coaches and Hemphill Brothers Coaches, a couple of the largest companies providing leasing services, evolved from touring gospel families. As children, the Hemphill brothers rode on tour buses with their touring gospel family. When the brothers grew up and started leasing buses, the operation grew to be second to none with one of the most modern fleets in the industry serving many Nashville acts as well as international entertainers. Their facility where they build their coach interiors is full of skilled, dedicated craftsmen. Just about every bus seen at a political rally is provided by Hemphill Brothers. They have even provided coaches for the President.

Leon Frazier was performing with "The Senators," a gospel group that had a customized Eagle bus when it caught the eye of someone in the rock 'n' roll business. The Model 05 coach turned everyone's heads with its mauve and silver exterior. One day in a suburb of Memphis, where the group had parked their bus, someone from the rock world approached Mr. Frazier about leasing the gospel group's ride to a rock 'n' roll band when they weren't using it. That was just the beginning of greater things. With that successful lease, Mr. Frazier started Senators Coaches and grew what has become a standard choice for many of the rock, pop and country acts. They were also able to acquire some of the best drivers in the business, who gave great attention to detail with their equipment. That only helped Senators earn more leases with the biggest entertainment groups.

Some of the companies are strictly corporate-minded with so many rules that it can make it hard for a driver to give the customers the level of service they demand. Large coach companies only consider the numbers and the bottom line, and to them, coaches are numbers, and drivers have become meat in the seat.

Other companies have colorful characters behind their operations. Naturally, some of those characters have musical leanings. The Calhoun brothers, Jack and Jerry, from central Florida are twins that few can tell apart if you don't know them. One brother owns Florida Coach and the other owns Florida Custom Coach. They are legends in the bus business as far as I'm concerned, and in the '80s, they had one of the most beautiful fleets. Everyone wanted to ride in them, and guys like me wanted to drive them. The artwork on the sides of their coaches, painted by an artist named Rainmaker, made them the envy of many. Willie Nelson gets his coaches from the brothers. Jack and Jerry recorded an album or two in the '60s, and rumor has it that Willie had written a song or two for them. They perform at the Farm Aid concert, which consists of many musical acts, every year with Willie, who is one of the Farm Aid founders.

The brothers leased their coaches to many of the major acts of the '80s and '90s and were in stark contrast to the corporate style of some of the other leasing companies. It's been fun to follow their companies and their spirited mischievous approach to the coach leasing business. The stories I've heard about those two would make an incredible movie, I am sure. They didn't invent the custom coach leasing business, but their approach set the performance bar high among all other companies.

Another impressive story comes out of Four Seasons Coach Leasing. Its owner, Mike Slarve, worked in the Los Angeles recording industry in the '60s during the same time some huge rock legends recorded. Mike worked at the Village Recorder, the largest independent studio in Los Angeles, where folks like the Rolling Stones and Fleetwood Mac recorded hit songs and albums. He promoted shows with acts like Rod Stewart and Deep Purple and managed a few acts before stepping into the coach leasing business. He started as a broker in the business, leasing other companies' equipment, and he has built a fleet of over 50 of his own coaches just outside Nashville.

Road House Coach in Texas puts the Texas touch to the business. Based in Lubbock for years before moving south of Austin, its owner Jay Boy Adams is a good guitar player and has recorded a few albums himself. He's provided nice coaches to the touring business for more than 30 years. Road House also had an artist who painted scenes on the sides of its coaches. A painter named Fitzpatrick (no relation) was equally as good as Rainmaker was for the Florida Coach companies. Fitzpatrick has a beautiful way of painting animals. I drove a couple of coaches that had his artwork on the side along with his "Fitzpatrick" signature. Of course a few people asked.

Nashville is often referred to as Bus City with dozens of companies like Night Train Coach, Music City Coach, All Access Coach, Roberts Brothers Coach and other quality companies competing for a slice of the business. More than fifty percent of all coach leasing companies are based in the metropolitan Nashville area.

I admire folks who have advanced from behind the wheel and gone on to establish themselves and their competing companies. Before Chip Huffman started Nigh Train Coach, he sang and played keyboard in gospel bands. In order to save money, it's common practice for gospel groups to share driving responsibilities. Chip would ride and drive thousands of miles in buses for various shows. I drove on many tours with Gaylon Moore, who now owns Music City Coach. He clocked hundreds of thousands of miles of driving experience before acquiring his bus company.

D&S and Taylor Tours, based in Phoenix, Arizona, are western companies that have been providing great buses to the industry for years and are the closest companies to Los Angeles. Both companies derived from drivers who bought buses and grew the companies to what they are today.

The people who build coaches are an important key to the whole system. How they build can make or break a fleet. Several of the large companies build their own interiors to meet the demands of their customers. Most of the smaller companies use one of the many independent builders. An owner's understanding the needs of his market and being able to have a builder accommodate those needs is very important.

Many interior coachbuilders are located in the Nashville area with several others located in Florida, Virginia and various states. Several builders specialize solely in conversions to the private market. Marathon Coach and Country Coach, both based in Oregon, and Liberty Coach in Illinois, among others, build some of the plushest coaches on the road that are sold worldwide. Racing teams use their coaches for drivers to live in at the racetrack. The race drivers rarely ride in them, though.

Usually, these private market builders build motor homes that cost one million dollars or more. The interiors generally won't meet the demands of the touring industry. Tour buses cover up to a million miles in their lifetime. Custom coaches built for Mom and Pop rarely accumulate more than 50,000 to 100,000 miles during their lifetime, with most being used for short vacations and winter living quarters.

There are financial people who invest in these sorts of things, since there are some tax advantages in investing in big equipment such as trucks, buses, tractors and the likes. Rarely are these people seen.

Bus maintenance shops are a vital key to the whole operation. Keeping the bus maintained so it doesn't break down and fixing things as soon as they do break are a must. And they do break. Put your home on wheels, and roll it down the highway and see what you would have to fix every day. The people who repair them are a key component to the equation. If a unit breaks down and an entertainer misses a show, it could be a financial disaster. Interior refurbishing, engine services and repairs are done when a coach has down time. Much of the maintenance is done before and after a tour.

It's the driver's responsibility to keep the bus in shape when the unit is on tour. Finding someone to repair a coach can be nerve-racking in some parts of the country. Parts and general mechanical knowledge of coaches is rare for a general repair shop that doesn't specialize in coaches. The large bus manufacturers have service facilities located in several states, but a break down cannot be planned in their area. Prevost Car, the primary supplier of entertainment coach shells to the industry, has facilities in New Jersey, Florida, Nashville, Dallas and Southern California. Everywhere else you either find someone to handle the problem or drivers fix it themselves. Things are always breaking or going wrong with a coach, so drivers have to be on top of it daily when not in the area of the bus owner's shop.

As a "Gearhead" I love working on a bus when I have the time. For me, fixing a small problem before it becomes a big one makes for a satisfying and relaxing time. Broken down on the side of the road trying to fix something to meet a demanding schedule does not make me a happy driver, however.

Drivers who are well known in the industry are requested often and their experience can help an owner to keep his fleet leased. These drivers are in demand year round. Many entertainers and their management know them and depend on them. Some of these guys and gals have just as many road-war stories from their experiences with different groups as the rock stars themselves. The police will kick in the hotel door of the driver's room just like they do of rowdy celebrities.

Drivers can face issues that can add to the spectrum of emotions on a tour. For a driver, it's a 24/7 job that starts before you leave the house and goes and goes until a few days after returning home. Once under way, you might be cruising along tapping your toes to Motown sounds one moment and the next tapping your fingers on the steering wheel frustrated by a traffic jam that might be cutting into your arrival time. Passengers can give you grief, wanting to stop here and there, cutting into your schedules. A phone call from home with a family problem that you really can't do much about can keep your mind off the details at hand. Working for endless hours and finally arriving to a hotel after looking forward to a hot shower and rest only to find they can't accommodate you because of corporate rules about check-in is just part of the job. Travel plans can change at the turn of a dime with a band wanting to go to a topless bar, a restaurant, store, or worse, some fan's house that they just met. So many variables can and do play into the mood of a driver.

With less than 1,000 vehicles in the industry, most feel the government rules should be applied differently to custom coach leasing and operations. In the early days of the business, there were no rules governing operations of custom coaches. Drivers could drive as long as they could safely do so. Sitting in the seat is how to make wages. Sitting there longer makes more wages. With up to a dozen passengers checking on you, bringing you coffee, talking to you, bothering you, it's not that hard to continue on for 10-plus hours. With the speed limit at 70, that's 700 miles covered in a sitting if needed. With the TV blasting a movie or sporting event, the noise and activity will keep you alert and going with the desire to get to the destination. Generally, if a coach is traveling more than 450 miles it is not a show day.

A major benefit for most of the lease companies is that coach drivers aren't the employees of the coach leasing company. Drivers are employees of the entertainers and the people who lease a coach. The group pays the driver's wages based on experience and the general rate that lease companies say their driver's work for. The coach company doesn't compensate the driver for any services whatsoever. There is no insurance provided by any coach companies or any 401K. Most good drivers consider themselves small businesses offering their driving skills and services to the clients.

The owners and companies have drivers who they only allow to operate their coaches, and they offer their clients these drivers with the coach they lease. Generally, good drivers get assigned to a coach for a period of time.

The coach company will try and treat you as an employee. They will give you rules and regulations to go by. Some will even give you a lecture. One coach owner gave me a class on how he wanted the beds made in his coaches. Of course once I left his office, I used my own system.

Many of the companies' coach owners and their office staff work eight to five and go home and sleep in their beds. Many have never spent 30, 60 or 90 days on a tour or even understand what a tour is. It's all about owning equipment with them. So just about every time one of these guys or gals gives you the run down on a lease or tour, they really don't have a clue who they're telling you to go pick up, how they're going to act and most importantly, how they will like their bus.

Just like bus drivers, bus owners can be a fickle lot. In years past, if you broke some of "their" rules, you might not get any work from them. In the past, some companies seemed to play games and lead drivers on by saying there may be work in the future. In the meantime, when a coach driver is not working, there is no pay. With a shortage of experienced drivers, coach companies and owners seem to have a different approach toward drivers these days. Earning the most for being good at my craft and away from my home and family is all that matters. The business side of life says that's what it's really all about, anyway.

Owners run the gambit from the professional corporate types to wealthy people who think it's a cool idea to own a bus that some rock or country star rides in. Some own buses because their accountants advised them to invest. Some are hard to deal with. Few are compassionate enough to understand the nuts and bolts of operating a bus.

When a bus breaks, everyone loses money. The entertainer, the bus owner, the employees of the entertainers and me, the driver – we all lose. When lights, stereos, toilets or whatever breaks, someone is not happy. Keeping one in shape and clean when up to a dozen people are riding and living in it is a mega job and expense that few understand. The bus owner is always concerned about the bottom line or the revenue, as are all business owners. How a driver spends money on a coach can be a point of contention between the owner and driver.

I've invested my money many times in a coach to keep it running and have had to argue with a bus owner to be reimbursed. If a moment arises and money has to be spent to keep the bus on time, I will probably do what has to be done to keep things on schedule. It's my strong work ethic.

I consider myself an independent, contracting my services, as all drivers do. With more than 25 safe years in the entertainment touring business, I have maintained quite a few contacts with folks who like my style and approach.

Several bus owners and bus brokers have known me for years, and I stay on their lists for possible work. A few entertainment management companies, tour managers and production managers know me and request me whenever schedules match up. I get a call once in awhile from them looking for coaches and offering work. When folks call me, I search through the various companies to find what they need, bid on it and put a coach together to meet their needs. Saving money for the lessee and making money for an owner is the goal.

An experienced, trustworthy driver who can generate revenue for an owner without being a liability to anyone is every coach owner's desire. A driver who damages the coach, scares the passengers and costs everyone thousands of dollars in liability issues, is an owner's nightmare. Not to mention the hassles of finding a replacement person and transferring them in and out of the seat when the coach is 2,000 miles from the shop.

Over the years, I've had to pay for my own insurance and cover my taxes, just like a small business. Like a small business, I try to put customer service first, giving my passengers the smoothest and safest ride possible and getting them to their destination on time no matter what. Giving passengers a smooth ride is a key to being a good driver. When passengers are able to get up in the coach and walk to the bathroom or prepare something at the galley and not be tossed into the floor, that will help them trust and trusting the driver is the ticket to good sleep in a tour bus. Would you crawl onto a shelf in a bus and go to sleep with just any driver? If a driver can drive without spilling their drinks, that's less mess you have to clean up when you get to the destination. Driving smooth and steady while passengers are sleeping keeps them in their bunks and out of my hair. The best part of waking up in a bus is already being in the next town.

Although my travels are usually based in the entertainment touring business, there are all types of customers who rent or lease coaches. It really doesn't matter to me who's riding in the coach. My motto: pay the rent and my salary and you're OK with me. Be who you want to be.

Besides entertainment based touring groups, I've driven individuals to sporting and racing events, corporate people to seminars and conventions, and private wealthy folks on vacations.

I once took a group of guys to a Notre Dame game. They had all known each other since grade school. Now grown and successful businessmen, once a year, they hit South Bend for their traditional game. I picked them up in Memphis, Tennessee, and drove overnight while they partied and slept. After parking the bus in the lot outside the stadium, I headed off to a local hotel. The group of guys tailgated all day until the game, and when the game was over and the celebrations finished, I checked out of my hotel room and came back to drive overnight to their hometown. I've had dozens of similar drives over the years.

Usually when I arrive to pick up passengers I'm meeting for the first time, someone asks, "Do you have any rules?"

I respond, "I'm the captain of the land yacht." I'm pretty easy going. You make your own rules to live by and if something doesn't seem to add up, I might remind you that the professional people I worked with last didn't do it that way. It is your house. Make your own rules; you get that privilege as the lessee of the coach.

There are a few common sense rules when living and traveling in a coach. The only rule I would have would be that I don't do your luggage. I will if you pay me, and I'll do it with a smile, but otherwise it's your luggage. If you're going to hand a bellman five bucks a bag every time we check in and out of a hotel, you can pay me, too. And with entertainers checking in and checking out sometimes two times a day, that's a lot of damn luggage. I'm working here, and after all, we live together. So, it's your choice.

Another very important unwritten rule to remember is to sleep with your feet forward, head to the back of the bus. Like a cat, it's best to land on your feet when you fall. It would be the same in a bus crash. I will never go backward fast enough to hurt you.

Other common sense rules are easy enough. Simple stuff like NO shitting on the bus. It's a given. Get your shit schedule right. You don't want to be the one making everyone late for work because you can't keep your shit together. No shitting on the bus. It stinks, everyone can smell it and there are plenty of other smells to deal with when you have up to 12 people in a bus living in less than 300 square feet. The air travels forward in a bus. I know when you go to bed. I can smell you take off your shoes. I know when you get up in the morning. I can smell your breath. Let's all try and keep the smells down as we ride around.

People always ask me to tell them the best tour I've been on. My response: there is no best tour. Every tour I've worked on has its memorable experiences. There are good times and tough times. Tours roll on no matter what, so you make the best of each day, take the good from them all and apply the lessons learned. I've had some tours that I didn't want to end. The 1988 Grateful Dead summer tour was a good time and their close-knit family lifestyle made everything seem so easy. Eddie Murphy's operation was first class and another tour that I didn't want to end.

Sometimes it's the activities between the shows on a tour that mean the most. After taking up golf in 1995, I considered myself very lucky that Chris, Ed and Michael of Queensryche made me their fourth in their golf outings. We made many treks to golf courses during the 1995 I Am I Tour. I was able to improve my game. I was so fortunate they put up with my bad playing and taught me many things I needed to know about the game. A funny sight, I thought, was me showing up to a country club with guys in a metal band to play a round of golf. There were a few weeks when we hit the course four times a week and we played some spectacular courses around the country.

MY SO-CALLED TYPICAL DAY

People often ask me what a typical day is like driving a custom coach on entertainment-based tours?

My response: "There is NO such a thing as a typical day. It doesn't matter what day of the week or month it is. There are show days and there are off days. That's the only typical in touring."

Just when you think you have it figured out, it's time for another tour. The only constant is the clock. Everything in the touring business works by the clock. Arrival times, load in of the equipment, rigging, staging, lighting, sound, sets, eating, SHOW TIME, load out, departure times ... repeat. The clock can be anyone's archenemy on a tour. Life on the road is a constant battle with this nemesis that churns with or without you. The clock is never late, and it never sleeps. With no personality, it just continues being the beast and master that it is. The ticking thing turns for you as soon as you have the assignment and are given a pickup time. Be there. Be on time. Start off on the right foot, the one you press the accelerator with, and here we go again.

I often drive alone from home or the bus shops to the pick-up destinations and back when an assignment is finished. Occasionally, a family member or friend rides along and we see the sites together when there are no passengers on board. Driving across the U.S. in a half-a-million-dollar-plus coach on my own schedule can make for comfortable travels. Stopping in obscure places to relax, regroup and recharge is fun. The middle of nowhere is the center of somewhere and it can be a peaceful place.

If you open the Rand McNally Map of the entire U.S., you will see the major highways of America. They are designated on the map with numbers and letters from the alphabet and have blue roads and red roads and a few green ones. I've driven every mile of the blue and green roads and many, many, miles of the red ones. I've been to and through every town in America with populations of 5,000 people or more and lots of small towns with populations much less.

I meet so many people I hardly ever remember a name unless I use it daily. If we talked for more than a minute, I can usually remember a face and match it with a where and when. On average, I see more than a million faces a year in my business. I see them as I travel the highways, and I see them at the events that most of the people who ride with me work. Each year, I see about 1.5 million people at various entertainment events. And I see thousands more doing the things you do between the events. Hotels, restaurants, laundry mats, parking lot attendants, people flipping me off on the highway.

As most tours roll over, the passengers in my coach will be in my life for less than 90 days, sometimes more or less, and by the time we finish our trip, we will have lived together, smelled each other and seen each other just about every day. And before it's over, we will have shared the many emotions of happiness, fun, laughter, sadness, anxiety, concern, anger and who knows what else together. For me, when it's all over, I will be able to review the trip and take what was good from it and use what I learned somewhere else.

It doesn't matter which direction I travel, along the way, I meet so many people in my daily activities. Wherever I'm traveling, inevitably when people see the bus stopped or parked they approach. Curiosity gets the best of folks. Many just walk up and start talking like we're old friends. A few even knock on the door. Some seem timid and nervous. That need-to-know look in their eyes is easily recognizable and noticeable from any direction I'm approached.

I can spot someone coming toward me with that typical first question every time. "Whose bus is that?" or "Who rides on that bus?" A common question that's been asked of me a jillion times. After a little banter many are concerned with how to drive such a behemoth. "Is it hard to drive?" Another very common question asked a gazillion times. I do it every day, and like to do it every day so it's easy for me. Gas mileage is usually the next question. I average it on paper to five miles a gallon. There are two motors, one pushes the bus, and one provides electricity inside just like at your home. Therefore, accurate mileage varies.

Just about anytime I stop, I can expect a conversation with someone. Sometimes I'm in the mood to yap it up. Sometimes I humor people and myself. Have fun with them and the moment, baffle them with bullshit. Sometimes the riggers of the job make me feel like just hiding somewhere and not talking to anyone.

"FUCK YOU, leave me alone."

People seem to persist. Human nature, I guess. The daily giggles of dealing with curious souls, sometimes is priceless. On one occasion, I pulled into a convenient store and when a curious person approached, I gave him all the wrong answers.

"Yeah, I'm just a rich guy living it up on vacation."

He asked, "What do you do for a living?"

"Brain surgeon," I tell him as I walk away. Harmless fun.

Another common example comes from a time when, after dropping off a band at a hotel, I went to a grocery store to grab some supplies for the bus. After shopping and loading my things in the bus, I looked out the window and caught a curious soul as he was headed my way. I immediately realized it was about to be question-and-answer time. Sometimes folks have such a determined look about them. I was in a good mood, so I decided to tease him a bit.

"YO, WHAT'S THE PROBLEM?" I said as he reached the door of the bus, darting eyes up and down, side to side, surveying the unit I'm driving.

And sure enough, he asked, "Who's on the bus?"

"Just some rich people," or any other goofy idea I might come up with, I say as he gave me a curious look.

"Are they famous?"

"They might be," I responded, as I positioned myself between him and the door.

"Can I see inside there?" the most asked question curious people can usually never resist.

This is a question that has always gotten me. Let's imagine for a moment if I was driving or walking down the street and went to the door of a random house and rang the doorbell. The homeowner comes to the door, we greet one another, and I compliment his nice home.

"Man! What a neat looking house you have. Can I look inside?"

What would you say? This vehicle may be mobile, but it is still a home. And just about anyone who questions me about it asks to take a peek inside.

Everyone who has an interest in the bus talks about a ride in it. On any given day, if I think they might be serious when they approach me, I'll give them numbers to some custom coach brokers, wish them well and go on with my gig or whatever I'm doing that day. If I'm in the bus, I'm usually on a schedule of some sort so I don't have time to yap it up all day. You never know who will be your next customer, so it's good to practice kindness, at least for a minute. After that, if they keep poking me for information, I use the "I've got things to do and a schedule to keep" excuse. That's my escape route.

Then there are moments that seem to be fleeting when they're happening, but they end up leaving those priceless lasting impressions. Like the time I stopped in the small retro Western town of Tucumcari, New Mexico, back in the mid-'80s. I was transporting the crew of an English punk band. We landed in Tucumcari to take a break from the excessively long drive the booking agent had arranged. The crew members, tired of being in the bus on a 1,400-mile ride, headed to a local bar as soon as we stopped at the highway hotel where I could get a few hours of rest before driving on. These guys never worried what the regulars might think of their punk star dress complete with earrings and tattoos in a small Western town. When it was time to travel on, the locals didn't want them to leave. Normal circumstance, extraordinary character. That's the rock 'n' roll touring business.

CHAPTER 1 | A FIRST TIME FOR EVERYTHING

The first time I saw the bus I would be assigned to drive, it was sitting on wooden blocks in a dingy garage that wasn't really a garage at all. Originally, it was a fenced acre for a couple of horses. It had a lean-to roof and an old horse stall that had been converted into a tool shed. In Pensacola, Florida, the sandy lot made for a cheap place for the bus owner to rig and repair. The Model 5 Eagle had been refurbished with a Model 10 Cap on the front and rear and was being leased as a Model 10. It was named Beachcomber after who knows what. All buses are named like yachts are named – land yachts that they are.

It was obviously a used line coach that someone like Greyhound had used and put a million-plus miles on. It had been refurbished a bit and sold to someone who had taken the windows out, paneled it and put an interior in it. Painted blue on top, the bus had a few bumps and scratches on it and a small ding in each of the corner bumpers. Corner bumpers on the old Eagle coaches were very expensive to replace, so many bus owners left them alone unless they were too damaged. Chances are that a driver would ding them up again.

It had all the wheels off of it and the guy working in the shop – another driver – was trying to install new brakes. I was instructed to help get it in shape and went to work as soon as I arrived after flying in from Little Rock. I worked all day helping to put the brakes back on and doing a hundred other things to get the bus ready to roll. It was filthy from years of use and had a stale, lived-in smell inside. The interior had been refreshed some with new upholstery but not the carpet. Who knows what germs lurked in its tightly woven trenches? When we got the brakes and wheels put back on the bus at the end of the day, I headed toward Atlanta to pick up my first group. North out of Pensacola, I took Highway 29 to Interstate 85 toward Georgia's metropolitan city.

In their day, late 1970s and early '80s, Eagle buses were just about the only bus that entertainers and their crews would ride on. The Eagle had what was called a torsilastic suspension system, which made it a very smooth ride compared to anything riding on air bags, which is the norm on today's buses. Air bags give a bus a side-to-side kind of motion when the coach is moving down the road. If you're in a bunk trying to sleep it can give you a motion of falling out of your bunk. Walking around while the coach is in motion is a different style also. Torsilastic suspension rocks you from front to back making the nose and the rear of the bus float up and down, head to toe with no feeling of sway.

Beachcomber rode like a dream and powered down the road just fine. The four-speed transmission was very sloppy, and, when I had left the shop, I had been given a 4-foot long 1x2 board that was put in the bay. It was explained to me that the reverse solenoid acted up once in awhile, and since they were a pain and big expense to change out, I was instructed that if I had to back up and the reverse didn't work to poke the solenoid a couple of times with the stick. This usually would get it back to normal. The best advice came from the owner when he suggested to park where you don't have to back up. I was so excited about driving that old bus I didn't give it a second thought.

I was sent to pick up Atlanta, the band, in Atlanta, the city. My first encounter with them was in a parking lot just north of town almost to Marietta outside the perimeter, as the interstate bypass around Atlanta is called. They were friendly and seemed like a great bunch of guys. Atlanta had been a hit band right out of the gate, so to speak, with several big country hits in 1982 to '83. They had played the big arenas and fairs, did it all in a very short time span and were about to go on hiatus soon after I drove them.

After loading everything, we got out of town after rush hour and headed to Nashville to pick up another player or two. There was a small truck following with the gear. They played a couple of small bars on the five-day run and of all places, the American Mall in Lima, Ohio for its 20th anniversary. That seemed odd to me, but, hey, a gig is a gig.

We arrived in Lima early in the morning before six. The tour manager gave me a leave time, and I got some rest. That afternoon I left the hotel with the band around two o'clock and headed to the mall for their show. The crew guys had ridden over on the truck to get the gear set up. The guys in the band jived well and played and sang awesomely together.

On the ride over to the gig, they warmed up with some tunes getting their voices in shape as most singers do before a show. I've heard many warming up in the bus driving over to a gig from the hotel, some singing songs that they would be performing during the show, or just scaling through notes. Atlanta sang together with perfect harmony and when finished with a song segued right into the old song "Sweet Adeline." They sounded like the best barbershop quartet I'd ever heard. No instruments, just their voices belting it out while I drove through Lima on the way to the mall. It was great.

When the short run was over I called the owner rep, Mario, and discussed some of the things that were wrong with the coach. By the time I got Atlanta back to Atlanta, I had a pretty substantial list of things that needed to be done to get this bus into better leasing shape.

That first run created a good memory for me and set the tone for my coming back for more such memories. There's nothing but good feelings created when you witness people singing together. I'm lucky to be the only audience member sometimes. I've heard some beautiful things over the years as I drive buses, even broken ones.

CHAPTER 2 | A WET DOG AND A CLEAN CARPET

As I've mentioned, it costs mega bucks to keep a bus in tip-top shape and clean. Humans can be messy enough. Try animals.

If I have been assigned to pick up you or your group, I have a routine that I will go through. I try to make contact with every customer several weeks before the pickup. The details are always the same, but it sometimes takes more time to explain to some people. Most of the information is the same from one group to the next: pick them up here, we're going there and there and there, drop them off and go get another group.

I'm a bit of a pessimist. I always expect the worst-case scenarios of what passengers might be like after the first phone conversation. I'm curious as to what demands they will make of me outside of what I normally do. Sometimes after my first conversation with a client, I may end up trying to find out just who they are. It's a normal procedure for me if I'm not used to hearing your name and what you're famous for. Of course I recognize AC/DC, The Rolling Stones, Janet Jackson and other well-known acts, but when I was offered work on Depeche Mode's 1986 first American tour, my first thought was, "Who?"

I've said, "Who's that?" on more than one occasion, having never heard of your "mega" group. In the '80s, record companies were putting hundreds of thousands of dollars into touring new bands, trying to see who would catch on and who would flop. I drove many small bands with one album to their name. The record company basically put them all on the road with small budgets trying to see if they could stir up some sales. Rent a bus and put band and crew in it, sometimes with a trailer, sometimes with a Ryder truck following and send them out to perform in the clubs throughout America. I've taken these bands to play in bars like Toads Place in Hartford, Connecticut, or The Metro in Chicago, the Whiskey in L.A., Leather Bottle in Lawrence, Kansas, Tipitina's in New Orleans, or First Avenue in Minneapolis. These clubs and bars and many others seem to be a must for bands if they want a chance at making it big. I've been to them all.

A band that got noticed received a few hundred thousand more dollars from the record company and usually got an opening slot on a bigger tour, one that would be playing old theaters and small-town arenas and armories. They also had to deal with small-town promoters trying to be the next Bill Graham. At some point, if all that money invested looks like it will pay off, the entire marketing department goes to work for your band, and if you play the game right, you're a "rock star." Most rock stars ride buses, which bodes well for guys like me.

I've started tours and picked up passengers all over America. Big cities like

New York City and Los Angeles are always good starting points. Starting in big cities can be very expensive for entertainers, though. Many start in other places, hone their shows and then roll into the big markets.

Consider yourself lucky if you drive someone who has played the game for a while. I was very excited when a bus owner's call came to take Emmylou Harris on a weeklong run. I had always admired her and had already driven several people who had run in the same circles with her during the '60s and '70s. I had been a Flying Burrito Brothers Band fan when I was younger and played a few of their songs when I was in a bar band. I had met and driven Chris Hillman when I was assigned to drive the Desert Rose Band, of which Chris was a member. Chris originally had played with The Byrds and also had partnered with Gram Parsons in the Flying Burrito Brothers. I also knew Emmylou would have some of the best Nashville musicians with her, so that was another reason to look forward to the run.

A few days before the pick-up date, I called her tour manager, Phil Kaufman, about the run. Phil is a legend. He was one of the Rolling Stones' first wranglers, and he's also the guy who in 1973, stole Gram Parsons' body from a California funeral home and set it on fire in the Joshua Tree forest in California. It's all written in his book, Road Mangler Deluxe.

Kaufman had a scruffy voice when we connected the first time. We went through the normal banter about how everything was going to be, where we were going, what the budget looked like, all the standard stuff. Then he gave me some more information.

"Emmylou has a dog and wants to know if you mind it riding in the bus," Kaufman said.

"I don't care as long as you include carpet cleaning in the bill when I drop Emmylou and the gang off," I said. I'm thinking something like that would run about $60. All of a sudden, he shoots through the roof.

"I'M NOT CLEANING THE FUCKING CARPET! WE'RE ONLY GOING TO BE IN THE BUS FOR EIGHT FUCKING DAYS!"

Now, we can discuss a problem all day long, but if you start yelling at me... well then, "FUCK YOU!" I almost got to the point where if they didn't want to clean the carpet, then they needed to leave the dog at home. But I let it slide.

"Anything else we need to talk about? I'm about to start driving toward Nashville." He was getting real prissy already for a rock 'n' roll guy, so I started to wonder if this run was going to work out or if it was going to be a miserable few days.

I went to Emmylou's house for the pickup around 9 p.m. Many of the Nashville acts leave Nashville on Wednesday and Thursday evenings. A person could get run over by a bus on those nights. There are so many headed out for the weekend gigs. When I arrived, it was pouring down – we're talking monsoon kind of rain. I pulled up in front of the driveway, and after a few minutes someone hit the door with a few bags while juggling an umbrella. It took about 20 minutes or so for most everyone to get his or her bags and bodies on board. Emmylou came to the door with someone carrying an umbrella over her head. I stepped back in my seating area and held out my hand to welcome her aboard. She looked at me hard.

"YOU'RE THE ONE WHO WON'T LET MY DOG GO!"

With that greeting, she started walking to the back of the bus. I was so bummed and shocked. I tried to right the ship.

"No ma'am," I said. "Your tour manager made that call." I didn't notice Kaufman standing to my left. He gave me a look. Then took off to the back of the bus with Emmylou. I sat down in the driver's seat feeling like shit and started to get ready for the drive to North Carolina.

After a few minutes, he exited the bus and came back with this Wolfhound type dog soaking wet and smelling like ... well a wet dog. As they went by, he turned to me.

"Let's go," he said. "Tomorrow the dog will move to the truck."

The dog ended up riding in the bus, the carpet got cleaned, and after a few days, Emmylou smiled at me. The dog, Bonaparte, and I became friends. And I got to enjoy some great music.

SORRY, CHARLIE

Everything in a bus is self-contained for any situation. You have to be careful what you throw away. You don't know its value to someone. It could have girls' phone numbers on it, so you have to look out for that kind of stuff. One man's trash is another man's treasure.

Charlie Wright, a good driver and friend of mine who passed away a few years ago, and I were on a tour together. Jerry H., another good friend and driver, and I were driving the crew buses while Charlie transported the band. The first night Charlie's passengers became upset with him and it didn't look like they would get over it. Crybaby rock stars are like that.

It was June of 1989, and the first show for the Howard Jones Tour. Howard Jones was an '80's rocker pop star from Great Britain. He had some American success with "No One is to Blame" and "Things Can Only Get Better." Both songs made it to the top five U.S. singles in '88 and '89. Another song, "Everlasting Love," made it to number 12. "Everlasting Love" had a video on MTV where two mummies went places together symbolizing their everlasting love. Several times when my wife visited me while out on the tour, the wardrobe people dressed us in the mummy outfits and we danced on the stage while Howard sang that song. It was fun, but our marriage wasn't everlasting.

On the first night, Charlie and I came back from the hotel a little early to prep for the short ride, see a little of the show and just be close in case someone needed something. When Charlie entered the bus, there were six bowls of wilting lettuce on his counter. He tidied up the bus and ended up tossing out the salads. When his artist came on board after the show, he was upset Charlie had thrown them out. I wouldn't have eaten the brown lettuce in those bowls myself, I thought.

To try and make good of the situation, a local guy told Charlie of a Denny's restaurant a few blocks away. Charlie checked and the angry tour manager assured him we were going to not be leaving for a while. Charlie headed out in the direction the local guy gave him, and I went to watch a movie in my coach, do some paperwork and wait for the load out to end. I offered to go with Charlie, but he turned me down.

Twenty minutes later, my door opened and the tour manager said in his British accent, "Where's Charlie?"

I told him where Charlie went. "Bloody great!" he explained, change of plans, "We want to go now."

We had no cell phones. How did we get along without those things? So we waited and waited and we were all starting to think something had happened to him when he appeared in a cab with a sack full of lettuce. The bowls he threw away were just Styrofoam bowls with plain lettuce in them. He returned with these really nice wooden bowls and also carrying a grocery bag with several heads of lettuce.

Poor Charlie. He arrived back thinking he was a hero with fresh lettuce. It turned out the lettuce wasn't organic so Charlie was in deeper shit than when he left. Wrong lettuce, and they had wanted to leave for almost an hour. Lesson learned: Be careful with what you throw away.

CHAPTER 3 | A TASTE OF MEAT AND A FUTURE LIFE

Before getting into the bus business, there was nothing more that I wanted than to get back into driving in the entertainment industry. I was driving trucks transporting general freight, which wasn't what I wanted to be doing. Show hauls were far apart, and the goal was to get back to something a little more exciting. An English band with a French name, Depeche Mode, played a big part in reaching my goal.

A trucking company representative called me one day and told me that his company had an entertainment division that was expanding. Paramount Transportation was a household moving company, and at one time, the busiest mover of military households. Jeff asked me to lease my truck to their company. He knew of my reputation with the Barbara Mandrell Tour. He explained his company was the main equipment transporter for country singer George Strait. He told me of all the work they were getting in the entertainment business and explained that I could be right in the middle of their growth plans if I would join their team.

Thinking this could be right where I needed to be, I leased my truck to his company. My first assignment, after handshakes, was to pick up equipment for the 1985 "Some Great Reward" Depeche Mode Tour. I had never heard of Depeche Mode and couldn't find out much about them at the time. But a band was a band, and I was grateful.

I met their crew at a shipping dock outside New York City where containers with the show gear had been sent. We spent the day unloading two 40-foot containers onto the ground and putting everything into my 48' drop-deck electronic van. It took several frustrating tries, but the crew came up with a suitable pack. I traveled that night to Washington, D.C. to the Warner Theater for a couple of days of rehearsals. The bus driver and I were the only Americans on the tour, and I met him when I arrived at the Warner. The crew went out after the first day's work and everyone was invited. I stayed close to the only other American as the crew attacked an Indian restaurant. Put an Englishman in any city and he will find an Indian restaurant. That's all there is to it.

We had fun getting to know each other, and the partying lasted into the late hours that first night. The Depeche crew had been touring around the world and had already established their inside jokes. The bus driver and I were readily accepted into their fold. We headed out through America having a great time doing shows and partying on the off days. I was pretty impressed with the way the band grew as we traveled. It was nothing short of amazing.

Their popularity exploded right before our eyes in the middle of the tour. Each show was a sellout with crowds exceeding the capacities of the venues they were playing. Their album, "Some Great Reward," was selling everywhere we went. We worked the East Coast, went into Canada for a couple of shows and then through the Midwest down to Texas, then west to California. Time flew, we were having so much fun. The friendships made on that tour have lasted ever since.

When the tour was over, the trucking company told me they didn't have any more shows at the time to transport. They offered me a load of furniture to deliver to Texas from California where I had ended the tour. Furniture? I refused that and explained I was in the entertainment division, find me some band gear to transport, I demanded. I wasn't going to get sucked back into hauling freight or furniture. Well, that didn't sit well with them, and after several arguments, I had to cave in order to pay for the fuel on my cross-country trip back to their office. Once I got to Dallas, I was cornered by a company manager. "You leased your truck to our company," he said in my face. "That means you haul what we tell you to haul. It's not your choice. You don't call the shots. You got that?"

I guess I could have fought back, but I noticed a shotgun leaning on the wall next to his chair. Who knew what this guy was capable of? During our "conversation" he had even touched it a few times. All I wanted was to get out of that office. Once I got home with an empty truck, he gave me a call. He had another freight load. I figured a few hundred miles was well out of shooting range.

"Go fuck yourself," I said and hung up the phone.

Depeche Mode made it back to the States for another short tour in bigger venues. They were getting bigger by the minute, and I jumped back on tour with them. Once again, they sold out shows everywhere we went with the band playing a packed-out gig at Madison Square Garden at the end of the leg.

I tried to find my own shows to haul while I was transporting gear for Arkansas company M.P. Productions to shows they had lined up. I had made a turn to the West Coast and got back home in time to pull a series of rhythm and blues shows. On one of the show dates in Mississippi, I was in the load-in area of the coliseum in Biloxi. It was a nice day out, and I had hand-washed my truck and was drying it off when a large guy with a loud voice approached me.

"That is a beautiful truck," he bellowed. I had the hood open, and he could see how clean the motor area was. The door was open with my stereo turned up. The inside was clean, and everything about the truck was sparkling.

"Damn, I wish I could get my drivers to take care of my equipment like this," he continued.

I smiled because I knew I always put extra effort into keeping my truck or anything I drove looking like it was brand new. He introduced himself — "Mario Martinez" — as we shook hands. He explained that he ran a fleet of buses for a company called Gristmill Coach from Pensacola, Florida. We yapped for a few minutes with him telling me he had a fleet, and a few of them were the buses that the crews and bands were riding in on this tour. I listened to him for a few minutes as I continued to dry my truck. Finally, he gave me his business card.

"If you ever want to drive a bus, just call me and I will put you in one in a heartbeat," he said.

"Trucking is my forte, and I enjoy it," I responded. He laughed as he walked away. I tossed his card into my truck and lost it somewhere. We finished our series of shows, and within a few days I was back to hauling freight to various destinations.

M.P. had another series of shows with several other different R&B acts several months later. While in Albany, Georgia, at the Municipal Auditorium doing a show, I had unloaded and started taking care of my truck when, over my shoulder, I heard Mario's unforgettable voice approaching.

"God damn! You're still polishing on that truck!"

He had a bus driver with him and started pointing to the various places I had cleaned my truck and making comments to him as he followed me around the truck. I think the driver wasn't that impressed and rolled his eyes a couple of times. Once again Mario made a comment about me driving one of his buses, and once again I explained I was doing what I thought was best for me. He gave me another business card.

"If you change your mind just call me." Yada, yada, I put his card in my briefcase and went on with my business. I finished that series of shows and hooked back up to a refrigerated trailer and took off hauling food and freight.

Times in the trucking business were tough, and freight rates were weak. Fuel prices had risen above a dollar a gallon. The interest rate was over 20 percent on loans. It seemed the harder I trucked, the worse it got for me. In less than two years I had trucked more than 200,000 miles and was worn out. After missing a payment on my truck, I started thinking trucking wasn't as fun as it used to be. Taking more speed to try and catch up only worsened the problem, and before long I missed a second payment. My investor called one day to ask what the problem was and gave me an ultimatum of keeping the payments up or losing the truck. After a few more weeks of struggling along, I started looking for a way to bow out of my deal with the investor.

I made contact with a company in Elk Grove Village that specialized in entertainment transportation. Upstaging is the largest trucking company in the world specializing in entertainment transportation. Upstaging had grown out of a lighting company that was based in the Chicago area. Robin, a young lady who was managing the company at the time, took my call and gave me the details of what it would take to be a driver for Upstaging. She was familiar with my name and what I had been doing and explained that I could fit in with the Upstaging team. My investor took control of the truck and within a few days I was on a plane to Chicago to start a new angle on this entertainment transportation thing.

Robin explained that I was going to go on tour with The Smiths, a British group whose lead singer named Morrissey. The tour was called "The Queen is Dead." I was driven over to Ryder Truck Rentals to pick up a tractor and head for Toronto, Canada, where the North American leg of the tour was starting. The truck was ugly to me after driving my beautiful Kenworth that I had tried to own. We argued about it for a few, and I felt stuck with it. I needed the work, so I loaded my gear into the truck and took off for Canada.

The Smiths' previous album had been titled "Meat is Murder." The band members and many of the European crew were vegetarians, so it was announced to the American crew members that there would be no meat served in catering. All the Americans on the tour were meat eaters and were not too happy. Eugene Holmes, one of the bus drivers, was a unique individual and said he had a plan for the carnivores. The crew bus driver on the Barbara Mandrell tour had been Jimmy Holmes, Eugene's younger brother. I had met Eugene a couple times. He was a large man with a beard who always wore overalls. He looked like something from a hillbilly farm. He was a great guy and had a good heart, always making jokes and playing innocent tricks on people.

Eugene went out and bought a grill, and every day someone would hit a store and buy steaks and burgers to go along with the great vegetables that were being served in catering. Of course, this pissed off the band when their bus would pull up and Eugene would be out cooking large slabs of meat on the grill. Eugene would tell them to "piss off," a British term he used whenever someone would complain to him. Meat was an issue throughout the tour.

We rolled through the Canadian leg hitting Toronto, Ottawa and Montreal before heading back into the states to Boston, NYC and other places, but the meat issue continued until we got to Cleveland.

The Public Hall in Cleveland is an older building that has a full theatrical style stage that splits the entire room. On the south end of the building is a theater where music or theatrical events can be performed. On the north side of the building is an arena-style room. The stage splits the room with only a sound-proof curtain separating the two venues under one roof. It's unique in its construction, and The Smiths were performing on the theater side of the venue. On the day of our show, a convention was going on in the arena side featuring... wait for it... outdoor grills. All the modern grills of the day were being displayed in the arena, and every vendor was cooking meat at their displays. Beef, pork and chicken were being cooked and with more than 50 or 60 vendors in the room the smell of grilled meat was overbearing, even to the meat eaters on the tour. There was a lot of complaining about the situation, but there was nothing the band or Belkin Productions, the promoters of the show, could do about it. When the band arrived, there was such a fuss that I thought the show would be canceled, but it went on as scheduled. The meat eaters on the tour laughed our asses off for that one.

Each night Morrissey took to the stage and would start encouraging people to come up on the stage with him about halfway through the show. The crews and local security would try to keep the crowds off the stage, but some nights it was impossible. This caused an incredible amount of drama with everyone, because as soon as someone would get on the stage, hundreds more would start heading for the stage just to get a touch of Morrissey and dance around like idiots. The band gear would get damaged, and some things would come up missing. As the tour moved west, the problem seemed to get worse as Morrissey seemed to make it a game. There were a few nights when the show had to be stopped all together, and there were a few more where the band never made it back to the stage because of the damage that might have happened that night. At the Irvine Meadows show in Laguna Hills, California, so many fans attacked the stage that the promoter and local authorities wouldn't let the show continue. It was unlike anything I had ever seen. The seats were empty and the stage was full of fans.

One of the problems with the truck I was driving was that Ryder didn't have too many GMC Generals for rent or lease in their fleet. When we had started the tour, the air conditioning in my truck broke. It was July and August, so the temps met the typical summer standard. The Ryder shops in America didn't have parts to fix it, and the international truck dealers around the nation needed a couple of days to fix the problem. Trucking management told me to just ride on with it. They were working from an air-conditioned office in Chicago. It became an issue for me, especially as we took the tour west toward Southern California and Arizona where the temps were topping 100 degrees every day.

After reaching the West Coast, the tour headed east again toward Florida with shows along the way in Phoenix, Denver, Houston, Dallas, and New Orleans. There were rumors among the crew that the band was partying a lot and they weren't getting along. In September, The Smiths had a show scheduled in the Bayfront Arena in St. Petersburg, Florida. Just before the show, word started spreading among the crew that a band member was missing and couldn't be found. When it was time for the band to take the stage, they didn't have a full band, and the show was canned. The crew reloaded everything, and we headed to Miami where the next show was scheduled. The band member was still missing, and rumors of what had happened to him were rampant. With all the issues before the band, the tour was canceled.

On the day the show was supposed to be in Miami, many crew members had met in the hotel bar. Few other customers were around and part of the crew was drinking their weight in booze. The bar was downstairs in the hotel, and behind the bar was a gigantic window that looked into the swimming pool outside. We could see all the bodies swimming in the pool as we sat there drinking. One of our crew guys, who everyone referred to as "Rooster," because of his red hair, left the bar. Not too long after, a woman sitting in the bar screamed. She was the first to notice Rooster in the pool sliding down in front of the window naked with his shlong pressed against the window. Everyone on the crew went nuts with laughter and hoots and hollers. Rooster was immediately arrested and taken away, and we were all asked to leave the bar. What a way to end a tour.

When I called the office, Robin announced that she had another tour to send me on right away. She said I would be driving the same truck, and I turned her down and told her I wasn't interested. I took the truck to a Ryder shop and headed to the house. When I got home, my girlfriend at the time insisted I get a job in town and settle down. I got a job right away that I wasn't really interested in and tried the home life. I felt like I was missing things, and one day while going through some paperwork, I came across the business card that Mario with Gristmill Coach had given me.

I called him and identified myself as "that truck driver who took such good care of my truck." I told him I had gotten rid of the truck, and he laughed.

"Are you ready to drive a bus?"

I told him I thought I was, and the next day I was on a plane to Pensacola to become a bus driver. Not too long after that I didn't have a girlfriend anymore.

SOMETIMES THE JOB BLOWS

When you work the night shift, your evening is in the morning. When that sun creeps through the blinds, many people rise, open the fridge and crack open some eggs. For those who clock out in the morning, cracking open a beer is more likely. Seeing a bus driver sip on a cold one at 8 a.m. to unwind is not an uncommon thing. In the 1980s, there were no drug tests for drivers, so occasionally I would sit back and relax with a joint.

One morning while on tour, I was sitting in the front lounge of a coach after a long and grueling overnight drive. Everyone was off the bus and headed into the arena to start his or her day. I did my normal cleanup activities and sat down at the table in the front lounge. There were some reefer roaches and unfinished joints in the ashtray. Common knowledge is you don't throw away passenger drugs. If weed is left in the ashtray, anyone can have it – a typical unwritten bus rule. I grabbed a half-smoked joint and fired it up. I was enjoying the subdued atmosphere waiting on the time to head to the hotel with the other drivers. That's when the real rest would come to gear up for our day's work – the coming night's run.

The quiet was disturbed when one of the roadies riding my bus abruptly swung open the door. He shot me a weird look as he passed me going into the bunk area. He returned shortly and sat down at the table across from me. A large clear bag of cocaine in his hand. With a coffee spoon, he took a scoop and spread it on the table. Roadies doing drugs in the '80s, whether to party or to wake up for work, was not an uncommon sight. He didn't say much as he chopped and prepared his lines. I sat there taking a few drags on the joint looking out the window.

My attention was drawn to him because of the desire he expressed as he prepared to top his morning coffee. His tongue was slightly sticking out in anticipation as he drew the two skinny lines with the laminate backstage pass hanging around his neck. He rolled up a hundred dollar bill, leaned over, and in one breath, snorted the first line down, kicking his head back and wiping his nose. I looked at him, not saying a word, and touched my nostril. It can be embarrassing getting caught with that little white ring around your nose or cocaine boogers, as the condition is called. I took another drag on the joint and was squashing it out in the ashtray when he took his other line. Snorting cocaine can be similar to taking a drag off a joint. You draw the blow into your nose and hold your breath a second and let it out like you would the smoke from a joint. As he raised his head again, the veins in his neck protruding from still holding his breath, he said, "People who smoke pot are STUPID."

He exhaled and licked the side of his laminated badge, straightened it around his neck and started to pack up his drugs. I just looked at him and said nothing as I touched my nose again. Another ring of residue outlined his nostril. He wiped his nose again, put his stuff away and hit the door. With the morning rush over, it was time for him to get back to work and time for me to go to the hotel for 12 hours of rest.

CHAPTER 4 | POWER OF A WOMAN

Burt Hasselton, a good friend and a well-known driver from Michigan, was assigned with me in 1987 to drive The Powerful Women of Wrestling, better known as POWW. Burt had been driving buses for years. Once I heard him tell another young driver that he had pissed on more highways than that driver had driven on. He had been driving coaches for years, taking care of The Beach Boys back in the day, among others. I hadn't been in buses long, and Burt gave me a few pointers about how to approach things.

POWW had evolved from the Gorgeous Ladies of Wrestling (GLOW) in Las Vegas, and after the split, POWW had moved its headquarters to Indianapolis, Indiana, where the producer and owner, David McLane, lived. McLane had thought this whole group into being and even performed as the ringside announcer.

I was driving Beachcomber, the older model Eagle that was my first bus to drive, and Burt was driving one named Mermaid. Beautiful artwork of ocean things, and of course mermaids, decorated the sides of his bus. How perfect for a bunch of lady wrestlers. That old Eagle was the grand product of two Greyhound buses that had each been in accidents. One had front damage, and one had rear damage. The bus owner had chopped them in half and made one good one out of it. After some refurbishing, he put it out to lease. Its crooked stance made the tires go through some tough times, but it worked. For a period of time, many Nashville companies pursued this practice.

We arrived in Indianapolis the night before having to pick up the group of women. Burt and I had followed each other up from Florida and decided to get to the pick-up point in the middle of the night before the next morning's traffic. We would just nap in the coaches until the next morning. We arrived at IUPUI, a college in Indy where the girls were living and practicing, around three in the morning. We weren't supposed to be there until 11 a.m., our pick-up time. We parked up close to a dorm we had been told they were in, and I started to do a little clean up on the old bus when there was a knock on the door. When I opened it, a couple of the wrestlers were staring at me.

"Is this our new bus?" one of them asked. They were laughing and giggling, obviously a little tipsy. I put on a business face.

"Why, yes it is."

"Can we see it?"

"Sure. Why not? It's your new house."

I pushed the door open and stepped back so they could enter. The second girl in the door reached out as she entered and grabbed the collar of my shirt, pulling me toward her.

"I'm going to fuck you before anyone else," she said in the way only a woman wrestler can.

I'm sure I turned three shades of red. She shoved me backward a little and took off, going through the bus, acting like a happy kid in a new playground. The girls hung out for a few minutes and then disappeared into the night. Burt and I thought it was going to be a weird tour compared to the normal rock 'n' roll tour, if there is such a thing.

After several days of rehearsals, the tour was kicking off in Dayton, Ohio, and I was walking around the arena through the backstage area. There, I met Queenie, the largest woman in the world, or close to it. Queenie was a passenger on Burt's bus. Queenie was so big she had to sleep in the floor of the bus since there were no bunks big enough for her. She was standing by the entrance about to make her appearance to the crowd. She had been in show business for a long time when I met her, the star of 25 films and hundreds of shows. She did roller derby and Slam-A-Grams... OUCH! ... in the Los Angeles area. She was a singer, comedienne and stuntwoman. Queenie did it all. She had been in movies like Mel Brooks' "Spaceballs" and in Aerosmith's "Love In An Elevator" video dancing with the world's smallest man on her shoulders. She was a hoot!

I was wearing a sports coat, starched white shirt, pressed jeans and cowboy boots. As I was walking by, she reached out, grabbed me by the head and pulled me against her huge boobs. She started beating my head against her chest in a Tarzan-style fashion, and I couldn't make her stop.

"Stop-op-op it-it-it Queen-en-en-ney!!"

And she is yelling right back at me.

"Why are you dressed up, you fuck?" I know she screamed a bunch of other obscenities at me, but I was more concerned about being tossed around like a rag doll. She pushed me away and I almost fell down. She then turned and charged out into the arena, and the crowd started cheering and sneering at her. Weird to be treated like a rag doll by a large woman! I learned from her later that she was just "getting into character."

We stayed in Dayton for a couple of days and then moved on to the next town. We stayed in each city for a few days at a time while the girls practiced their moves for shows and that week's taping. As the days went by, several of the girls and I started hanging out in the towns we were staying in. We would eat and go out to the bars, museums, and parks together. We made some outings to lakes in South Carolina and Georgia.

We spent several weeks in Florida hotels that were on or near the beach as we made the rounds through the Sunshine State. As the time went on, one of the girls in the group and I started getting close. We enjoyed each other's company, and in every town, we were hitting the streets seeing all the sites together. Philly, New York City, Cleveland, everywhere we went. We spent many nights dancing and days sightseeing when not working. Most nights there were no driving duties for me.

In Atlanta one night, about eight of the wrestlers and I went to the Limelight

Club, a popular party spot, and partied for a few hours. Everyone was drinking heavily, and one of the wrestlers named Pocahontas started to get sick.

One of the girls yelled, "Let's get her out of here!" We headed for the door, a girl under each of Poco's arms. At the door, bouncers saw us coming and the look on Poco's face and they swung open the entrance as fast as they could. As everyone crossed the threshold, Poco heaved chunks at least 20 feet in front of her and down the entrance way. There were dozens of people waiting to get in, and they were positioned along the side of the wall. When she blew chunks, they all hugged the wall to avoid the mess.

"EEEEEEEWWWWW!" everyone screamed.

A bouncer, who had probably seen it all before, yelled out, "ANOTHER SATISFIED CUSTOMER!"

This was the way it was with this group – a great time had by all. The tour went on for several months with TV tapings of the matches and interviews of the wrestlers, all the things you would imagine in a wrestling world. We traveled the country with the girls doing their work in big venues like the old Omni in Atlanta, an armory in South Carolina and Hammond, Indiana, a big wrestling town. Much fun can and was had traveling the country with 24 women wrestlers.

When the tour was over, I went out on a run with a country band. We traveled to a bar in Four Corners, Texas. Find that one on the map, friend. No, not the one close to Houston.

Michelle, the wrestler I had befriended, drove out from California and met me. She found Four Corners, which was pretty impressive. She followed me back to Atlanta where we parked her car at a dealership, and she hit the road with me for several more days on tour.

The next year we went out again to film a second season with POWW, but the practice facilities had been moved to Miami Beach, Florida. I went down between tours and stayed with Michelle in an Art Deco hotel right across the street from the beach. A delectable location, and what fulfilling times I had living on Miami Beach, hanging out with the wrestlers, partying and seeing the sites for several weeks before we headed out across America again to start a new season. Michelle was starting to become more than a friend. A year later she became my wife.

CHAPTER 5 | STEALING THE STAR

One thing you have to realize about driving buses for celebrities is that like any other business where the goal is making money, someone will come along and cut your throat to get ahead. Sometimes this is not a "do a good job, work hard, get paid" kind of environment.

Every industry is like this, and I saw my share of shady deals driving trucks, but the ability to rub elbows with all types of celebrities and to be paid while doing it can turn some in the business into monsters. Being able to service the biggest acts gives one mega bragging rights, and in the '80s, it seemed it could trump even the money being made.

I hadn't been driving coaches for long when I got the call to see bus owner Mr. Grist about an opportunity that I would have been crazy to turn down. Mr. Grist was the head of Gristmill Coach, and on top of that, he was a prominent figure in Mississippi government. A wealthy Southern businessman and a politician? That isn't always a good combination. I went to see Mr. Grist and his manager, a man named Mario, who hailed from New Orleans and was the one who had given me his business card.

Mario is a very loud man who must enjoy his loudness because he cannot stop talking. He talks so much that you want to buy whatever he is selling just so he'll shut up. Within a few months, I came to know him as a loveable guy, and we shared some great times. But that didn't mean he wasn't above getting his cut of money by any means necessary.

I walked in and saw both of them sitting, waiting for me.

"Sit down, Jerry," Mr. Grist said.

As much as Mario loved to talk, Mr. Grist was almost the opposite. He didn't waste time, and he didn't mince words. I hadn't sat down for more than a second when the offer came up. "How would you like to go on the Eddie Murphy tour?"

What? Eddie Murphy? Those two words, especially uttered in the late '80s, were about as big as one could get. Murphy was the hottest comedian and on his way to becoming one of the biggest movie stars in the world. This was a man who revived *Saturday Night Live* and became an icon before he was 25 years old. I think the first words that came out of my mouth were, "Holy crap!"

Eddie was about to head out on the "Raw" tour, which wound up turning into a huge concert movie, which in turn made him an even bigger star. Hearing those words sent my mind racing. Not only would I be involved with a first rate tour, driving one of the biggest celebrities in the world and his entourage, but I knew I would instantly be upgraded to a better coach and a better lifestyle. This could only lead to better things. How could I say no?

I didn't get a chance to say anything before Mario chimed in.

"If you want to do it, Jerry, you'll give me five hundred dollars."

There's always a catch.

"You give me $500, and I'll put you on the tour right now."

Everything I was just thinking stopped in midair. Five hundred dollars? I was thinking that these guys wanted me to pay them in order to get the job?

"Wait a minute." My mouth finally caught up with my brain. "You want me to pay you to go on tour?"

"Oh, yeah, baby!" Mario had a way with words.

I hadn't been thinking about negotiating for a driving job. I was definitely put on the spot. So I said the first thing I could think of.

"Well, I better think about that."

Mario jumped right back in.

"You better not take too long 'cause there is a long line of guys that would jump at this chance."

Was there a long line? There had to be. If I got this excited about the tour, there had to be plenty of people that wouldn't even consider not paying Mario. Still, I needed some fresh ears. I went into the next office to call my girlfriend.

"How long is the tour?" Michelle asked.

I told her.

"How much do you get paid a day?"

I told her.

"For how long?"

I told her.

"Then go back inside and pay the man his $500."

It was that simple. I paid Mario, took the job and learned a mega-lesson about the new career I had chosen, mainly that I was going have to find a new bus owner to work for, one that didn't charge me to make him money.

So it all came together. After the money changed hands, I was assigned the Murphy tour. I was introduced to George Fitzgerald or "Georgie," as everyone called him. He had been Eddie's first bus driver ever since Eddie had become a big touring act. The Raw tour would be his third go around with Eddie, and I was now along for the ride.

I knew I didn't want to screw this up, so I listened to everything Georgie told me. I knew what was expected of me and what I should expect from my passengers and how to respond. That could be the most important advice.

So the assignments were handed out. I was to drive Eddie's brothers, Charlie and Vernon. Charlie became famous in his own right a few years later, appearing on Dave Chappelle's show and writing with Eddie. But for now, it was his brothers, two security guards and a couple luggage handlers on my bus. The five-bus convoy started in Florida and headed to St. Louis to get our passengers at the St. Louis airport. At the time of the pickup, it was just about getting our passengers from the airport to the hotel along with their luggage. It ended up that there was so much luggage, we needed a truck to come back and transport it.

We then went through general introductions at the airport and back at the hotel. Needless to say, everything was going according to plan and I thought everything would be just fine.

The next morning, we had our buses in line along Market Street outside the Omni Hotel located in the old train station in downtown St. Louis. Everything was ready for the hundred-mile drive to the first show in Carbondale, Illinois. All the drivers stood on the top of the steps of the train station to admire our fleet, while waiting for the "talent" to come down from their rooms. We were standing around, talking the standard operational bullshit waiting on our passengers when a brand new incredible looking Eagle bus drove by. It slowed as it cased the other buses in line. Then it sped off and around the corner.

"Wow! Who the hell is that?" one of the drivers asked, goggling the beautiful coach. "I think I recognize him," Georgie said, adding, "He's probably not lost." That put a concerned look on his face.

Joe Mooney, AKA Mickey Moe Johnson the Social Director, wasn't lost at all. He was driving in circles doing what his bus owner told him to do. The coach was owned by one of the Calhoun brothers' Florida Coach companies. Joe had been driving entertainment coaches for years and knew the ends and outs of the business very well. He knew what he had to do that day to turn Eddie Murphy's attention to his beautiful new coach.

As the Eagle rounded the corner and slowed, passing the fleet again, the doors opened at the hotel, the security came out, and soon after, the entire posse emerged. Eddie was flanked by his troops, and we all began heading for the buses.

As I walked across the sidewalk to open the bay doors on the passenger side of my coach, Joe's Eagle passed my coach on the other side one last time, slowly creeping along. I was third in line behind Eddie's bus and the management bus.

Eddie's bus was first and was driven by Chris B., a friend and fellow driver who was about to shake hands with Mr. Murphy and welcome him aboard. The Eagle came around the front of Chris' unit pulling into the empty space in front of Chris' bus in a jackknifed angle, the door opened, and Mickey Moe jumped out onto the sidewalk after setting his brakes.

"Hey BOSS! You shouldn't be riding on that bus! You should be riding on this one!" Eddie was on the steps of the Van Hool bus driven by Chris. His personal items were on there along with his luggage. All he had to do was step on, close the doors, and the tour would be under way. But he looked over at Mickey Moe and his beautiful shining bus, and for a second, all bets were off.

Eddie looked inside the Van Hool and then walked over to the Eagle. There was no comparison. Our buses were nice, real nice, but they were no match for Mickey Moe's brand new bus. The artwork made it a lot flashier than the one he was standing in front of. Eddie walked to the door of the Eagle, looking at the beautiful artwork on the side as he walked toward the door. He went inside and never came out. In a few minutes, Eddie's belongings were transferred to the Eagle, and Chris was left with his bus, as we pulled away and headed to the first show.

The rest of us followed the Eagle out of town and started the tour. Chris headed back to where he had come from without being able to dispute what was happening. I couldn't believe what had just happened and realized even more what a tough business I had adopted for a career choice. Joe pinned the phrase: "No one ever said the life of a rock 'n' roll bus driver was going to be easy."

Florida Coach and Mickey Moe had taken advantage of a situation that wouldn't exist today. Now there are agreements, contracts and cash deposits. But back in the '80s, it was just about making the sale. Mickey Moe made it. And I learned many lessons from the tour and from Joe. Years later, he told me, "I was just following orders." I never did find out if Chris paid $500 to get on that tour.

THE FULL MONTY

As I started working on larger tours, I jumped onto the American Music Tour, a country gig with a rock show attitude. It wasn't the Rolling Stones, but the crew clicked as well as one for a big act like the Stones. The tour featured five or six acts such as Janie Fricke, T.G. Sheppard, Sylvia and a few other up-and-comers from Nashville. It was a short run – 10 to 12 days or so – but it had a big production complete with big sound, big lights and dates in Louisiana, Texas and Oklahoma.

When the tour headed to Texarkana, Texas, for a show in the city that borders Arkansas, Janie's bus broke down, so they had to improvise. A rented camper from a local Texas RV dealer helped them at least make the show on time. The onslaught of jokes from the crew and drivers was inevitable.

At the time, T.G. Sheppard had a couple of the nicest buses on the road, one of them being a Marathon. They were all dolled up with starry space scenes painted on both sides and T.G. I and T.G. II painted sharply next to the entrance doors. T.G. I was for T.G. Sheppard, and T.G. II was for his band. Before the day was over, someone had grabbed a pillowcase and taped it to the camper with the logo T.G. III painted on it.

It seemed that Janie and her band were the brunt of many of the jokes on this tour, all in good fun. By the time we arrived in Lubbock, Texas, the jokes were getting out of hand. The crew guys emptied a rigging case just before Janie was to take the stage and convinced a well-hung local guy to get naked in it. How they figured out he was well hung was not information I'd been privy to. They constructed a sign proclaiming, "WE LOVE YOU JANIE!" and they wheeled the case to the side of the stage. The venue had seats and a walking area between the stage and where the crowd was sitting in the front row so they could look up without getting neck cramps.

Janie was in the middle of one of her hit songs when four crew guys rolled the case between the first row and the stage. Just as she was hitting a high note, the case was opened, and the well-hung local guy sat up and put the sign over his face. The crew rolled the case from stage right to stage left. The crowd, not being able to see into the case, never caught a glimpse of the well-hung local guy. Janie, however, got the full monty without missing a beat. She just smiled, pointed her finger and kept singing.

Hard work with a little play is a good way to earn a buck.

CHAPTER 6 | ROLLING WITH ROCK ROYALTY

1988 was a very good year for rock 'n' roll. I got to roll with some of the biggest acts around. In addition to jumping on tour with R.E.M. for a stretch, I got the call to work with Van Halen. You didn't like rock 'n' roll if you didn't like Van Halen, and I love rock 'n' roll. They were definitely a favorite of mine by the time I had joined the tour.

One reason Van Halen was so awesome, at least to guys like me, is that they had the perfect music to blast in your car while driving. A friend at home, affectionately known as D-Day, blasted them non-stop on his car stereo, and he had one of the loudest and clearest in the neighborhood. Getting stoned and riding in the back seat of his car while he drove like a maniac was like a rite of passage. We cruised around town, looking for the parking lots where kids congregated, and he would always be playing Van Halen at the highest levels he could. It rocked! When we listened back in those days, David Lee Roth was the lead singer, but when I joined the tour, the front man was Sammy Hagar. When I got that call, I thought, "I wonder what D-Day would think about this?"

I had dropped another tour and headed to Lexington, Kentucky, where the band was rehearsing for their second leg of the tour. Van Halen had just finished up the Monsters of Rock tour with groups such as Metallica, Scorpions, Dokken and Kingdom Come. After that tour finished, they went out on their own to support their album, "OU812." It was going to be an American trek and then over to Japan.

I was assigned to take care of the backline crew and some sound guys from Audio Analysts, one of the best sound crews in the business. You knew it would be a good tour if these guys were working on it. The backline crew consisted of drum and guitar techs, and one of the techs on my bus was Zeke Clark, Eddie Van Halen's guitar tech. Zeke was tall and lanky, and since he was the man behind the man, the world seemed to revolve around him. Since I was the new guy, I was going to be assigned backline, and since I had only been with this company for a year, I thought I was getting thrown under the bus, so to speak. The other drivers wanted a more mellow experience. I was going to drive the party bus.

When I talked to the lead driver, he started giving me the lowdown. Basically, he gave me the lowdown about Zeke. Oh joy! A sensitive roadie! Zeke was the one who designed Eddie Van Halen's most famous guitar, now named after its player.

"If Zeke ain't happy, nobody's happy," was the company line.

I got an earful about how weird and sensitive Zeke was and how I needed to take care of him and the other party animals. I was unimpressed.

"As long as they walk out on their own, I don't care who rides back there," I said. "I'm here for the check. As long as the check doesn't bounce, be as weird as you want. I'll take care of anyone. The normal way I do my job."

There was a joke going around with our crew that if Zeke hadn't been born, there would be no touring industry. Basically, Zeke invented it, came up with the idea one night at a party. Despite the joking, I started thinking of ways I could get him on my side. Anything to make a tour run better. I didn't need a sensitive roadie worrying about my driving skills or my habits.

I was lucky in one sense because I had a fairly new Florida Coach, Model 10 Eagle. It was in mint condition, was smooth and had a strong motor. I loved it. There were these absolutely eye-catching murals painted on the side, and the interior had slightly dark wood and brown carpet. It was a beauty. No matter what the ride looked like, my main concern was Zeke. I needed to figure out how to make this relationship work, and I was working on a way to offset any aggravations he may send my way. Hell, I was just stoked to see Van Halen live.

I arrived at Rupp Arena on a Thursday and got myself acquainted with the tour management. I got all my credentials, and I was able to watch a rehearsal. Van Halen was tweaking this song, rehashing that one, and I, along with a few members of the crew, were lucky to be getting a personal show. This was definitely one of the perks, seeing something that no fan gets to see, the band goofing off and playing great music when no one else is around. The next day was show day.

My day started late since we weren't on the road yet, and I had to take the backline over to the gig. I grabbed nine guys and introduced myself and made my first run. With that out of the way, I went back to the hotel for some sleep. I wanted to get a nap so I could come back and see the first show. The upcoming overnight's drive to Cincinnati was a whopping two hours. I wasn't in any danger of being exhausted. I got back for the show and was reminded of another great aspect of the Van Halen experience – beautiful women, who didn't hesitate to flash their breasts. Many sat on their boyfriends' shoulders, which seems a bit odd to me to let your girlfriend show off her breasts to a rock star, who could snatch her up with a nod of the head or a point of the finger. Either way, it was a good show.

I got back to the bus to prep and got my pizza ration for the night. Pizza on a tour bus after a show is a given. I sat in the front lounge table of the coach when Zeke walked in. We had shaken hands already, but this was the first one-on-one time I spent with him.

He gave me a look... a roadie look. On a regular show day, drivers don't usually return until the hour before they are going to drive.

"What are you doing here?" he asked in a way that only Zeke could ask. I just smiled.

"I came to watch you do your gig, man," I replied. "I heard you were the best guitar tech in the business." I had added a bit more Southern twang to my voice as we engaged in a bit of a staring contest. He tossed a few personal items on his bunk, grabbed a piece of pizza and plopped down at a table across from me. He took a bite and with his mouth full of pizza, he asked, "So how long have you been driving a bus?" He had the King Roadie tone in his voice, and so all notions of kissing his ass flew right out the window. I had to have some fun. I mustered up as much hillbilly in my voice as I could.

"Shucks, dis mah first day-uh," I said. "Way-ell, I mean my sec-unt day-uh. Yes-tir-day-uh wuz mah first day-uh when I drove hee-er." Then I grinned. Big Cheshire grin. Zeke dropped his pizza.

"What? You never drove a bus before?"

I kept the twang, but maybe not as severe as before.

"Naw. Last week, I was at a truck stop in Arkansas with a load of goats on my trailer when one of these fancy buses pulled up. I went over to look at it, and I told him how pretty it was. I said I wish I could drive something that pretty. Well, he must have been mad about something because he said he was quitting, and if I wanted the job I could have it. So we walked over to a phone and called the owner. That guy quit on the spot, and I drove the bus over there, and he told me to drive it over here, and now I'm here, and I'm real glad to be here." I put the twang back in my voice. "What'chur name agin?" I even finished with a traditional Scooby Doo giggle.

Zeke just stared at me for a second. He took another bite of pizza, threw the rest of it on the table.

"You're fucking joking me."

"Naw, it's all true!"

Zeke quickly walked out the door.

It was fun, but now I had to figure out how I would approach him when he came back. He didn't come back immediately though, so I walked around to see how the load out was going. Before a tour rolls away from its first show, it can take some time to get a hold of the truck-packing routine. Rupp Arena is also a pain to load and unload from, not a concert-friendly building.

I walked past the production office, and Frank, the production manager, yelled over at me.

"Bus driver! Come here!" He didn't know my name yet. He had a big crew with him. That was cool. But I could tell he was stressed.

"Listen," he said. "Do me a favor, and don't get Zeke all excited, will ya?" I should have figured Zeke would come here first. He made a beeline over to Frank to complain about me. Frank tried to assure him that I hadn't been a goat hauler the day before, but Zeke didn't seem that convinced. Apparently, he was tracking down the other passengers on my ride and informing them of my driving history. I figured that I wasn't fired, so I headed back to the bus. I sat down and waited for Zeke. When he showed up, I went right back into my newly donned persona.

"Dang, I wish they would hurry up. I want to drive this thing again."

"Shut up," Zeke said. "I know you're not new. So quit fucking around."

For some reason, my little interplay with him worked. We had a good relationship after that, and I was filled in on some of the great rock 'n' roll backstage stories that only a roadie like him could tell. He really is one of the most famous roadies I've ever driven. Just ask him.

Another tech that rode on my bus was Kevin D., Michael Anthony's bass guitar tech. Kevin had worked for a lot of bands, and he is respected in the industry. We had two shows in one town, and since I knew the bus wouldn't be moving at all, I decided to join the party for one night. I got to see the show and have more than a few drinks. Kevin knew I had seen plenty of shows from off the side of the stage, but I had never seen one from under the stage, so that's where we headed. That was where Kevin tuned the bass guitars while the show was going on.

Like a lot of big rock bands, Van Halen had an elaborate stage design. Kevin was under the stage, but he was off the floor. There was another part of the stage that was elevated above the rest where the musicians could run up, tower over the crowd and get them riled up. In Kevin's work station were racks of bass guitars. On the other side of the stage in a similar position was where Zeke worked. Kevin was like a surgeon for bass guitars. His carefully prepared workstation consisted of a table with a tablecloth draped over it. This gave him a clean slate to use his high-tech tools and do his work on the guitars.

As he did his job, he mixed in fun, too. There were two bottles of Jack Daniels sitting next to his cases, and they were easily accessible for Michael. He would reach down and grab it, take it on stage and take a swig or two during a song, all to the roaring approval of the crowd. This happened every night, and I was convinced that it wasn't 100 percent whiskey.

So this happened again. Michael grabbed the Jack bottle, kicked it back and bent back down to the area where Kevin and I were standing. He then handed me the bottle and gave me the universal "kick it back" sign. I turned the bottle up and tried to equal his input.

It wasn't tea!

Michael and Kevin had a hearty laugh at my expense, and Michael ran back out on stage while I was still coughing and choking.

A real rock 'n' roll show. I loved every minute of it.

CHAPTER 7 | THE LIP-SYNCER IN THE HAT

Did I know?

When people find out that I drove Milli Vanilli once upon a time, that's the first and only question that leaps to mind. The duo of Rob and Fab was the top selling musical act in the late 1980s. Then there was the scandal that broke out over their lip-syncing tour and the acceptance of a Grammy based on false pretenses.

Of course I knew. The day I arrived for the tour, I had to sign a contract, along with others, about keeping my mouth shut. Keep my mouth shut and make some good wages or blab blab and go looking for more work. I know lots of secrets if you want to call them that. I don't have a problem being quiet about what's going on behind or under the stage when the world is being entertained. What difference does it make? In my opinion, being entertained is the most important part. Fooling the public is what keeps them coming back. I had already driven several legs of the New Kids On The Block tour along with a few others who had drawn accusations of lip-syncing.

On the Milli Vanilli tour, I was assigned to drive a coach that had a recording studio in the rear. I transported the band that played on the stage with Rob and Fab. The front lounge was a normal tour bus setup with bunks in the hall, but the rear lounge was loaded with the most modern recording equipment available at the time. Assigned to drive the other bus on the tour with me was a good friend and mentor, Larry C. He had been T.J. Sheppard's driver a few years earlier on the American Tour.

After the shows each night as we drove to our next destination, Rob and Fab would usually get on my bus with the band and a tech and work on new material until the early morning hours. They had a great remix of a song by Deep Purple called "Hush" in the works. I would drive into the night while Rob, Fab and the band worked on new songs. Of course, there was partying, too. When they were tired, we would pull over, and the two stars would move to the other bus where they slept.

The tour started in Louisville, Kentucky, and after several days of rehearsals and a big ol' lip-syncing show, we headed east toward the bigger markets. Milli Vanilli was one of the last shows in the old Richfield Coliseum in Richfield, Ohio, just south of Cleveland. They were very popular, but of course, the question was always there. We had 60 shows on the bill, and all but one was sold out. There was even a festival show in Moncton, New Brunswick, Canada, which played to over 60,000 fans.

Some days, Rob was really working his way toward being a rock diva. One day in Shreveport, Louisiana, he grew a massive frown after I had laughed out loud at one of his insane ideas. The show had played my hometown the night before in a cow barn known as Barton Coliseum. Barton, along with several other arenas, was built in the early 1950s as some type of work project. Oklahoma City, Albuquerque, Shreveport and other Mid-South cities all have practically the same designed buildings, usually located at their fairgrounds.

One of the many teen fans that passed through the dressing room area that night had swiped one of Rob's favorite hats. It was shaped like the one Dr. Seuss' Cat in the Hat wears, but it had a rainbow of colors. He was furious, and he called for a meeting of all the people who pretty much were associated with him: tour manager, production manager, wardrobe, a couple of others, including me and L.C., the drivers.

I was in the back of the room with L.C. listening to Rob chew everyone out about the missing hat. He and I hid behind the others. Rob had a plan.

"I want a helicopter!" he screamed.

What? Everyone just sort of looked at each other.

"I want a helicopter that will fly me back to Arkansas. I want a car that will take me to this girl's address. I have her address. I am going to kick in that front door and get my hat back. Then I'm going to fly back to Shreveport and do the show tonight."

I laughed envisioning that happing in Conway, Arkansas, where apparently the thief lived. Unfortunately, when I laughed out loud, Rob got the crazy eyes, the "I'll kill you, motherfucker!" look. L.C. and I have had a good laugh about that one a time or two.

Maybe if Rob had known how their careers would come crashing down in a few months, he may have not worried about a hat. They did entertain the masses, but everyone behind the curtain, including me, yeah, we knew.

CHAPTER 8 | THE SHORT STRANGE TRIP

Not only did 1988 provide me the chance to work with Van Halen, the rock 'n' roll kings to me at the time, but the year gave me the chance to work with the jamband kings, the Grateful Dead.

I knew who they were. I enjoyed their music, but they weren't in the forefront of my musical tastes at the time. I'd heard it was one of the best tours to be on. When I got the assignment, I was looking forward to the run. I didn't care if they played polkas. A good tour is a good tour.

I arrived in Bloomington, Minnesota, the day before the show. First days are always crazy with everyone doing his or her best to get started on the right track. The Dead had many of the same crew for years, so everyone was comfortable with their jobs. Just like the band, they were easy going and laid back.

I was assigned to drive Robbie Taylor, the Dead's production manager. Robbie's regular driver wasn't available for some reason, so I was assigned the seat. Robbie is well known throughout the industry and has years of touring experience. We left Bloomington after midnight and headed for Alpine Valley, Wisconsin. Once we got out on the highway, Robbie came up to the jump seat with his glass of wine and stretched out. The jump seat in a Florida Coach Eagle was very large and designed in such a way that you could stretch your legs across the entryway. The windshields on the Model 10 Eagles were large, but overhead cabinets blocked the sky from the passenger's seat. He leaned back, drank his wine and observed my driving skills. By now, I was starting to notice the Deadheads en route to the next gig. I had passed enough of them to figure it out – hippies in beaten-up cars and vans weighed down with camping gear. I brought it up to Robbie, but it seemed to be an old hat for him. He started sharing the history of everything and everyone involving the Grateful Dead as he drank his wine. I asked him a few questions on things I'd heard over the years and drove on into the night passing Deadheads along the way.

Bob Dylan was already at Alpine doing a three-night stand. The Dead was then moving in for three nights. It was craziness like I have never seen at Alpine compared to the many times I've been there since. Thousands of people were camping in the parking lots. The roads getting into the venue were being closed for long periods of time to allow traffic to use both lanes going the same direction. It was a nightmare getting in and getting out. During our four days there, The Dead used a helicopter to fly the band and crew out to Lake Geneva Airport. From there we used cars to get to the hotel.

In 1988, the backstage area at Alpine was a bit of a pain. The load-in area has a steep ascent, which makes it tough on the trucks and buses to get to their positions. And it was all dirt at that time. But once you get the production in, everything is worth the effort. Alpine is a great place to see a show, and recent years have seen improvements to the venue.

The bus company whose bus I was driving also had the buses on the Dylan tour. The daughter of the owner was one of the drivers, and as we arrived, she was getting her golf clubs out and ready. You have to drive across the Alpine Valley Golf Course to get to the backstage area of the amphitheater. Several other people were following her lead and heading out to the course. I had yet to take up the game. Several other drivers didn't go, so I followed them around for a few minutes before heading out on my own to investigate the masses.

After the first show, we stayed over at the gig and slept in the buses. Sometime late in the night, Robbie and several others decided to head out to Barter Town. They named the camping area, where all the Deadheads camped, after the city in the Mad Max movie. We took golf carts out for fun and headed out to the camping area. It was easy to understand where the Barter Town name came from. Besides the constant roar of music on stereos and from people playing their own instruments, many of the Deadheads made things to sell to support their travels following the band. There was everything from food to shirts to jewelry and hats. And of course drugs. There was alcohol, acid, mushrooms, marijuana and almost anything else you could think of. The rumors were true.

There were Deadheads everywhere, and at two or three in the morning, the parties seemed to be peaking. Many were tripping on drugs and booze. It looked like a party from a '70s movie scene. As we rode around, many of the people recognized Robbie and some of the crew guys. We stopped at various parties and wheeled and dealed with the partygoers, getting our favors and trinkets. Girls seemed interested in our positions with the band. It was easy to strike up conversations with just about anyone. I watched all four of the shows at Alpine and got hooked on the jam sessions the band performed that weekend.

We went to Buckeye Lake after Alpine, and the convoy of Deadheads went with us. I passed many of the same ones remembering their vehicles. Some were very unique – converted buses and campers and many loaded down cars with supplies and people. After the Buckeye Lake show, we went to Pittsburgh, Saratoga, New York, Rochester, New York, and we finished out in Oxford Plains Raceway in Oxford, Maine.

At that time, I couldn't remember a tour that I had ever done that was more organized than the Grateful Dead, or more fun for that matter. I learned a few new approaches to touring, and it made the gigs after that easier to accept. The entire time was perfect. The crew, the catering, and the crowds were all just an amazing thing to be a part of. I learned to appreciate the spontaneity of a jam band compared to the rehearsed and canned shows from factory bands. It's music for the moment, not for the masses. This Jerry says thanks to that Jerry.

ANOTHER JERRY STORY

Traveling with Bruce Hornsby, a jamband musician in his own right, was a really good time. Throughout his stellar career, he has had some of the best musicians in the business in his band. Of course, Bruce is an incredible one himself.

I've been privileged to work on two Hornsby tours. On one, Bruce was opening for Bonnie Raitt, and the other one was a headlining tour. John Dearth and Bobby Reed, two great players from Charlottesville, Virginia, played with Bruce, with John Molo doing drums. Debbie Henry was singing background on the tour. I knew her from some of the Patty Labelle shows I had worked. Jimmy Haslip, an incredible bass player, well known for his work with the jazz-fusion group, the Yellow Jackets, did a series of shows with Bruce. Several other bass players sat in after Jimmy left. Bruce and the band rode on my bus.

It kind of worries me when passengers won't sleep in their bunk, especially when it gets late. Some are like that, though. I feel like they don't trust me doing my job. The way I see it, if we crash, you'll be hurt either way.

Jimmy wouldn't spend time in his bunk, instead opting for a seat on the couch right behind the wall that separated my driving area from the front lounge area. He would play his bass all night long, jamming on things I had never heard a bass player play. He can play like no other. It may seem strange, but just about every musician or band I've ever worked with that came out of Virginia are what I call "real musicians." These are people who can play and read music, and just about all of them have a music degree of some form. Many bands out of the big coastal cities, where the star canning factories reside, can hardly read a book much less read notes on a page.

One night at a show in North Carolina, I had walked up to the side of the stage in a theater where Bruce was playing. I was standing behind the curtain watching the show. I was facing Bruce but standing in the shadows a bit in an area where I thought he, the other musicians or the crowd wouldn't see me.

When he finished a song the lights grew brighter before the next one as he sat at his piano. He was making small talk to the crowd of 3,000 or so in the sold-out theater. I couldn't make out too much of what he was saying. Voices can sound muffled when all the musicians are playing and you're standing behind the speakers. Then he looked right at me and said to the crowd, "Hey, guess what? Jerry is here tonight."

Bruce had a long association with the Grateful Dead, even having played many shows with them over the years. The crowd started yelling and screaming and showing their love. They thought that's what he meant, and they knew who Jerry was. Even I started looking around for Jerry Garcia, thinking I hadn't heard that he was sitting in tonight.

After a minute or so, it got quiet. Then Bruce leaned into his microphone and said, "Jerry Fitzpatrick … my bus driver." Everyone laughed, me included.

CHAPTER 9 | TRICKS OF THE TRADE

As a younger driver, sometimes you want to drive for certain celebrities, and sometimes you may want to drive certain buses. I had a chance to drive a 1990 Marathon Coach for a bus broker. It really didn't matter who would be on it, the chance to drive a Marathon was special. Marathon builds incredible coaches with plush interiors, and when this one was new, it was one of the nicest lease buses in the industry.

Like so many other opportunities that came to me by chance, so did the one to drive this top-notch bus. But by the time I got behind the wheel, this particular Marathon already had half a dozen drivers who had improperly operated it. There were dents and scratches, and many of the interior functions... well, they didn't function. Most of the bus owners I have dealt with through the years know that I take "pride in their ride," and I will keep things in top shape. I will even try to fix things. I might have a run-in with an owner who whines about the expense of fixing things, but I usually just take care of it and worry later. No matter what breaks or doesn't work on a bus, it reflects on me in most cases. Most passengers don't know the bus owner and expect the driver to work like they are the owner of the equipment. This particular Marathon I volunteered to drive was owned by Robert Van Winkle, better known as Vanilla Ice. When Mr. Ice wasn't using the bus, a bus broker leased it out to other entertainers.

A promoter in Texas booked it for a weekend to use as his office while he managed the entertainment for the KSCS Country Fair. KSCS was and is one of the largest country music radio stations in the United States. They promoted an annual event known as the Country Fair. It grew and grew over the years until finally, it was placed in and around Texas Stadium in Irving, Texas, where the Dallas Cowboys used to play. The carnival rides were placed out in the parking lot, and it resembled a midway at your standard county fair. But inside the stadium was a 40 x 40 stage that was placed on the 50-yard line facing the south seats. They would do everything in their power not to damage the field that the Cowboys played on, so you would routinely see large sheets of plywood laid out across the field from the access tunnel to the stage for equipment to drive on.

I knew the promoter, Glen Smith of Glen Smith Presents, from my staging days. GSP had rented from Concert Staging Services where I had worked as a stagehand. GSP mainly promoted country shows in Texas. My first contact with GSP was when I worked some shows at a new venue called The Oil Palace in Tyler, Texas. Jimmy, a GSP assistant, and I had become good friends. Jimmy was the one who did the work in the trenches for the promoter, and I think Jimmy was the one who came up with the idea of parking a coach behind the stage to use for an office.

The fair was Saturday and Sunday, so I took off from my Arkansas home Friday for a leisurely five-hour drive to Dallas. To a bus driver, five hours is a breeze. My plan was to arrive in Dallas, get the bus washed up and looking good just before I drove it to the field next to the stage. The tens of thousands of people probably weren't there to see a bus, but for those who would notice, I wanted it to glow. At least they would think, "I wonder who is in that beautiful thing?" The way the stairs were positioned on the stage, I knew it would look like every star on the bill would be coming out of my bus. This would be an easy gig – set up shop, enjoy the show, and head back home to be with the family. For the time involved, it was to be a profitable run.

Dwight Yoakam, one of my favorite singers, was on the bill as was Mary Chapin Carpenter, another singer I admired. I enjoy country music, and yet, I don't care for working in the country music touring business. I have avoided it whenever possible. Nashville accountants are scrooges, and Nashville wages don't compete with pop, rock and other tours where pay scales for skilled tradesmen are much better. With Nashville acts returning home every week, accountants consider it a benefit for you to return home every week. But I've never lived in Nashville. I have, however, driven Nashville acts on short three-day runs and have had to wait two weeks or more to be paid for those three days of work. The pay scale for those three days only equaled two thirds of a pop or rock tour pay scale.

But, like I said, that weekend in Texas, I had a Marathon custom coach rented to a country music festival. The weekend looked promising, and I skipped into the Dallas area by 8 p.m. I figured I would grab some dinner and head to the stadium by 10.

Finding the right gate was not a problem at Texas Stadium nor was maneuvering the parking lot or reaching the service entrance ramp. I parked the bus and walked down to the field. It was an impressive sight seeing where the Dallas Cowboys played ball. A lot of heroes on this field. I wandered to the stage and announced my presence. We figured out where the bus should go, and I planned on washing her up, driving her on the field and then taking a nap. Everyone else was heading out to the hotels.

I was impressed with the layout. I had worked in stadiums before, and I knew exactly where to find water to clean my bus. Halfway through the tunnel headed for the field is a level where all the big service trucks can enter and bring their beer and sodas and everything else sold at a stadium. Garbage bins are in these areas too. And next to any garbage bin is usually a water connection. This time was no different. I had my own hoses and tools of the trade. No big deal. Everyone has his own way of taking care of equipment, and I have argued with other drivers about various products, ideas and techniques to get the best shine on chrome. Anything works if you have enough elbow grease. I stuck that bus in the tunnel and worked it over, washing and drying it by hand in about three hours. By 2 a.m., I had everything put away and slid into the driver's seat to move the coach onto the field.

Then I noticed some water had pooled on top of the shift pad. It had dripped in because the seal around the window was leaking. I grabbed a towel and soaked up everything I could. When everything appeared dry, I turned the switch. All the proper lights came on. I then turned the motor over. The computer did its check, and I figured there was no damage. All buses with Detroit motors and transmissions have a computer that checks fluid levels and other key components for the bus when you turn on the key. All appeared safe.

I put the bus in reverse so I could back up enough to pull forward through the tunnel and onto the field. As I started to move, the transmission slipped out of reverse and jammed into first. Then it slid back to reverse and back to first. I tried to push the keypad to get it into neutral, but it was not working. I killed the engine. After jerking back and forth, the bus sat across the tunnel in such a way that I was blocking everything. No one would be able to get through the main ramp to the field as long as the bus was sitting there. My one saving grace was that it was 3 a.m. and there was not a soul around.

With necessity being the mother of invention, I grabbed a hair dryer — didn't everyone have a hair dryer in the '80s? — and started blowing as much hot air as I could on the keypad. I tried that angle for over an hour. I just wanted to get it out of the tunnel so I could fulfill my rental obligation. There was also the embarrassing factor of blocking every other single vehicle and possibly shutting down the entire fair.

After drying the keypad with a hair dryer, I was able to move the bus to the bottom of the ramp where the field was before the transmission started to act up again. I was still blocking the tunnel when I spotted a forklift driver. Frazzled, I convinced him to pull the bus into its designated position before anyone else got there.

I slept until noon, and when I woke up, the gates had opened, and the first acts were about to take the stage. The bus was filled with production people from various bands. The bus was in place, and no one needed to know how it got there. I took the opportunity to slip out and grab a shower in the Cowboy locker room. I called a local repair shop that came out before the show and fixed the bus as good as new.

When I walked back and entered the bus, I heard Jimmy say my name.

"Well, there he is now," Jimmy said. "Why don't you ask him?"

I walked in. "Ask me what?"

"Is this coach for lease?" said a woman sitting at the table inside the bus. She was blonde and was wearing a gray college sweatshirt and some baggy sweatpants. I figured she was someone's assistant. Didn't feel like the glamour of a superstar.

"It sure is," I responded.

"How much?"

"Depends on who wants it and for how long. Who would it be for?"

"Mary Chapin Carpenter."

"Awesome," I said. "Has she seen it yet?"

"She sure has. I is her."

I was obviously embarrassed, but I didn't care and showed her around. The coach was mauve and purple inside and out... girl colors, I guess. I gave her some details about the bus owner and my card.

At that point, I was allowed to hang out all afternoon to watch the show and the country stars milling around backstage. There was one guy on the bill named Toby Keith. He had one hit on the radio, "Should Have Been A Cowboy." It was catchy. I could relate. I know I should have been a cowboy. Toby only sang about four or five songs that day. He was on early, and the announcer proclaimed, "Here is the next Garth Brooks, ladies and gentlemen... Toby Keith!" Next Garth Brooks? I guess if the radio man says so.

When he came off stage, I was standing next to some road cases where water and towels were available. He walked over to me, alone, with no extra pampering that you might see with bigger stars. He picked up a towel and wiped his face when he looked up at me.

"Good job today, Mr. Keith," I said with a smile. He smiled back.

"Thanks."

"I drive this bus here."

Without looking at it, he said, "Yeah nice bus." He then caught those girly colors, and his face changed. I could tell he wasn't that impressed. The man had just walked off stage, and he was still sweating and flustered, but I didn't care. I handed him one of my cards.

"If you ever make it to the big time, call me, and I'll be your driver."

He gave me that "you must be the dumbest person in the stadium if you think I am getting on that pink bus" look. Then he turned and walked away. It seems he did make it big, real big. I saw him a few years later at Farm Aid. A great guy helping a great cause. Haven't gotten a call from him yet, though.

CHAPTER 10 | AMERICANS VS. RUSSIANS

In the 1980s, the record companies, or the canning factories as I like to call them, were investing money in promising new bands. After each newly discovered band recorded an album, companies would invest thousands of dollars for the up-and-comers to tour the American bar circuit. I had my share of driving these types of bands during that time. One of the fun ones I traveled with was a group from the San Francisco Bay area, named Vain. The band and the crew all jumped into my bus with a trailer behind it, and we hit the road promoting their new album, "No Respect."

This was the height of the hair band genre, led by mega groups such as Bon Jovi, Def Leppard, Cinderella, Poison and Motley Crue. It was hard rock but with a bit of sheen to it. The musicians wore makeup and of course carried blow dryers, but they still attracted the ladies ... lots of them. Maybe it was the makeup they wore.

I picked Vain up in San Francisco on the first day, and we headed to the first show at University of California at Davis with several other bands, one being Drop Dead Gorgeous, also from the Bay area. The Drop Dead singer had a ring through his nose and a chain attached to it that led to another ring in his ear. He had a Clockwork Orange style hat and tattoos everywhere. I remember thinking he was beating himself up as he jumped around singing, more like screaming, with that chain hitting him in the face. It wasn't a fad that caught on with me. After the show, we headed east toward Chicago and on to the East Coast bars.

When we got under way and had a few shows behind us, everyone came together in a nice team fashion. Every day we were getting the word out and selling a few records. It felt like a nice underground movement. Our tour manager, Frogmore, had toured with Engelbert Humperdinck and was a pro at his job. He was easy going and knew how to keep everyone motivated and everything going smoothly. Vain shot several videos that climbed the MTV ladder. When we were in New York, the band made the rounds including some of the MTV shows. In 1989, that was a big deal. Does music television play music anymore?

After several months of touring, there was a small break of a week or so between Minneapolis, Minnesota, and Austin, Texas. Once we hit Austin, it would be back to the grind – six shows a week. Sell, sell, sell. The original idea was to go to Texas, have some days off lying around, and wait for the next dates. I had been on the road for months before picking up Vain, and then we had been at it for several months with several more to go. I heard the tour manager talking about what the band was making for small club shows, and at the time it was less than a thousand dollars with the promoters covering production costs, hotel rooms and amenities.

I talked to my wife about us promoting a show in Little Rock with Vain so I could come home for a few days and still make a buck. It took some talking, but she got behind the idea, and we started putting the wheels in motion to make it happen three and a half weeks before the break. I booked the show through the agency and paid the deposits. While I was still out on the road, Michelle put together a little army of kids and got a local radio disc jockey named Carol Kramer on our side to help promote the show. Working for Magic 105, the biggest rock station in town, Carol was instrumental in promoting new rock 'n' roll in Little Rock. At the time, it seemed the Arkansas station didn't care about promoting new rock 'n' roll. Songs like "Freebrid" were in the rotation every hour. She worked tirelessly for the station. Some days she didn't even go to bed, she worked so hard. In those days, Little Rock wasn't a regular stop. The scene was passing our city by. There wasn't even a descent club for a band to perform in.

Michelle made flyers and tickets and secured the building. We decided to have the show at Rick's Armory, a National Guard facility located in the War Memorial park area of Little Rock. The building had a round glass room that gets rented for just about anything you can think of. We hired local sound and lighting companies, hired off-duty police for security and planned to have a concert in the "megadome" as we called it. Safely, the place can hold about a thousand people.

The group my wife recruited to pull off the show helped her find an opening act by hosting a battle of the bands the week before our show was to take place. Stacie "Mack" McIntosh, a young black girl who loved (and still loves) rock music, befriended Michelle and assisted her in putting the show on with a local rock band named Onyx, who won the competition. Stacie helped do it all – passing out flyers and using her connections to get the word out. The McIntosh family was well known in Little Rock. Stacie's uncle, Robert "Say" McIntosh, was a popular political activist who challenged many of the local officials, including Bill Clinton.

Vain continued to travel the country doing shows while all this was going on, and the tour manager just added the Little Rock date into the schedule. I had become good friends with the guys in the bus, and they did their part helping with newspaper and radio interviews.

When we arrived in Little Rock from Minneapolis, we had a day off and the guys staggered off into a hotel that Michelle and I had secured for them. My wife and the team she had assembled all worked hard to make the event a reality, but before the show happened, we had $8,000 on the line. The show went off as planned for the most part, with a good walk up on the day of the event. Carol Kramer came through like a champ, getting away with everything she could at the radio station to help promote the show. Carol was on top of it all and her help made our show a success.

When the bills were paid and everything was covered, my wife and I made $43. Everyone had a great time, and I made some new friends in the process. I also learned some fun lessons about being a promoter.

After the show was over, we packed it all up, I kissed the family and headed to Texas for the next Vain show. A few days later we were in Dallas where Vain had been booked for a show at a club named City Limits. Also on the bill was a band from Russia by the name of Gorky Park. The Russian act apparently was big in the Eastern Block and was trying to break ground in America as one of the first Russian bands touring in the U.S. after the wall came down. The morning we arrived at the club, the Russians showed up about the same time. From just about the time both doors opened on the buses, one group was arguing with the other. I don't think anybody even shook hands. The main tension of the day centered on who was the headliner and who would play first. Then there were disagreements about gear placement. Who's using what microphones and anything else you could think of … just a bunch of bullshit. I heard them yapping about it, figured they would work it out, so I went to the hotel once the disagreement over who was parking their bus closest to the door was settled. There was no chance of working it out with their bus driver. I didn't know him.

The show wasn't until eight or nine that night, and around seven the tour manager called and asked me to come back because tension was escalating enough for a fight, and he wanted me near the bus in case some kind of trouble erupted. I got over to the bar 15 minutes before the show started and wandered out to the front of the house to see what was about to go down. The Russian band ended up playing first, which they were not happy about. They felt they were a bigger act than Vain.

Sure enough, "shit happened."

One of the Russian guys threw his bass guitar through Vain's bass drum, and the war was on. All of our band and crew hit the stage, along with their crew. There were 20-plus men on stage under spotlights and everyone was throwing punches, hits and kicks. Guys at the soundboard were pushing and shoving, trying to save the gear. It was mega chaos for more than a few minutes.

The crowd didn't have a clue what was going on or why. It turned into a mess, and a lot of equipment got damaged and a little blood got spilled. When it was over and the paperwork was done with the police, we took off for El Paso for a show and headed west to California with the camaraderie among us tighter than ever.

In the rock 'n' roll world, at least for one night, the Cold War heated up.

NO PACKING FOR ME

I'm not a big gun advocate. I certainly support the right to have them, but cognizant of the damage guns can do, I just don't participate much in activities involving guns. I'm not saying ever.

While en route with a famous rock star on a day off, it was arranged to stop at a ranch and visit some friends who were visiting friends who knew somebody. I drove all night after the show and arrived at the designated rendezvous point in the middle of nowhere in Colorado. Around 8 a.m. someone came down and met us and we went another 30-plus miles off the main highway, traveling on small country roads and finally came to a dirt road. I might mention I hate dirt roads or any road that gets my bus dirty.

We pulled through the gate of this secluded ranch and a half dozen people were there to greet us. The ranch was spectacular with incredible views of the wilderness, mountains and endless sky. We all joined in on a big breakfast laughing and getting to know the crowd that was expanding because word spread quickly that my star was at the ranch. Several of us then went out on horseback for a couple of hours riding through the countryside. A good time and the weather was perfect. (Weather always stands out to me, because knowing the weather is knowing everything that could affect the drive, the day or the show.)

When we returned to the main house, a ranch hand took the horses from us and we hopped on four-wheelers and rode to a gully where everyone had gathered with a large collection of guns and ammunition. There was everything, from large caliber hunting guns to military-styled weapons like M-16s and even pistols of every shape and size, some with scopes. A couple of machine guns were also in the pile. It was an incredible arsenal of over 50 weapons. Across the small valley were several things that had been placed on the side of the hill like a bell and other metal objects in various distances with several really far away. The owner of the ranch gave us free range to shoot anything except each other, which made everyone laugh as we started heading over to the table to choose weapons. We spent the next couple of hours blowing the crap out of the side of the hill and the targets. At one point there was more than a dozen people firing different types of weapons.

It was loud and obnoxious, sounded like war but fun as all get out. We broke for a short period when some of the ranch hands showed up with some incredible food in a chuck wagon pulled by horses. After food and a ton of laughs, we went back at it until the sun was starting to set over the mountains, and I started encouraging us to get out of the country and back on the highway before dark. We still had miles of travel to our destination. We said our goodbyes, and as we were pulling back onto the dirt road, my rock star was sitting in the jump seat excited about the awesome day we just shared.

As we pulled out he said, "I hate guns and everything they stand for but GOD DAMN I LOVE TO SHOOT THEM." I could feel the logic in that.

CHAPTER 11 | BREAKING IN THE NEW GUYS

You sometimes come in contact with a band that gets its breaks because of being at the right place at the right time. Breaks are a part of the business.

I got a call to drive a band named Dada from Los Angeles. I thought they might be up-and-comers touring in clubs and bars, but these guys had secured the opening slot for a Sting tour. Dada had signed with IRS Records, which was owned by Miles Copeland. Miles' brother is Stewart Copeland. Stewart was the drummer for The Police, whose lead singer was Sting. There you go. Easy to see how they got the slot. Good for them.

I was married backstage on a bus during Sting's 1988 Nothing Like The Sun tour, so I knew I would be around friends.

I was excited about the run and headed out a day early, aiming for the desert and eventually the West Coast. I drove to Pasadena to visit some in-laws, rest and freshen up after the long drive across country. I was told by the production manager in a phone conversation a week before to contact the band's manager at the record company when I arrived in the L.A. area. I obliged and called him when I got to my in-laws' home. He wanted to see the bus right away. He's in Burbank. I'm in Pasadena.

"No problem," I tell him. "Come on over" and I gave him directions.

So he shows up at my in-laws' zipping up in a convertible sports car. Seemed like a nice enough guy, and his low-down on the band made it seem like they were good guys too. He wanted to see their bus first and tell me their big secret... they hadn't ever ridden in a bus.

"Any of them?" I asked.

"All of them," he said. "They've never toured in their lives."

That can be a good thing, I thought. Blank slates can be wonderful in my hands. I had a chance to convince these guys about the way "real rock stars do it," at least in my eyes. My only worry was that they would have some preconceived notion on how to act when traveling on a bus.

"No problem," I assured him. "I will take care of them. I guarantee it." After some discussion, the plan was I would grab the guys the next day at a sound studio in downtown L.A. I spent the rest of the night relaxing with family.

I found the pickup location easy enough by my designated time. That's what I do, I find places. They were on time, which surprised me because who is ever on time? I spent the next few minutes packing the bus and meeting the band and crew. These were all L.A. guys. They didn't have an overboard sense of flash. They didn't look like they were trying to be rock stars. They looked like excited kids going on a field trip. They got on the bus with Mr. Manager following them on. When everyone was settled, Mr. Manager went into a speech.

This guy went on for 20 minutes, preaching the pitfalls of life on the road, the temptations, the horrible people. I'm surprised he didn't cast a glance my way. He talked about the young girls and how those harlots would be after them. "Don't give in!" he exclaimed.

"Preach it," I thought.

He talked about drinking. No drinking on workdays... better yet, no drinking at all!

"This gig is important," he said constantly. Then he started into the drugs... yada, yada, yada. I sat in my seat and had never heard anything like it before. I looked out on these kids, and I thought, "Overprotected." They had to be. This manager had to be working on orders from this group's parents. That was the only conclusion I could come to.

I will say this about them, they listened. They didn't roll their eyes or pretend to fall asleep. And I listened. I waited for him to wrap it up, and then I escorted him off the bus. He was shaking my hand, and I almost thought he was going to cry. He really seemed to like these guys, or maybe he wanted to be on the road with them. Either way, it was a big moment for him. I understood, but all I could think about was the traffic building. I didn't want to get trapped inside the L.A. rush-hour bubble.

He stepped out of the bus and as I walked with him to his car, he had one more request of me. He wanted me to drive them by the IRS Records office. Of course, that meant doubling back and dealing with more traffic, but you do what you are told to do.

I closed the door and turned to face everyone. They were quiet as could be, maybe thinking they were going to get another lecture from me. I surveyed the crowd and said the first thing that came to mind.

"Man, I'm glad that jerk isn't going with us."

They were stone-faced. I continued.

"Chop 'em out, fire 'em up, crack 'em open. I know where the girls are in North Hollywood. What kind of fucking rock band are you?"

I think they got the joke, and laughter started building. I slid into my seat and kept mocking the things he said. At least they knew when a guy was making a joke.

That was me trying to have fun at his expense.

The scene outside IRS Records was like a crowd rallying around a high school football team going to the state championship. "Good Luck Dada" was attached to the roof, and all of the office was outside waving. A nice gesture, but I didn't stop. I got on the freeway, and we headed out of L.A.

I finally got to hear them, and they produced tight sounds. Good three-person bands can make it sound like there are many more than three people on stage. Dada did just that. Plus, they were easy going, and that's always a blessing on a tour. I bought several of their albums over the years, and although they never hit the grand heights of selling out arenas, they still put out good music. My children and I laughed at their lyrics and dig the music. Their biggest hit, "Going to Diz

Knee Land," is not exactly what you think it is about.

This was going to be a good tour. I was looking forward to watching and working with them for a long time as well as my friends on the Sting tour. I received a call from the bus owner just as we were starting to gel as a team. The bus owner needed to fill a slot on Aerosmith's "Get A Grip" tour and was offering the slot to me. It was kicking off in Kansas in a few days, and he wanted me there. He planned for me to swap out with another group's bus. It was better for him, better revenue, and he wanted his bus to be on that big tour. It was a no-brainer for me as well. Aerosmith would be all over the country to support this album, but because they were so big, there would also be plenty of breaks between stints for me to see my family. I had to go with the steady paychecks. I'm glad I was exposed to Dada, though. To this day, Dada is still one of my favorite bands to listen to.

We swapped out buses in Memphis, and I never saw that band again. It was a bummer to leave these guys because the short time left a good memory. But good times don't pay the bills.

CHAPTER 12 | THE POWER OF THE POLITICIAN

A part of my life has been spent with rock stars, but you don't necessarily have to make music to be one. Polished politicians and religious leaders can be just as captivating as the Rolling Stones. The term "rock star" can be attributed to more than a few politicians. My state's own Bill Clinton is as bona fide as perhaps Martin Luther King Jr. or John F. Kennedy were in their time. But few know how to speak to a group of people like Jesse Jackson. The power of Jesse can be felt the moment he enters a building. I was in such a building once when I drove a truckload of production equipment to Memphis for a PUSH (People United to Save Humanity) convention. At the time I was on a break from driving buses and filling in by driving a production truck. I didn't know at that time who was trying to destroy humanity, but I paid that no mind.

Several bands were on the bill and played before Jesse even arrived at the Mid-South Coliseum. I was sitting on the side of the stage watching the Bar-Kays do their "funk" thing. They were one of my favorite bands back then. I had worked many shows with them throughout the Midsouth and enjoyed their style of music. They had a drummer, Willie Hall, who was incredible, playing a double bass drum set up. Many of the big hair rock bands hadn't made their mark yet, and the two-bass drum style wasn't very common with bands.

After the Bar-Kays performed, the road crew hit the stage to make the changes for Mr. Jackson's speech. Besides driving the equipment there, I was a gopher for whatever anyone needed. I helped grab a couple of the guitar amps and push them to the ramp at the back of the stage. Weird as it may seem, as I was finishing up, I felt something different in the air. There seemed to be a presence as I walked back over across stage right behind the monitor mix console. I took a seat on one of the road cases and could see the arena floor entrance and a crowd gathering. As the lights went down, I stood up, and I could definitely feel the tension in the building. The crowd began to cheer, and a commotion behind the stage picked up when the man, who many considered the most important voice for black America at that time, rounded the corner headed for the stage. When he climbed the steps, the noise was deafening. The feeling of power was tangible, and as he walked to the front of the stage waving a little and smiling, it was something like I had never felt before.

And then, as quickly as the crowd had been roaring, it got deathly silent. I mean quiet quiet. Looking out over the crowd from my side of the stage, I could see every face staring at him. With the stage lights placed on the audience, I witnessed a sincere concentration on everyone's face.

After the silence, he raised his right hand, made it into a fist and said his first words into the microphone.

"Say I am."

Everyone in the room, including me, responded.

"I am!"

He said it again a little louder.

"Say I am!"

Once again, the crowd shouted back.

"I am!"

A third time he yelled it.

"SAY I AM!"

I could feel the vibrations through the stage as everyone screamed back.

"I AM!"

The power in the room was electric, different from any of the rock shows I have witnessed. I believed at that moment he could have directed that crowd to do anything, and it would have happened. Me included! Good, bad, anything, the command that he had was overpowering. Obedience was his, and you could feel it in the coliseum.

He then launched into a great speech that applied to everyone: black, white, red, yellow, purple and green. He just wanted everyone to make our world a better place. I agreed with him on pretty much everything that day. I had only known him through the media, but he definitely seemed to portray a different image in person.

When the event was over, I was thinking heavily during the two-hour drive back to Little Rock. I gave a lot of consideration for Mr. Jackson and what I had observed. No matter what anyone has said about him, I truly believed this was a man with good in his heart trying to get the best result from everyone. Maybe I could have been fooled, but I was a willing fool that night. Mr. Jackson's presence is so powerful. Being in the presence of his power that night was a long way from those who influenced me as a youth in a racially divided community.

I felt the good in his heart that night in Memphis, and, that's what I got from him and his speech. Well, that and a small paycheck, of course.

HYPNOTIZED

Feeling that emotional connection with Jessie helped me recognize it with others down the road. Very few entertainers can grab an entire crowd and hypnotize them. The ones who can capture that moment and express themselves, their music or comedic form are truly meant to be there in my opinion. That Zen-like moment can creep up at shows, but it is rare. The feeling is incredible and there's nothing like escaping through and soaking up its power. It all has to do with the entertainer, the crowd and the moment.

I felt it with Journey during a show in Detroit. I felt the crowd making contact with the band and vice versa. I felt it after Black Sabbath blew the roof off the Alamodome in San Antonio one night. Depeche Mode had a knack for catching crowds by surprise and putting them into some kind of bouncy dance trance. One night at Brendan Byrne/Continental Airlines/IZOD arena in New Jersey the crowd was shaking the entire building so much that the speakers hanging from the ceiling were bouncing on the chains and management and riggers were going nuts over safety issues.

While touring with Aerosmith we went into Pine Knob a day early to tape a segment for a BBC Television show called "Top of the Pops." Aerosmith had a hit on the charts in Europe, and, on a day off, the crew had loaded in gear so the band could play the song. A radio station gave away several thousand tickets for the taping at the venue. Whenever cameras and tapes get involved, usually hours are spent taping the same thing over and over. After a near dozen takes to get things right, playing the song over and over, a director called it quits. When the taping was over, Aerosmith started a jam session, playing an hour worth of songs that I had never heard them play before. Some old stuff and some new. The several thousand fans got a great private show. I got one too and enjoyed every minute of it.

Marilyn Manson's production and music was a bit hypnotic as was the inspiring feeling that Ricky Martin gave to the masses. I have felt it many times … that moment when forces come together to create a euphoric state of reality. It feels orgasmic. All things are forgotten except that moment.

JAZZY PIZZAZZ

Entertainment hypnotism probably can be traced back to the very first entertainers. George Shearing, whose career spanned from the '30s to modern day, was possibly the most influential jazz piano player in the world. Joe Williams was one of the best jazz and blues singers and crooners. He was a mega-legend during his time when the music and crowds dressed differently compared to today's events. Joe's stories of the old days of performing and how life was during mid-century America were so surreal, and his humor added so much to the stories that sometimes I wished I lived back then. Joe and George were wonderful to be around, and I believe I could listen for hours to these their tales from the trails from long before I was even born.

George became popular when he developed a piano technique known as Shearing's voicing, a type of double melody block chording, with an additional fifth part that doubles the melody an octave lower. I know. It sounds weird to me too. Performed live it sounds incredible. That's why he was the best.

George performed for three presidents and the Queen of England. He recorded with Nat King Cole, Peggy Lee and Mel Torme, among many others. I picked them both up along with several other musicians for a short run through the upper Midwest performing at older theaters where everyone used to go to see shows. There were no arenas back in the day when these two were at their prime.

The run was a short one only lasting a few days, with the musicians and a couple of crew guys all riding in one bus. The schedule wasn't very tough since George was in his late '70s at the time. Joe was closing in on that age as well. There was no wild partying of today's standards going on, and it turned out to be one of the easiest tours I had ever done as well as a history lesson about days of old. George was as sharp as ever, and even though he was blind, he could fool you with his antics.

One day we were in the bus getting ready to depart for our hotel. Mrs. Shearing was sitting on the couch in the front lounge of the bus, and George was sitting at the table.

Someone said, "Okay, it's time to go."

"Wait a minute, where's Fred?" Mrs. Shearing asked. Fred was one of the roadies. "Without Fred, we're dead."

Without missing a beat, George said, "What about Chuck, honey? What are we if we don't have Chuck?" Chuck was another crew member. She tried to answer, but it didn't matter. Everyone started laughing. George was so witty.

I enjoyed listening to their stories of the old days. Seems like we all long to have lived in a time before us. Those times seem golden and magical to me. Today's touring bands and crews have such a different life compared to the older traveling acts. They didn't have the luxury buses or the high-tech production equipment of today. In their day, the music was all that mattered. Amenities that touring groups experience now weren't even thought of in the prime working days of George and Joe.

At the Pabst Theatre in Milwaukee I stood on the side of the stage behind

George and watched the show. What an incredible thing to hear and see these two masters perform. Standing behind George I could see his hands moving all over the piano keys. He was so smooth with his playing as he sat straight and proper in his tux. His hands seemed to open wider than any other pianist I had ever seen. He could catch notes that no one else seemed to be able to reach.

The crowd of men and women from older generations always arrived to the show wearing their Sunday best. As I looked out into the audience, I saw several crying as they felt the emotion in the music. I imagine they were reminiscing of days gone by and how the music had touched them at earlier periods in their lives. George and Joe were probably the classiest entertainers I've ever seen or had the pleasure of working with. Hats off to them. They definitely knew how to capture a crowd.

From children's shows, like Barney, to the acts that older generations enjoy, I've witnessed the broad spectrum of entertainment hypnotism.

CHAPTER 13 | NOT READY FOR PRIME TIME

I'm an unknown behind the scenes, but I've had my share of newspaper face-time. For instance, I was in a small town once in eastern Pennsylvania doing my laundry on a day off. In the alley where I had to park, a guy showed up with a camera and took my picture in my dirty clothes. A little embarrassing. He said it was going in a local paper. I can't even remember where that was. Allentown, maybe?

I try to keep up with the world that doesn't tour by reading local newspapers and watching local newscasts. While Americans on the East Coast think of ways they're different from those on the West Coast and vice versa, I see how we're alike. The news in one town is the same as the next – death, destruction, do-gooders and happenings.

I couldn't imagine what my grandfather would think of the modern news. The newspapers and the CBS Evening News were so important in the 1960s when I sat watching with him. It was there that I learned how to study the news. Nowadays, I have lost faith in getting the right news. Giving it to the public straight doesn't seem to happen anymore. Influenced by stockholders and the corporations that pump millions of dollars into advertising on the networks, it's no wonder that we now get such a filtered version of the news.

I've had to deal with the media on more than one occasion, mainly in connection with the celebrities I've transported. The paparazzi have staked out hotels where my passengers stay as well as chased my bus as I've driven down the highway. Once I got in toe to toe with the media... and I wasn't even on a tour.

In late 1996, I tried to go from the traveling life to home life once again. I wanted so much to spend time with my wonderful family, so I prayed for an opportunity. My prayers were answered when I received the chance to get out from behind the wheel and back into the staging business. Mike "Bean" Pinner, a friend, mentor and the owner of Concert Staging Services, where I got my start in entertainment production, called me one afternoon. He needed a salesman to sell staging to fairs, festivals and concert promoters. Tired of the road, I readily took his offer to help increase sales. I knew lots of people in the industry, and I wasn't afraid to approach them. He was designing a mobile stage that was self-contained on one trailer, and when it was finished, I was able to book it with the Ozzfest Tour. I started approaching all the festivals and promoters in the country trying to drum up more work for the company.

For many of the events that took place in Little Rock, Concert Staging Services was hired to provide equipment. From outdoor concerts, speaking platforms, river festivals and anything that required outdoor or indoor staging, CSS provided in the Central Arkansas area.

In August of 1997, Mike and I went downtown to Little Rock Central High School to scope out media locations for the 40th anniversary of the integration crisis. In 1957, National Guard troops escorted nine black students to the school despite objections of white protestors. My mother, pregnant with me at the time, had been one of those who had protested integration. She had graduated from Central the year before.

Dignitaries from the city, state and around the world would be attending the anniversary event, including President Bill Clinton, who at the time was embroiled in the Paula Jones lawsuit.

After a few hours at Central High taking measurements and doing calculations, Bean asked me to accompany a media person to the Legacy Hotel downtown on Capitol Avenue. He mentioned taking some measurements to see if we could set up staging a media event. Why the Legacy Hotel? Because it was directly across from the front door of the Federal Courthouse building where the President was expected to go to trial. CNN wanted to build a tower in the parking lot of the hotel about two stories high so they could broadcast and have the perfect angle on the front door of the building where the Paula Jones case was going to be heard. En route to the hotel, the representative from CNN explained that ABC had already rented the best floor in the hotel to anchor their nightly news coverage of the trial. Other networks were in negotiations for the other prime floors. They were going to rebuild the windows in the hotel so their cameras would have the perfect shots.

It was all basic stuff, calculating how much space verses the height versus the weight. As we were measuring the property lines, my mind started racing with an idea that almost got way out of hand. A year before, I was in Los Angeles on tour and during a day off, I had passed by the O.J. Simpson trial. It was insanity. Reporters were camped all along the sidewalks across the street from the courthouse, and there I was, stuck in the traffic jam caused by the sensational trial. The L.A. police were trying to keep it in order. From what I could tell, they seemed to have little success.

While we were measuring, I suddenly realized that the media spotlight was about to descend upon Little Rock. As a staging company, the bigger the structures, the more everybody makes. Building a temporary structure to handle the weight of all the equipment needed to broadcast the news meant we were going to use a lot of equipment. I had an idea that if we built a press riser in the middle of Capitol Avenue (blocking off that particular part of the street), we could rent out space to more than 100 media sources, offering each a 4 X 8 space big enough for a camera to sit on and shoot a reporter with their back to the courthouse. It would provide a perfect scene from which broadcasters could report back to their hometowns. And everyone would have an equal spot. Who could have a problem with that?

I took out my pad and wrote on both sides: one for the CNN folks and one for myself. I wasn't about to let this idea leak out. I had already been involved with several thousand concerts, festivals and events, and it was easy to imagine how a media compound could be set up so everyone had a fair shot at coverage. Every second that went by, the CNN idea was added into the mix of the larger media compound idea.

As soon as I got back to Bean, I could hardly contain myself. I must have looked like a little kid at Christmas with the urgency to talk to him right away. No time to waste. I had already run some preliminary numbers and it looked like a very profitable idea, especially if the trial went on for a long period of time. When I finished my presentation, we went back over to Capitol Avenue to measure the streets and sidewalks to be sure we could build something special.

CSS started business in Little Rock and had a good working relationship with the city. The company had even custom-built the area in front of the Arkansas Old State House, where Bill Clinton gave his acceptance speech after being elected president in 1992. I wasn't in Little Rock that night but watched all the festivities on TV and could see the great job the company had done. This was just going to be another feather in both our caps. Within a few weeks, Bean had approached the right city people with our idea. They gave us a permit to block the street and build a media compound. A day later, our phones started ringing with news outlets discussing our contraption.

I was in Bean's office after lunch one day when the secretary came in and said there was someone on the phone from Australia wanting to talk to someone about the media compound. Bean told me to deal with it.

"Hello, this is Jerry. Can I help you?"

I noticed his accent right away and noticed some tiredness in his voice. A 17- hour time difference made it in the morning hours where he was. After my sales pitch, I started receiving calls from as far away as Tokyo and London. I was giving them all the same line. "Prices were coming soon along with diagrams of the compound. We will have a place for you," I would say. If all conversations went this well, this could be better than I had imagined. I gave everyone the dimensions, explained there would be a roof to protect against weather, security, port-a-potties, etc. With the layout, we had more room for two separate towers similar to what CNN had requested.

Yeah. CNN. Forgot about them.

All seemed to be going well when I received a call from some lady from CNN headquarters in Atlanta. She was real pissy from the start of our conversation.

"Hello."

"Do you have any idea what the hell you are doing?" she firmly asked.

I resisted being a smart ass.

"I'm not sure what you are talking about."

"You don't control the media. NO ONE CONTROLS THE MEDIA BUT THE MEDIA! You can't charge space on your little riser for this! You're not going to be able to build a riser when I am through with you!"

"We do have a permit, and we are providing a service to the media. We're not trying to control them—"

"You don't know who you are dealing with!" Click.

She hung up. "For fuck's sake!"

The phone rang again. Someone else from CNN wanted to meet with us. The phone rang again. It was the New York Times wanting a quote about the battle to control the media at the trial. A couple of days later, the Times ran a little story how a scaffolding company was ripping off the media in Little Rock, Arkansas. That story got picked up by news services and sent around the world. Bad news for Little Rock. Bad news for us. One day, we were building stages and media risers and the next we were being chastised by the national press in our own hometown.

If the trial had actually come to pass, every news agency would have had a place on the riser. We're talking more than a 100 anchor positions. They would have stood on a safe, engineered structure with safety rails and weather protection. And most important, everyone would have had a camera angle of the front door of the Federal Courthouse.

In the middle of this mess, Bean and I were then invited to dinner with a media representative by the name of Bill Headline. Seriously! Bean told me he was some bigwig media rodeo person that corrals the press when there's some sensational event that draws worldwide attention. The guy who rodeos the media is named Headline. "Ironic," I thought.

Hearing that name reminded me of a funny story centered on another name. A friend of mine who worked in a record company office in New York City once told me they got calls every day from people saying they had a demo and wanted to be the next big star. It was kind of funny at first, she explained, the things people would say to try and get the record company's attention. But having to deal with it every day, all day long, it gets annoying. They had a code word they laughed about: Mercedes. They would tell these goofballs to send their stuff to Mercedes. Apparently, someone had made a comment about buying a Mercedes when they became famous, and it had stuck. So I was laughing at Bean telling him Headline is a "bullshit" name. He was swearing he's a real person and smiling back at me. Sure enough we ended up at a table in an upscale pizza place on Kavanaugh in Little Rock with a man that was insisting his name was Headline. Bill Headline.

He was a nice enough fellow, but after we ordered he told us how it was going to be from his perspective as if he was already in charge.

"The media was not going to be corralled by you or anyone else, for that matter," he explained to us.

We sat there and listened.

"I like your ideas, and maybe we can use some of your equipment, but definitely not on this scale."

He said everyone would have a good camera angle, but no one would be able to rush to the door every time it opened and that had to be a possibility.

"That's how the media get their stories," he said. "By pressing the subjects. Putting pressure on them yelling obnoxious things to get them to respond with the wrong answers so the media can get more dirt." He smiled as he finished.

He definitely didn't like the idea that gave everyone an equal chance to hear everything. Only the major networks would have access to that sort of thing.

CSS still had the city permit. The city people could easily see how things were being manipulated. Between having all these media people dancing in the middle of Capitol Avenue every day during rush hour for who knows how long or having an organized event, we felt we knew where the city stood.

The garbage continued, and on Tuesday, March 10, 1998, a story ran on the front page of the B section of The Wall Street Journal. Right there in the same article was my name next to the Pope, Mother Teresa and Princess Diana. The article explained how the media were suffering financial loss and cutting back on expenses, and "Jerry Fitzpatrick, a scaffolding company manager," was ripping them off believing they had bottomless pockets. Apparently, the American media had closed their offices in Paris for financial reasons, and it cost them an arm and a leg to go back and cover the Princess Diana story. Then they had been shamed into covering Mother Teresa's funeral because they had gone overboard with the Princess Diana funeral. There were also the millions and millions of dollars the media lost when they had suddenly left Cuba after paying the Cuban Government for the rights to cover and broadcast the Pope's visit there. Was that legal? The article itself explained how each of the networks had lost over $2 million they had paid the Cubans. To me, that was one of the biggest stories of my life. My dad had spent countless hours on alert status because of the Cuban Crisis, and the thought that Cuba might be loosening up its stance and allowing someone like the Pope to visit was very interesting to me. For the media to pull out and run to D.C. to cover a blow job story seemed pretty ridiculous in my opinion.

Sometime during the process, we were called into a conference with the city of Little Rock and Dale Nicholson, the top dog of the local Little Rock ABC affiliate KATV Channel 7. We being myself, Bean and Red, another guy who has worked production events in Little Rock. Dale had been a familiar voice at the affiliate for years and had worked his way up through the ranks. He had this deep baritone voice that is soothing and easily recognizable to everyone who has lived in Arkansas.

Dale walked in, avoided handshakes, sat down and got right to business. According to him, we were, as he pointed his finger at us, "ruining the city's reputation" with the plan to corral the media. Over and over came freedom of the press issues. Bean and I responded several times that we weren't trying to control the media, only provide a service to them. Then he hit the exclamation point.

"No one works in my city without my approval. Period!"

Years ago, a couple of brothers started a sound company. Bean started the staging company, and a good friend named, Byl (pronounced "Bill") Harriell had started a lighting company. All these guys knew each other and worked events and shows together for years. One day, rumor had it, Byl was arguing with someone over a bid dispute when he said, "No one works in my town without my approval. Period." Occasionally, someone would make reference to it in a joke about something, asking if Byl knew of it or had given his approval. This is Byl's town, so watch out. Byl even joked about it. So as soon as Dale said what he said, Bean, Red and I looked at each other and almost busted out laughing. I could hardly hold my tongue.

We all thought, "Does Byl know that?!"

What made it funnier was that Dale was so intent on himself and his point. I don't even think he cared if we were in the room — after all it's his town. He just kept explaining it was going to be his way in his town or no way. The city decided to take back our permit. It had become a public relations nightmare. A few days later Federal Judge Susan Webber Wright dismissed the suit when a settlement was reached between the parties. The trial never came to pass, after all.

Not long after that, the office pressure was getting to me, and the road was calling. With a pregnant wife and the possibility of seasonal lower wages, I hit the road to escape from the pressure. A coach company offered me a run with the first call. Getting back on the road has always been a good way to relieve life's pressures.

CHAPTER 14 | THE MISSED BEAT

I never know where an entertainer or passenger might have me stop and what we might encounter.

Many types of people lease custom coaches and use them for different applications. Surprisingly, many folks use them because they won't fly. It's not uncommon for actors to take a custom bus when they travel across country from L.A. to New York City and back. John Madden, an NFL commentator, stayed away from airplanes and went via coach all the time, as do other prominent figures and Hollywood stars.

Such was the case with Lenny Kravitz. I had the opportunity to move him across country several times from Los Angeles to Miami, to New York and back to his various homes. On one drive to New York in the same Marathon coach that caught Mary Chapin Carpenter's eye at the KSCS Country Fair in Dallas, Lenny requested we detour through Dallas. He went shopping in Deep Ellum and found a couch for his New York flat in Soho. It was a royal pain to try and figure out how to get a couch into the bay of a bus. It was even more of a pain to get it out of the bus while blocking a street in Soho in Lower Manhattan. The trip up the stairs and the elevator to the floor to Lenny's place was not fun either.

One day on a ride, Lenny came up to the jump seat beside me and called Robert Plant to discuss Robert's opening act position on an upcoming European tour. I couldn't believe Lenny was talking to one of my heroes. Even more, I couldn't believe Robert Plant was going to be opening for Lenny. In 1991 that was crazy to me. On another ride from Los Angels to New York City when we had taken a more northern route, Lenny came up to me as we neared Detroit and said, "Let's go to Toronto."

I took the necessary turns and crossed the border at Windsor to head for Toronto. Upon arriving we checked into a hotel and stayed until the following day. As we were leaving town and driving on Young Street, there was a young man with his drums set up on a street corner. The setup was similar to how a horn player or guitarist plays on the street with cases in front of them to collect tips. It was hard to miss the man's music as he pounded on his drums. We headed up the street and Lenny yelled, "STOP," as he came up from the back of the bus to investigate the rhythms.

I pulled over at the corner and put my flashers on. Lenny got out of the bus and went over to listen to the guy. He walked around the street man, putting his hand on his chin, standing, looking and listening. He would move to another angle and assume the same stance, hand on chin, looking and listening. After a few minutes, Lenny spoke to the man. The guy didn't have a clue at the time who Lenny Kravitz was. I was sitting in my seat watching for the police to come and tell me to move. Parking on Young just south of Bloor Street is very limited, and I was thinking of things I could tell the police to stall them while Lenny did his thing. Suddenly, Lenny came back into the bus and as he passed me sitting in the seat, he said, "Help him get his drums in the bus. He's going to New York City with us."

He then disappeared to the rear lounge, his favorite riding place. I followed orders, helped the guy pack up his things and found a place for them in the bay. There was no tour manager to assist with any of the questions I had like whether this guy had proper credentials to cross the border. As we started to head out, Lenny came up to the front lounge and gave the guy a tape of a song and told him to learn it, that when we arrived in NYC he was going to have to play it, and if he did well he might be considered for Lenny's touring band.

I was confused about Lenny's intentions. I already knew that Cindy Blackwell was Lenny's drummer for the upcoming "Are You Gonna Go My Way" tour. But that's not my business. As we made our way out of Toronto after eating dinner, it was a little after 7 p.m. I headed for the border at Niagara Falls where I had made many successful crossings. The drive to NYC from Toronto is almost 500 miles. Driving at a comfortable speed would get me there around five or six in the morning before rush hour. Just the way I prefer it. That night, the border was no hassle. I think it was close to shift change. We showed our IDs and were allowed to pass without a major inspection. This was pre-9/11.

After Lenny gave the guy the tape of the song, he had retired to the back lounge again. The man put the cassette tape in the machine and started listening to the song. Within a few minutes he had gathered some of the pillows on the couch and started banging out the beats to the song. He sat on the couch in front of the stereo/cassette machine and played the song over and over and over trying to learn the licks. He finally passed out by 4 a.m. and I was happy to have some peace for the last few miles of the ride. More than 400 miles of "Are You Gonna Go My Way" being started and stopped over and over while this guy beat on the pillows was enough to drive me crazy for the night.

As we approached the city, I called back to Lenny and told him our location. He came up and sat in the jump seat and called Craig Ross, his guitar player, and Tony, the bass player, and directed them to meet him at the rehearsal studio where the band was practicing for the upcoming tour. Several techs were called to get the equipment fired up. The studio was in Hoboken, New Jersey, just outside the Lincoln Tunnel and traffic was picking up as we arrived just before 6 a.m. Craig and Tony arrived within a few minutes of our arrival, as did the techs. I went into the studio thinking this could be one of the greatest rock 'n' roll stories in the making, a guy being a street player one day and the next drumming for one of the biggest rock stars in the world. And it was unfolding right before my eyes.

The guitar players warmed up a minute while the drummer did a couple of rolls on the kit that was already set up in the studio. Drums are like cars, I guess, and it seems strange to sit at a kit that is not yours, no matter who you are.

Lenny said, "Lets do it!" and started the intro to "Are You Gonna Go My Way."

In my experience with Lenny, I had learned he could be a bit moody once in awhile, and as the guy missed the first intro everybody stopped playing. Lenny took his guitar off and slung it across the room and into a case that was sitting next to the wall. Several parts of the guitar broke off.

He screamed, "Fuck this shit."

He yelled for someone to send "this motherfucker" home. Soon after, Lenny headed toward the bus and said for me to get him to his home in Soho. I never saw the guy again and have often wondered if he realized that he was one beat away from the big time and just how big of a chance he had missed.

CHAPTER 15 | RUN FOR THE BORDER

You never know when you're going to get to work on a tour with someone you admire, but it happened to me when I landed the Lou Reed tour in 1989. I had been a fan of his hit "Walk On The Wild Side," and "The Last Great American Whale" is one of my all time favorites. I also was excited to watch Rob Wasserman, who was going to play bass for him. Watching Wasserman up close was always a treat. The end of the run was going to culminate at Alpine Valley with a mini-festival featuring Cowboy Junkies, Edie Brickell and Elvis Costello.

The tour would only be about 35 days or so, and I knew some of the crew guys from other treks, so it looked to be an easy way to make some money and have a good time. We were going to start in the south and work our way toward Canada. I got to Atlanta in an older model Eagle bus the day before the first show at the Civic Center. Although Lou was a big star, he was working under some tight budgets this go round, so we had older model buses for the crew. Lou and the band would fly for most of the dates, and the crew would take to the road. Two drivers dropped out, and Jerry Harris and I were picked up. Harris was a good driver and a good friend and that made things even better.

After Atlanta, we actually took a dip south before heading up the East Coast. We headed to Orlando and then to Sunrise for a day off. With most groups working on a budget, the hotel rooms aren't ready until at least after noon. Sometimes they can work you in. Most times they can't. Corporate policy! It can be a pretty horrible wasting a day off waiting on a hotel room in Florida.

When we got to Sunrise, it was about 4 a.m. — no way we were getting in our rooms yet — so I headed over to the beach. Most of the guys on the bus were still trashed from drinks and drugs when we arrived at the beach, so we just hung out there until late morning. Watching the sun come up over the ocean made up for no hotel bed.

We worked our way up the coast hitting all the hot spots – I-95 through North Carolina and Virginia and Maryland – doing shows the whole way. It was a good bus. It was a good crew. It was a good group. Everyone was a pro. Everyone was doing his job. Everyone was getting along. No stress. Not yet.

With the tour were two girls from England. They worked for a catering company, one of the best around working with touring groups. They, of course, served Lou and the band. The crew ate from local caterers. They were fun girls, Denise and Michelle — and they loved working their way around with different entertainers. I moved from band to band with a bus, and they went from band to band with their cooking skills. As the tour headed to Canada, it was made apparent they had working visas for the United States but not over the border. We were going to be in Canada for six days, three for work, so the girls didn't bother with any paperwork. They decided they would fly in as tourists and jump on the bus in Ottawa. We were traveling from the Merriweather Post Pavilion in Maryland to Ottawa — about 550 miles or nine hours of driving. I traveled up I-83 to Harrisburg, Pennsylvania, then on north on I-81 to Syracuse, New York. I dropped the girls off at the Syracuse airport early morning, and we teased each other about who would make it to Ottawa first. Sometimes the border is a wave-through, "Glad you're here kind of thing." Sometimes it is a hassle.

When we reached the border, I collected everyone's passports and showed them to the immigration officials. On this trip they wanted more detail. They wanted to see everyone off the bus. I showed them my ID as the driver, and they cleared me through. Not much to worry about, it seemed. Before 9/11, I never had a problem getting to and from Canada.

Everyone else had been sent to the immigration office. As I lit a cigarette, a customs officer approached me and asked if I drove the bus. I acknowledged and she requested a quick search. I had stopped a few miles before the border and made sure nothing was lagging around. I had gotten assurances from the bus "mom" that no one had anything on them. I didn't have anything on me either. You don't have to take drugs to Canada. They're already there just like in America.

The customs officer started in the bay, pulling out bags, then dug into the bus. She asked me to turn on the lights, and she proceeded to open cabinets and the bathroom door. Then it was back to the bunk section. We had 12 bunks so all 11 people in the bus had one, and we had a "junk bunk" where people threw their bags. Looking into the junk bunk, the agent pulled out a bag. It was Denise's. Or Michelle's. I couldn't remember. She unzipped it reached in and pulled out a 35mm film canister and shook it. There was a small tinkling noise so she opened it. The second that lid pried open, I could smell it. Hashish. Fuck! Most British men prefer hash to weed. I guess British women do, too.

The customs lady was having a fit. She came toward me, yelling and screaming at me to "GET OFF THE BUS!" and "KEEP YOUR HANDS OFF EVERYTHING!" She acted as if she had found the mother load and was telling her partner. My assurance that she hadn't really only made her angrier.

"SHUT UP!" she barked back.

The bus was under a canopy, and more agents got word of the find. They started pulling the luggage off the bus and placed the crew and me in a secured area. I tried to explain what was going on, but this feisty one wasn't having it.

"We're bringing a dog on this bus," she crowed. "It's going to sniff every last inch." We were going to have to wait for five hours for the dog to show up. "So get comfortable," she smarted, as we sat in the not-so-comfortable secured area.

The agents took everything out of the cabinet and threw it on the floor of the bus. Everyone's bags were emptied and thrown into piles. The bus was a disaster. Then while we waited on the dog, it was our turn. Strip search. Bend over. Spread 'em. Ewww.

The dog arrived. He sniffed every single thing and found nothing. I knew he wouldn't. The bus was clean, as we all knew it was, except for one of the girl's canisters. We wanted to get to Ottawa by noon, and we were leaving the border at 6 p.m., which left us arriving at our hotel after nine. What a miserable way to spend a day off. The girls got an earful when we arrived. It was a bad scene for them. I love Ottawa, the capital of Canada. So beautiful and historic. I've tried to get out and see some of the city every time I've been. This trip was not one of them.

The show was at the Capital Congress Center, a large convention hall with a theater and large banquet rooms. A river runs through town, and, across the street, large luxury boats tie up when they come off the lake. It's quite a picturesque sight. The drive out of Ottawa that night was only 130 miles to Montreal. I planned on napping, watching the show, driving to Montreal, and getting ready for the longer run to Toronto. I ate dinner with some of the crew guys and got ready for the show. It wasn't sold out, but it was pretty full. As the lights came down for the start of Lou's performance, I was out at the front of the house where I could hear and see everything.

The intro music started and the other players in the band took the stage first. As Lou approached the stage, he tripped. He wound up breaking his foot. No one knew what was going on just yet. After a minute, the sound and lighting guys started to rustle. I could tell something was up. I waited another minute and then headed backstage. Lou had been taken back to the dressing room and a doctor had been called. Rumors were already swirling about the show being canceled and then we quickly found out that the entire tour was canceling.

There was still three weeks worth of tour left — and there was the possibility of a tip — so I was not happy to hear this. After about 30 minutes someone announced to the crowd what had happened. Details on a new show or refunds would be forthcoming and so on. I got with the production manager, and we made a plan to return to New York City. Most of the crew was from that area. We got out of the venue by 10 p.m. and headed south for about 450 miles. I had phoned the bus owner and the bus broker as soon as I heard we were dropping out. It was middle August, the prime season of touring. I knew I would be redirected soon.

The next day after dropping all the crew in New York City, I found a pay phone on Staten Island on my way out of town and got my next gig. This actor — Dennis Quaid — was doing a short run of bars through Oklahoma and Texas, which wasn't far from home and meant I could spend a couple of days with family before the assignment started. I would be far from the Canadian border. Lucky me.

CHAPTER 16 | BROTHERLY LOVE

Oasis was one of the United Kingdom's biggest bands. They had broken all ticket sales records in the U.K. and other European countries. They flew to New York City in October of 1995 for a series of shows, I assume, to break ground in America.

Sonny, another driver, had been assigned to do the run but had pulled out at the last minute due to some scheduling conflict with the band he was already working with. Sometimes that happens when a band extends its tour or adds some extra shows or duties at the end of their scheduled tour. I got the call at the last minute and had to hustle to be on time. I almost always enjoy working with English and European groups, so I readily grabbed the gig to cover for Sonny.

When I met Oasis in Manhattan to take them to a show in Baltimore at Hammer Jack's Club, they seemed like just another bunch of wankers to me. Another English invasion, they come one after another, you know. On our first ride we headed south out of New York City to get the first show in. Rumor had it that the two brothers in the band, Liam and Noel, didn't like each other and couldn't seem to get along. Those rumors I found to be true as we started our run through the states. Those two would argue about anything.

Hammer Jack's is a neat club I have been to many times over the years. A lot of bands in the '80s made the bar a required stop on their way to fame. The club could handle over 1,500 people on a good night. When we arrived on a Monday for a sound check and a show, only several hundred people came to see them. The drive down to Baltimore was pleasant enough, getting to know the tour manager and the guys in the band. The ride back to NYC wasn't quite as smooth as Noel and Liam were arguing the entire time. Several more trips had the brothers arguing every minute.

The show at The Orpheum in Boston rocked the place pretty hard. The Orpheum seems to be a great venue for English rock bands to perform. Lousy load-in for the crew, but once the gear is in place, the old building is a gritty place for rock 'n' roll. After the Boston show we headed to Pittsburgh for a day off and a show in the Strip District at a bar called The Metropol. Heading over to the gig, the brothers once again were griping at each other and of course about all the things wrong in America. Typical Englishmen.

It's pretty amazing to me that someone can visit the United States and within a few days know all the problems with our great country and have all the answers on how to solve them. The show in Pittsburgh didn't do that well with ticket sales. It was a Monday, perhaps one of the slowest days of the week for people wanting to get out and party. The group seemed to be annoyed with the small venue and lack of fans so the ride out of Pittsburgh to Buffalo had them all in the front lounge whining and griping about the situation, among other things.

As I headed north toward Buffalo on I-79, the brothers and the band got into a heated argument about something. I'm thinking, "Great! Don't these guys ever stop bitching and moaning?" To this point everyone had been pretty nice to me. Their tour manager, Margaret, seemed to have a way with the guys, getting them to do the things required to help move their career forward. I hadn't been in the middle of their arguments, choosing instead to just listen to them. Sometime after an hour or more of listening to these guys piss and moan about every little thing they could think of, I yelled at them to give it a break. Trying to be funny with my tone I added a little British accent to my voice and yelled at them, encouraging them to share some love with each other. Liam made a comment, and I smarted off at him in response. He pulled the curtain that separates the driving area from the living section and stepped down on the step. With his arm held out, he yelled pretty loudly that he wanted to arm wrestle me.

I asked if he was fucking crazy as I was driving him at highway speeds. I told him to take a seat before I slammed the brakes and tossed him out of the front windshield and ran over him for bothering me. He was holding his arm out wanting me to take his hand and when I let off the gas a little, he returned to the back making smart-ass comments. We all laughed with Noel telling him not to "fuck with the bus driver." The guys continued with their heated argument as we rode through the night.

A stop for fuel in Erie, Pennsylvania at the Pilot Truck Stop had them out of the bus and into the store. Truckers recognize an entertainer coach whenever it pulls up to the fuel island, and several always approach and ask, "Who's in the bus?" At 2 to 3 a.m. with a whiny, pissy British rock band, "Who fucking cares?" People ask all the time, nonetheless. While I was fueling, the guys went inside and were doing some shopping when I noticed them arguing in the store.

Whine, bitch, whine, bitch, whine, for hours it seemed. The guys were still going at it when we arrived in Buffalo. While we were sitting in the bus waiting for Margaret to check us into the hotel and get our keys, one of the musicians in the band said, "Fuck this. I quit," grabbed his bag from the luggage bay and left. Craziness ensued with trying to find him when the tour manager returned. By mid-day I was notified the tour was canceled since the musician had caught a flight back to England. I notified the bus owner and dropped the guys at the airport heading to the West Coast to pick up another entertainer.

In 2001, I received a call from a bus owner wanting me to drive Oasis again. My schedules matched up so I took the gig looking forward to seeing the guys and the band. I do like their sloppy style of English rock 'n roll and have many of their records. The 2001 tour was aptly named "The Brotherly Love Tour" and featured three bands that all have a history of brothers not getting along. The Black Crowes were the headliners with Oasis co-headlining and another group, Spacehog, as opening act. Each group had brothers notorious for fighting with each other.

It was a short 30-day tour that started on the West Coast and finished in the Northeast. It all worked out to be a great time with little bickering on my bus for that entire tour. I prefer it that way. Peaceful rides are the way to go.

CHAPTER 17 | DEALING WITH DIVAS

If you sit behind one bus, you don't exactly sit behind them all. Each one has its own age, its own style, and its own problems. So moving to a bus named the "Baby Bus" may not be the most rock star thing I could do, but it was in demand.

In truth, the baby bus was built for Garth Brooks' family. Garth had his own bus, as his schedules were pretty tough with tour promotion. Baby Bus with Garth's family on board followed the tour at a slower pace. It was built while Brooks' children were still very small. The bus itself was a 40-footer. Most coaches are 45 feet in length. The bunks were made small for the children, and it had extra safety features. The coach was painted baby blue with polished aluminum along the bottom.

Baby Bus had gone through several drivers before I sat behind the wheel of it, but it was still in really good shape. There were no major dents and the miles were low. Because it was shorter than most coaches, it was lighter, and it had a good, strong motor. That meant it would travel through the mountains without major headaches. It was seen more as a family-style coach. I was able to use it with Ann and Nancy Wilson of Heart when they took an acoustic tour. I drove Courtney Love, of all people, on it. And I drove members of the band Smash Mouth.

Smash Mouth was part of the indie-rock craze in the 1990s, coming out of the West Coast. The band was known as punk ska, using elements of early '80s punk with a reggae feel. You could call it happy-punk. It wasn't aggressive or mean spirited. It felt fun. Smash Mouth was beginning to be a recognizable name and that meant more buses on bigger tours.

I needed to do a test run to see if we would be a good fit with the band so I took a quick shag across the nation with Steve Harwell, the lead singer, and tour manager Scotty the Hottie... well, that's what he's called. Scotty is a lover of all things baseball, especially the Chicago Cubs, and he's an excellent wrangler of wayward musicians. He's a solid tour manager. If we all liked each other, then I would be assigned to drive guitarist Greg Camp and his family on Baby Bus while Steve rode in another coach with another driver.

Being able to handle a tour bus from the driver's seat is only one detail of the job. It's imperative that you can get along with your passengers. There are always politics that play out, drama that needs to be averted or egos that need to be soothed. A clash of personalities between musician and driver can result in some long tours, even if the time spent touring isn't that long. A group may work their way through several drivers before everyone is comfortable. This had been the case with Smash Mouth.

When I got the assignment, the bus owner told me they were great passengers. But the bus owner doesn't make the trip, and I had found out there were more than a few drivers who were refusing the tour. So I did my own checking. Mickey Moe relayed the hours he had spent with the group on the side of the road in Kentucky after Steve was shooting fireworks out of the back window of the bus. He was so fed up with their childish behavior that he encouraged police officers to arrest them. Fireworks I could deal with, but things other drivers said bothered me, like their lack of cleanliness and their disregard for being on time.

Being on time is essential during a long tour run. Getting to the hotel on time just to get enough rest instead of sitting behind the wheel is driver issue number one. So this test run was a chance to see how the punctuality issue would affect me. My first pickup was in San Jose at the management office where I met Steve and Scotty. Then we zipped down to Los Angeles. Easy first day with general pleasantries and first-day niceties. Steve did the morning radio show at KROQ the next morning, one of the most famous radio stations in the nation. From there it was an easy drive to Phoenix.

All the places were the same. We raced across the country so Steve could hit all the morning shows. Here is a thank you plaque for making "Walking On The Sun" such a big hit, and by the way, here is our new album "Astro Lounge." Blah blah blah. All the bands had to do it. All the stations had to do it. Promote, promote, promote.

For Steve to make the morning shows in all the major markets, we had to haul ass from city to city to make each of them on time. From Phoenix, we trekked to Dallas, an all day-and-nighter. I passed the test. We got there just fine. Dallas to Houston was a breeze, but Houston to Atlanta was tough because of the horrendous traffic. After Friday morning's radio show we had the weekend off before D.C. on Monday morning. We picked up Greg Cramp, the guitarist, who would be my passenger if I passed the test for the upcoming Smash Mouth tour, and headed to Bristol Motor Speedway for a NASCAR race. Greg was a great guy, and I had decided almost immediately, stories be damned, this could work out well doing the family thing for the tour.

We got to the racetrack, and Steve had an announcement.

"Jerry, I decided you're gonna be my driver for the tour."

"Well, that's not the plan," I said. "I'd been planning on driving Greg and his family, and we need to stick to that plan."

"I don't really care about that," he returned. "I really want you to be my driver." With that, he was off to the races.

I grabbed Scotty.

"I don't care what he says, this is not what I signed up for," I explained. "I prefer to be driving a family, not the chief partying guy of the group." It seemed to be settled, and I strolled into the Speedway. Met Dale Earnhardt and had a good weekend. Sunday we headed up to D.C., worked the East Coast for a few dates before heading back out west. Then it was a few weeks off before the real tour kicked off.

A common belief is that bands all ride together in one bus. That may be the case when budgets are small, but when they become more successful, more famous and have a bit more in the bank account, they tend to stretch out their comfort zone and acquire individual buses. It becomes a home away from home. After all, the average person doesn't go home with their co-worker. With new government rules in place and being a family person myself, for Baby Bus, I wanted to drive a real family. My want was fulfilled but not without the hassles.

When the tour started, the first few days with Greg and his family were smooth sailing. It was exactly how I thought it would be. The only problem was Steve. He wouldn't leave me alone. He kept thinking I was going to switch to be his driver, and it was causing a rift between him and Greg. I tried to laugh it off, but the hassles kept coming. He agonized his own driver; he wore out Scotty and me and kept acting like a child on and off the stage. During his drunken antics, it seemed he put more effort into that than the energy needed for putting on a good show. Then there was the partying. It seems we went to millions of nightclubs, and all the drivers spent countless hours waiting behind the wheel for the games to end and the tour to roll on. When a driver takes a band to the bar in a bus, it's usually no fun for the driver. Being the "DD" means no drinking and no partying. From bars, fans are typically brought onto the coach. Big messes are made and when it's all over and all the drunks go to bed, there is still the drive to make to the next town.

It was a tour that was filled with needless drama. I just wanted to yell, "For Christ's sake, do what you're supposed to do! Entertain the masses and count your money!"

There's a lot of talent in Smash Mouth, and there were some good times, but the good times that they offered seemed more like work.

CHAPTER 18 | CRASH

Every day at my job is another chance to meet new people. When they see a million-dollar bus pull up, however, the questions are nothing new.

It's just normal curiosity of the human kind. People can be so gullible when a clown crosses their path, and sometimes I feel like a clown. I can usually tell by the looks on people's faces if I'm going to tease them a little and give them a story that might stick with them for years. So many people are absorbed in their routines where nothing too much out of the ordinary happens. Then the circus comes to town.

The question that comes my way the most from people I meet can also be the most sobering.

"Where are the worst drivers from?"

My response is always the same. "AMERICA!"

People drive badly no matter what state they're from. Those lines are blurred almost immediately. When I first started driving, I had my opinions, but after nearly 30 years behind the wheel with so many people operating vehicles on the road, it's hard to pinpoint the knuckleheads anymore. I've seen bad drivers in Kansas and in Los Angeles, in the streets of Philly and on the back roads and highways through the Heartland.

Morning rush hour is the same throughout the entire U.S. Everybody gets up at the same time; they go through the same routines to get ready, dry that hair, drink that coffee, and hit the road. And it's these same assholes who clog up the streets in the same locations at the same time every single day, causing wrecks.

I've seen so many automobile crashes that I've become cold to them. It wasn't always that way, but now I am almost cynical. They are always caused by the same thing – people not paying attention or driving beyond their means. When I drive a few hundred miles a day, I will see at least one crash. Some of them happen right before my eyes. Even though I can be numb to them, I can still remember them, and sometimes they shake me. Then there are those wrecks that cause me and my passengers to be backed up for hours. When I was new to driving for a career, I was programmed to be in this help mode. I wanted to assist anyone I saw in a wreck … very Good Samaritan-like. But I'm hardened, and now I usually don't care when I see one.

A Virginia Tech study showed that nearly 6,000 people die in car crashes each year involving an inattentive or distracted driver, and about a half million were injured for the same reason. I've driven more than a million safe miles. Every mile that I drive, my risk of being involved in an accident increases, because of some driving fool. Eighty percent of crashes are related to driver inattention, and those distracted drivers who use handheld devices are four times as likely to get into wrecks that will injure them. Let's just say I am a bit of a hard ass about this. If I had my way, I would ban phones, radios or anything that is a distraction. Radio-controlled speed censors for vehicles traveling in metropolitan areas are not a bad idea to me.

You might have the same thoughts if you've seen horrible collisions like the ones I've witnessed. The memory of one of the first crashes I encountered still lives in my mind today. It was early in the morning, and I was traveling east on I-40 in New Mexico. Heading up a hill that curved to the left, I saw a Kenworth Conventional truck that had crashed in the median, on his side of the road. This particular area had a stretch that was all downhill, and toward the bottom of the descent, the highway turned to the right. The truck didn't turn. He kept going straight. The truck was pulling a loaded trailer, and as it crashed into the median, the trailer swerved over toward the driver's side. The driver was thrown from the vehicle. The truck then slid over him, and half his body was trapped under the sleeper part of the truck. It was like a scene from *The Exorcist*. His chest was facing up, but his head was turned completely around, buried in the dirt. It was not family viewing. I drove by slowly, almost stopping, as there was no traffic during sunrise that morning. I saw the police approaching. I knew I couldn't help. I pulled off the highway when I reached the top of the upgrade and caught my breath. I said a prayer. I sent some good thoughts. God bless that man. He rides with me even today.

Another time, I was in Jessup, Maryland, just outside of Washington D.C. enjoying a day off. I had come into the area to fuel up, wash the bus, get some supplies and get back to the D.C. hotel for a relaxing evening. I can remember so many details on this day, but damned if I can't remember what band I was driving at the time.

I was sitting in the turn lane at the intersection of Waterloo and Washington Road just east of I-95 in Maryland. Across the intersection was a moving company truck sitting in the left turn lane waiting to head the opposite direction from me. Traffic was light, and both of us sat waiting for the light to change. The trucker had an impatient driver behind him in a big ol' Buick Roadmaster. He wasn't happy that he couldn't get going and obviously fearful that once the light did change, this truck would casually saunter into the intersection and leave him to sit through another series of lights. When he had enough of waiting, he accelerated around the right side of the truck. Watching him I already knew what was about to happen. Instead of driving through, he pulled into the intersection and cut a hard left in front of the truck. The Buick tilted, and one of his hubcaps came off, he turned so sharply.

The light was still green for thru traffic on my side. A cement truck traveling west was going toward the intersection at speed. Since my bus was just as big as his truck, there was no way of seeing that Roadmaster pull out into traffic until the last second. All he saw was a green light, and he was continuing on through the intersection.

The cement truck driver saw the car just as he was passing me. His back axles were going by my entrance door on the right when the car pulled out in front of him. He locked his brakes as he was swerving to the right to avoid this nut in the car with no patience. The cargo in the truck – wet cement – shifted and as he crashed into the car, the truck tipped over and slid on its side toward the light poles just stopping short. No other traffic was around. A lazy Saturday afternoon, peaceful one second, chaos the next.

Glass and car parts flew everywhere, like a bomb had been dropped on the intersection. Then all was still. Both the other trucker and I, who sat there and witnessed the entire thing, locked our brakes and jumped out of our vehicles. Running for the car and the overturned truck, it was a crazy sight from my end. The mess missed me only by several feet. The other trucker just missed being a part of the accident by a foot or two. The car was hissing out of every crack. Smoke was filling the air. The man in the car, an older black man, was still sitting upright in his seat, his head tilted back. He was losing fluids. He was dying. Actually, he was dead. What a waste.

The cement truck driver was climbing out of the blue cab screaming and cursing the entire time. Someone shouted to him that the other driver was dead. He quieted down after that. I got back into the bus and cleared the intersection, heading south on Highway 1 so I wouldn't be caught at the scene for hours. I told my story to the police and was on my way. I still had things to do, but watching a man die in front of my eyes... that made the rest of the day and the rest of the tour seem surreal.

One night I was driving down I-95 from Baltimore, heading to the Carolinas for another show. It was about 1 a.m., and as you leave downtown Baltimore, you travel through various suburbs and towns and burghs between there and D.C. Then you jump on the Capital Beltway and travel around the nation's capital. It's anywhere from four to six lanes wide. Depending on the time of day, the traffic can move real slowly. That's why I like hitting these places in the middle of the night. It's amazing how the freeway works when no one is on it. One of the strangest sights on this trek is the Wilson Bridge, which employs an actual drawbridge on it, a weird sight on a freeway. Just south of Alexandria, Virginia, the freeway splits turning west and back north, while I-95 continues on south. In those years, the freeway interchanges were rated at 30 miles per hour.

The curves on that area are sharp, so I was taking the junction slowly and carefully. I took one curve when a dark green minivan zipped around the corner so fast, he overcompensated for his error and almost slammed into me. He was trying to slingshot around me on the outside corner, and then in an instant he was drawn to the bus like a magnet. Of course I hit the brakes and swerved to the left shoulder, just trying to avoid a collision. Man, did it piss me off that this idiot was driving like this in the middle of the night. I could see that the van was overloaded with people and luggage. The guy couldn't even see outside his rearview mirror. And since most of his cargo was in the back, it pushed the headlight beams up, seeming brighter. I did my usual bit of cursing at him, and he corrected himself, got into the passing lane and gassed it into the night. New

York plates. This asshole had to have been taking the family south to Disney World or something. Wish he would take better care of his cargo.

I put it out of my mind, got the bus back on cruise control, and continued my drive south. Inattentive drivers do this kind of crap every day. They feel as if they are in control, they understand their autos and can handle them in any situation. The general public averages between 12,000 and 15,000 miles a year just from driving from home to work, taking the kids to school or to Grandma's and maybe a vacation. They just don't understand the danger they are in when they are driving. Once you put that car in gear, your biggest fear shouldn't be the drug dealer, the robber or the murderer. Your biggest fear should be the soccer mom talking on her cell phone while putting on her makeup because she is running late with screaming kids in the back. Fear the idiot who thinks driving fast and swerving between the traffic is going to get them ahead of some imaginary line. Everyone wants to be the leader.

As I-95 heads south past the Quantico Marine Corps base, it strides past a couple of rivers, and on past Fredericksburg, Virginia, and the terrain begins to level out. I was in the middle lane, just about 60 miles south of the Beltway Junction, when I saw brake lights come on in front of me. I started moving over to the left lane as cars from all around were stopping in their spots. Dust and smoke filled the air, and I figured out in a moment that an accident had just happened. I came to a stop in the passing lane.

In my lane, sitting overturned, was a baby seat with a child still in it. There were other children scattered on the freeway along with a couple of adults. Every car had stopped, and people were rushing out of their cars to help in any way they could. But for a second, I didn't. I was just looking ahead at the child seat. I will never forget the sight. I couldn't see the baby, but I could see the blood.

I could see over to the right that the minivan was the one that had crashed, the same one that cut me off earlier. It had flipped over several times, throwing its passengers out onto the freeway, and came to rest lying on its side in the middle of the freeway. Traffic was backing up, and now everyone was outside the cars. The emergency vehicles snaked their way through. There was a crowd gathered around the baby seat. I saw that someone started to move it, trying to turn it over, but someone stopped him. The child was dead. A cover was placed over the seat as well as a few other bodies, and everyone else tried to help the living. Dead bodies in the road always stick in my mind. I never forget them. Seeing a dead child in the road because someone was driving carelessly fills me with rage.

Auto accidents are not accidents at all, in my opinion.

In 1984, I was traveling north on I-75 between Cincinnati and Dayton, Ohio. I was en route to the Nutter Center with a load of production equipment for a Barbara Mandrell show. There are three traffic lanes heading north from Cincinnati. I was about to pass a semi-truck that had parked on the shoulder of the road with its hazard lights on. It appeared the trucker had stopped behind the line on the shoulder of the road for an emergency. I moved over to the middle lane when I saw a car zooming up on the right side headed straight toward the truck. It slammed into the rear of the trailer. It was so loud I could hear the collision from the cab of my truck. I saw the entire crash and immediately pulled over. I was just a few miles from my exit, seven hours early before my load-in time.

I ran back to the accident. The trucker was heading back to the car as well. A woman was still in her car, moaning and bleeding everywhere. No airbags, not in this car, not in '84. Also no cell phones. The other driver and I didn't know what to do. The woman was bleeding and injured badly. Another car had stopped, and the driver was going to head to the nearest pay phone to call the police. All we could do was keep her comfortable. The ambulance arrived and carted her away. I got her name and checked on her a day later. She was in bad shape, but I spoke to her family and left an autographed picture and T-shirt of Barbara Mandrell. I hoped she would recover enough to see them.

If I think about it hard enough, I can still hear that crash, I can still see it. I see them all. I may not feel the same way I did when I started, but they always stay with me. So it keeps me thinking, "Pay attention, you fucking idiots!"

I see a need in the near future for speed sensors and computer equipment that won't allow you to speed in certain areas. I imagine a device that alerts the police when you are actually doing it so you can be identified. I've wished for that invention many times. Let's just install it when we buy a new car. I know people would complain about their freedoms being violated, but having seen what I've seen, I know that bad apples can rot the entire bunch, so let's get 'em out of the barrel.

Traffic is just another line in our lives. People don't cut you off in the grocery or movie lines. You're not going to swoop in and steal someone's seats in church. In a restaurant, everyone waits their turn, and we have survived based on common courtesies. But you put these same people behind the wheel of a car in control of thousands of pounds of steel, and they become society's nightmare.

CHAPTER 19 | FLASHING BEFORE MY EYES

Ann and Nancy Wilson are the sisters that fronted the fabulous rock group, Heart, and in the late 1990s, I got to drive them as a duo instead of as a band. The girls were on an acoustic tour, Nancy playing guitar and both of them singing. They both rode the bus with Ann's children and nanny. A real family atmosphere. We had many long runs on that journey, and the girls were real riders. I beat them up pretty badly on the East Coast where rough roads and short buses can make for a bumpy ride. But the three months we were together was an honor. I got to circle America with the Wilson sisters!

One of the perks of this tour was listening to Nancy's other work while she was touring. Nancy's husband, at the time, is film director Cameron Crowe, the man who wrote the immortal words, "Show me the money!" While Nancy was touring the country, Cameron was filming *Almost Famous*, a great flick about a rock band touring the country. Nancy was scoring the movie for her husband, so, throughout the tour, she would get to play dailies from the movie on the television in the bus. As I drove, I heard these actors who I couldn't see say their lines over and over while Nancy figured out where to place the music. Never got to see a frame of the dailies, but when the movie came out, I figured I knew every line and every scene.

On the West Coast, we were headed from San Diego up to a resort in Northern California. Konocti Harbor on Clear Lake is absolutely beautiful, and quite a getaway, but it's treacherous to get to. You leave the comfort of I-5, cruise control and head west on Highway 20. That road curves through the mountains where buses and show trucks are not recommended. If you can make it there unscathed, the amenities are second to none, and a family can have a blast there. With a stage on the water, a summer concert at Konocti Harbor can be a great experience. I was able to hear the show from my cabin. I shuffled down to the stage for the last part of the show and to get the bus ready for our trip to Las Vegas. The duo was playing a show at The Joint in the Hard Rock Hotel the next night. It would take an hour just to get back over to the interstate and make tracks across the Sierras.

After driving out of California on I-80, I headed south on Highway 95 at Fernley, Nevada, toward Las Vegas. It was creeping toward daylight, and I had made a stop for fuel and a snack and then got back to the grind. In 1999, Highway 95 didn't have a lot of the modern upgrades it has today. There were no passing lanes for this particular stretch of road.

I rounded a curve to the left, and I headed down a steady decline for the next few miles. As I came around that curve, I saw what every driver would dread –

a semi in my lane heading right toward me. The asshole had decided to pass a slower truck as they headed up the hill. The semi he was passing had nothing but mountain on his right. He couldn't get over anymore without clipping a few rocks. Then there was the road with his truck, the passing truck and my bus, three of us on a two-lane highway. On my right was the rest of the mountain with a steep drop down. In other words, I was driving next to the side of a cliff. The drop off was absolutely terrifying.

I don't know if the passing truck clipped the other one's mirror, but they were extremely close. I pulled over as far to the right as I could. I know I could have reached my hand out and pulled a strip of dirt off his trailer with my finger. I could hear the bus grab the gravel on my right side and then slip. In a split second, I pulled it back, and I found my bearings as I pulled back on the road. What they say is true. Things go in slow motion when you are on the verge of an accident. I saw a highway sign jiggle in the rearview mirror where I clipped it, and I saw dust flying off in the air as if in some Western, all of it in the span of a half second that seemed to last a lifetime.

As soon as I got straight, I reached for my CB radio. I was ready to curse the guy out, but as those words met my lips, I changed my mind. It didn't matter, and I rolled down the hill. A few seconds later, my right leg started shaking uncontrollably, and I burst out crying. The adrenaline of all types of feelings after a truly near-death experience was something I had never experienced before or since. All I could think was, "At least I didn't shit my pants."

The sun came up, and I got my composure back. Then the girls woke up.

I can't remember which one talked to me, but I heard, "Did we hit a bump back there? I felt us jerk around." She didn't say anything else. I don't think they ever realized how close they came to being two more rock 'n' roll legends. In fact, I don't think any rock star, cozy on the bus, is aware of the dangerous situations around him or her. If that's the case, it's a job well done for me.

CHAPTER 20 | WRONG NUMBER

Just about every day when I'm working, I am around rock stars with fans who would do just about anything to get close to their favorite entertainer. They practically melt at the sight of their celebrity, and rules get tossed aside when they are trying to reach out and touch their rock star, if even for a second. Rules of the road tend to go out the window for them as well. Road rules are number one in my book. Mix that with securing the safety of my precious cargo, and infatuated fans sometimes give me a run for my money.

Along with roadblocks and potholes, I have to constantly watch out for starry-eyed fans whose desire to see their rock star up close could result in injury. Fortunately, their actions mostly just produce smiles and giggles.

One day I picked up singer and guitarist Dave Matthews in Seattle for a drive to the Gorge Amphitheatre where Matthews and his band were doing a three-day run of shows over Labor Day weekend. We were traveling on I-90 eastbound and passing through Ellensburg, Washington. I was cruising along when I passed a car that had five women in it. When they saw me passing and (more important) saw Dave sitting in the jump seat they all started yelling and waving and the worst of it all, they started driving like ding dongs. They sided me for a couple of miles; Dave had waved back a couple of times. They were snapping pictures and screaming when one of the girls had recorded her phone number on a piece of paper and held it up. I dialed the digits on my phone. The girls' squealing outside the bus and on the phone were like sounds blasting through the stereo. I handed the phone over to the boss, and he chatted with them a minute. We learned they all were in the Army and stationed at Fort Lewis, Washington. Of course, they needed a ticket or two. We got their names for the tickets and said goodbye.

We arrived safely at the gig, and it was a great weekend. The Gorge is one of the most beautiful places on earth to host a musical event. It's a well-known facility, and you're lucky if the job takes you there. Surrounded by campsites and nature, fans are more relaxed than the rock-out scene in big city arena shows while they enjoy the electric energy created by the music.

I never saw any of the screaming girls or talked to them again until January the following year. I was home lying on my couch on a cold, wet Sunday afternoon watching a football game when the phone rang. I didn't recognize the number but answered anyway and a girl's voice on the other end said, "Hi Dave, how are you today?" Me, being old school, said, "Dave's not home, man" like Cheech and Chong said in their Dave's Not Home skit. The girl laughed and said, "You're so funny, Dave."

I told her I was not Dave Matthews. We debated my identity for a good while. I didn't mind, the football game was lousy, and I was having a giggle waiting on the next one to kick off. She said she knew I was Dave because she had seen Dave dial her number, and she had kept the number of the incoming call all this time. She had even had the number tattooed on her arm. I said, "YOU DID WHAT?" She repeated that she had my number tattooed on her arm, and she said it was OK we were talking, because she wouldn't tell anyone that she had spoken to Dave. It took another bout of banter to explain to her whose number had called her that day and why it was mine. We had a good laugh about it once she believed my identity.

In our conversation, she explained she was heading to Iraq or Afghanistan for a tour. God Bless that child. Another young brave American following government orders. More than a year passed when one night the phone rang. When I answered, someone said, "Hi Dave!" It was a different girl, so I went through the spiel again: "Dave's not home, man." We bantered about it for some time when she tells me she is at a tattoo parlor in Washington. It was the same tattoo parlor where the other girl had my number imprinted on her arm.

She knew the soldier who will never forget my number. We had some more good laughs about the whole thing. Most important to me is I found out that the girl had returned safely to America from her tour of duty with, hopefully, only the mental scars to heal, and of course, my phone number on her arm.

CHAPTER 21 | LOVE AND LEWD

There's no telling what the world thinks of Courtney Love. Even those who haven't listened to a note of her music or seen one frame of her film work have an opinion on the brash and brazen diva. She is what some would consider a "real" rock star. Or at least a stereotypical one.

I spent a few weeks driving her in the Baby Bus, and during that time I came to admire her. In my opinion she is genuine, and I admire that in a person. No bullshit with Courtney... or maybe all bullshit, who knows?

In rock circles, she was a musician and an actress, but most people will always remember her as the wife of Nirvana's front man, Kurt Cobain. Rolling Stone magazine even dubbed her "the most controversial woman in the history of rock." That, my friends, is saying a lot. When Cobain committed suicide, Courtney was on her way to rock stardom in her own right, recording the album "Live Through This" with her band, Hole. The title couldn't have been eerier.

Unlike other assignments where I had just wanted to drive in the most professional manner possible, this seemed a little different. I was excited about being able to work for a well-known, hard-to-deal-with rock star and completing the mission where others had failed. I had worked with many in the industry whose public persona is not the same as how they are in private. Maybe I wanted to see what made her tick. Having witnessed much of the crap tossed her way, especially in the media, it was easy to see her struggles with life. When I got the assignment, I was a little cautious, but the tour manager, Nick C., is one of the best in the business and that comforted me. Also, my friend Gaylon was driving the band, so I knew I wouldn't head down this unknown trek alone.

The first day I met Courtney, she was late getting to the bus. I'm sure she was playing rock star or something, but it had me waiting for an endless amount of time blocking a main thoroughfare during rush-hour traffic and dealing with the police threatening me with jail if I didn't move. She came through the door of the coach and shot me a weird look. I had nothing to lose. I figured I'd play the game and shot her the same look right back. She was wearing this pink... thing... and the first thought that entered my mind was if she turned out to be as bad as everyone had said she was, I would just leave her ass on the side of the road somewhere, maybe a truck stop. I had already been out for a year, and some time off was looking better and better. Heck, maybe kicking her ass out in Nebraska would give me 15 minutes of fame. Probably no money, though.

It never came to that, and actually, I came to respect her, although she was as predictable a rock star as they come. There has to be a book somewhere that gets passed around to all the wannabes telling them all the stupid things they are supposed to do instead of concentrating on music.

Because of her habit of being late, we were late pulling into Seattle one night. The fans were still there at the back of the Four Seasons hotel, where I had driven to try and avoid them. Some were tried and true fans, but a few were pros looking for autographs to sell. So in addition to driving the bus, sometimes I assist with playing part-time bodyguard. Usually it's just blocking the adoring fans while the star can get into the hotel. I look at it this way: That's my paycheck. If she gets hurt, especially when I am there to prevent it, I gotta look for another paycheck.

So we were pushing our way to the hotel when one of the pros — wearing a flannel shirt in Seattle no less — sticks out a guitar in one hand and a black marker in the other. Courtney lived up to her rude rock star role. My girl snorted up a loogie as well as any man could muster and sends it hooting right at the man's cheek. It hits the bull's eye and drips down his perfect grunge shirt. But she ain't done.

"The grunge era is over, and I ain't signing some cheap-ass guitar for you to sell," she screamed.

He was stone-faced when a voice yelled out, "Save it!" I think they were referring to Courtney's snot rocket. At 4 a.m., she was right on her mark acting the way everyone thought she would, and she pushed her way into the hotel, not missing a beat. I had only known this woman for a few days, but I instinctively yelled out, "That's my girl!" I then helped usher everyone else into the hotel.

On her first night performing, I checked out the show. It didn't seem to be more than fifth-generation punk. They knew what they were doing. As was the case, she played the evil rocker to the hilt. She bared her breasts a couple of times, pulled on her panties while she straddled the stage barrier, and yelled a barrage of "Fuck Yous" to the crowd. Yeah, it was punk. It gets kind of boring after a while, a lot of people out there trying to imitate the original sound. But one thing I can spot is musicianship, and her back-up group, Hole, was really good. Eric Erlandson was the guitarist, Samantha Maloney played drums, and Melissa Auf der Maur played bass and backing vocals, what vocals there are in a punk-type band. Samantha was one of the best rock women drummers I have ever seen. She even took Tommy Lee's place in Motley Crue for the "New Tattoo" tour in 2000.

But while Courtney was doing what she was supposed to do on stage, she did that same type of stuff off stage. I walked onto the bus one night when she was throwing food at her traveling chef. I think she complained that something in her sandwich was not fresh. The chef felt terrible, but so did I. I knew I would be the one cleaning it up the next day. The chef cried, and of course Courtney was rude to her, but hey, that's the way it is. We are all paid to do a job and do it right. I tried to do mine right so she wouldn't throw a bus at me.

Hole was touring with Marilyn Manson, so I was interested in seeing both bands perform. I was so busy after Hole's set on opening night that I missed out on the main act. That didn't happen the next night. The Beautiful Animals Tour, which was the name of Manson's tour in 1998, was one of the most amazing shows I have ever seen. Say what you will about his antics, his anti-religion bent, his bizarre look... the man puts on a captivating theatrical event. That didn't stop the two most polarizing figures in rock at the time from coming to blows. Having Courtney and Marilyn on the same tour was like throwing two fighters in the Octagon. After antagonizing each other, sooner or later they are gonna go at each other.

It happened in Nampa, Idaho, just outside of Boise. Courtney rushed the stage during Marilyn's show and attacked him. Each night on the tour, they both had made crass remarks about the other. Each night the rhetoric escalated. At this particular venue, the Idaho Center, the dressing rooms have speakers where you can hear what's going on from the stage. Not even into their first song, Marilyn made a crack about Courtney. This time she was ready to put up a fight.

I was standing in the hallway with one of her bodyguards wondering when I could start moving things out of her dressing room to the bus. That was when she stormed out and started a full sprint to the stage, the whole time screaming, "Motherfucker! Motherfucker!" In a flash she was trailed by nearly everyone else in the hall with me bringing up the rear. Needless to say, by the time I got to the stage, she was already being carried off, a couple of guys on both ends, carrying her while she was in full crazy mode. The crowd was screaming — maybe they thought it was part of the act — and Marilyn was standing there dumbstruck trying to regain his composure. They let Courtney down as she continued her fit away from the stage, and once again, as if by instinct I said, "That's my girl!"

Although there were more obligations, Hole was asked to leave the tour after the Nampa event. Due to contractual duties, we headed to San Francisco and Sacramento to finish, during which time plans were already being made to send Courtney and her band out as a headliner. After Nampa, Gaylon and I made our journey to California, during which I almost witnessed my friend's death.

Pulling out of Sierra Sid's Truck Stop in Sparks, Nevada, where we topped off our fuel tanks, an 18-wheeler almost crushed Gaylon. A construction zone was at the end of the on-ramp to the freeway and the speed limit was 35 mph. A trucker must have been doing 70 or more as he swerved into the zone where we were getting on the freeway. He locked his brakes, and I could tell that the truck was fully loaded from the sound and the smoke and the way the truck was tilting. I can hear it all if I think about it enough. I don't see how the guy missed Gaylon. He would have plowed right into the left front driver's side of the bus, right where Gaylon was sitting. As the truck approached Gaylon, I was warning him over the CB radio. He was braking and nearly scraping the barrier wall. His expert driving abilities saved the day. So goes the occupational hazards on the road. We headed on to San Francisco for a day off.

San Francisco has so many great concert venues, and I've been to them all. Meeting Bill Graham at the Shoreline Amphitheatre was one of the highlights of my life. The man was the best promoter in the business, and every time I was at a venue in the bay area, I would almost always catch a glimpse of him — at the Fillmore, the Warfield, the Fox in Oakland and the Greek in Berkeley.

The Cow Palace is another great one, and the final show of the Marilyn Manson/ Hole partnership was probably one of the best concerts there. I just didn't know about it. Being the driver for the band kicked off the tour, secured areas once granted access to become restricted. There was a short break for production coordination and time for ticket sales, and then we took off on the Celebrity Skin Tour. The new headlining tour was smaller with the group Imperial Teen as opening act. The tour really started to find its groove, especially without another Alpha Dog around to push Courtney's buttons.

The first week of April, someone associated with Courtney flew to our locations and brought her some personal belongings. A few days later, I took her to the Detroit airport from where she flew to Seattle with the items. I arrived at the airport early and parked in the Bob Evans Restaurant lot just outside of the airport so that folks awoke to coffee or eats before the early flight. Courtney was very quiet and mellow that morning as I dropped her off. She even gave me a concerned smile as she departed for the plane. A couple more days passed, and I picked her back up at another airport in another town. She seemed to be her old self as we finished the tour. She was back to typical Courtney antics.

A year or two later, I was driving for another band and staying in a Hollywood hotel on Sunset Boulevard. The Hyatt is a hotel where many road crews stay. Hollywood is a pain in the ass for bus drivers. Parking is always an issue, having to unload in the street and blocking traffic. While we were there, one of the roadies riding my coach called and said Courtney was in the Star Bar across the street in the La Mondrian Hotel.

I went over and flashed my pass to get in the door. As I approached where she, Drew Barrymore and another actress were sitting, a bodyguard stopped me from getting close. When I explained who I was and how I knew Courtney, he went over and spoke into her ear. She looked over at me and gave me this little wave and then turned away. That was the end of the relationship.

"Ah! That's my girl," I thought. I wouldn't expect anything more or less from Courtney Love.

THE BACK OF THE BUS

Some fans can go to extremes to meet their favorite stars. I've met many groupies of bands and entertainers along the way. These women have walked through the door of tour buses I've driven, waved at me and headed straight to the back of the bus. Ziggy in the Midwest, Caroline in Texas, girls from Florida to California, most of them have reputations with roadies and musicians.

During a chance meeting with Pamela Des Barres, a popular West Coast groupie from the '70s, I found myself listening intently to her stories. By this time, she had written multiple books about her experiences as a groupie. I enjoyed hearing firsthand how her stories came to light.

There are so many groupies in the Northeast. There's no way to remember all their names.

Certainly, one of the most famous groupies in America is Sweet Connie (Connie Hamzy) who is from my hometown. In Grand Funk Railroad's song, "We're an American Band," there is a verse that refers to Connie working the band over backstage in Little Rock. I've known Connie many years but never had the pleasure. She is a friend, and I admire her for being real to who she is, living the way she wants.

Connie's not afraid to speak her mind and challenge the status quo. She's even stuck her neck out there and run for local political office. She's a person not afraid to tell the truth. Her boldness may be shocking to many people, but having known her for many years, she's probably one of the most real and honest people I know. What you see is what you get.

There were even reported antics with Arkansas's former governor and our nation's President Bill Clinton. I know she has no reason to invent any of her stories, and I admire people who can walk the walk.

In the 1980s, Connie was well known with bands and roadies. Her memorabilia is fascinating to go along with stories of Jon Bonham, Led Zeppelin and dozens of others. Just about anyone who rode on my bus and asked where I was from would follow up with a question as to whether I knew Connie. Many a jaw would drop when I would say, "Of course, I live next door to her." Well, not really next door to her, but close enough.

CHAPTER 22 | SEX SHOW AFTER THE ROCK SHOW

It was always interesting to me that for many rock stars, rock 'n' roll took third place behind those other two vices, sex and drugs. But when you're on tour, the music is only part of the experience. And the band members usually aren't the craziest ones around.

The characters you meet on tour vary in extremes from normal working types to the absolutely insane. Don't get me wrong. Everyone does his job, but it's what goes on after the jobs get done that always pique the interest of the concertgoers. So when you run across those insane types, you just have to understand that if you respect the job they do, you can tolerate the insanity... a bit.

A typical crew bus might have up to 12 people on board, all with different personalities, religious beliefs, and approaches to fashion, sexuality, hygiene and ways to self medicate. Throw them into 300 square feet of living space and see how it goes. That's the unique thing about touring: When it all works, everyone pulls together as a team and you march across the country. It reminds me of the TV show M*A*S*H. When it's time to work, you go to work. The rest of the time, you just have to laugh.

Someone I laughed a lot with was Biker Bob, a rock 'n' roll truck driver. Bob was a scruff individual who always wore scruffy jeans and scruffy white T-shirts with riding boots – usually scruffy. His normal attire included several jackets with bike patches and emblems on them. Bob never really supported any one motorcycle group's colors. He was a friend to them all.

He was really a friend to the ladies. As rough looking as he was, he always knew which buttons to push to get the girls. Almost every night I would see Bob with a different woman, many just drop-dead gorgeous. Heck, sometimes there was more than one, and they swooned all over him. I never understood it. The rest of us would just give him a look every now and again saying, "Let us have your extras, please." I remember a night in St. Louis where Bob got on a roll. He already had three in his truck as I was coming back during the gig to get ready for the night run. I walked by his truck, and as the curtain opened ever so slightly, I could spy a large-breasted woman standing up in the sleeper area trying to get her bra back on. There were two more girls in the front. All of a sudden, all three caught my eye, and as is the custom, either in New Orleans or any rock show, they gave me a flash. I have seen a gazillion breasts in my day, but it's always nice to admire. I paused, looked, smiled, waved and went on my way. Bob was the master.

Many times, names are changed to protect the innocent. In this case, I need to change the names to protect the guilty. But the next story, with slight changes, has probably happened thousands of times to hundreds of bands. I have a feeling Bob was involved with a lot of them.

After arriving at a gig, a bus driver always has a few chores to batten down the hatches before rolling to the next city. Empty the day's trash, clean up the day's drinks and do paperwork. Once in a while, I get my stuff done and head in to catch some of the show. This was one of those nights. I love standing to the side, hearing the music and catching the energy of the crowd. Most amphitheaters are the same. There is a long hall that leads to the stage and along those hallways sit different rooms, some for business, others for pleasure. While walking down the hall this particular night, I passed Bob, made my standard comment about his haul of women and started to move by. He stopped me.

"Fitz, you might want to be close to the dressing rooms when the show goes down."

I knew this was one of Bob's shenanigans, and I knew to always be around if invited for Bob's shenanigans. I raced back to the bus, got my work done and headed back to the dressing room area. As I got there, the hallway was a mess with people, band members and crew, all sweaty, most dirty, trying to get where they needed to be. I was just trying to figure out where I needed to be. That's when I saw Bob.

"Get to the opening act dressing room now." No need for further explanation. I headed down the hall and saw more people slipping into the room. Inside were about seven crew members. "Aren't they supposed to be working right now?" I thought. They were just standing around.

They were waiting for Bob when he burst into the room with this... well, to say she was a nine would be a bit of an injustice. She had on tight blue jeans and a leather halter-top. No matter how good looking she was, she still looked like Bob's type. He led her to a table toward the back wall of the room and zipped back out again. Seconds later, he came in with another girl, this one just as good looking, and brought her to the table. Just about that time, the lead singer of the night's main act walked in. He was joined by a couple of other band members, and the sight of him made these girls melt. It was almost as if they would do anything for him. And then they did.

There was a table in the room normally used for catering, but the food was gone. There was a blanket that was draped over it, and Bob came toward them. He pulled them close, whispered in both their ears and backed away. They started to undress each other. The second girl pulled the other one's halter top down and started kissing her breast. Then they paused, got naked, climbed onto the table, looked in each other's eyes for a second and got after it. It was something like I had never seen.

One moved down between the other's legs and started kissing while the first girl moaned and moaned. The rest of us stood there watching. Of course with this crew, there was plenty of grunting and comments, but for the most part we just quietly enjoyed the show as the room seemed to warm up. The girl getting serviced was leaning on her elbows and making more noise, shaking and sweating. When it seemed over, they switched positions, and the other one got to do her moaning. This caused more catcalls from the peanut gallery, and after a few minutes, it was over.

The lead singer then casually walked up to the girls and thanked them for the show.

"That was great, but did you know that I have never seen two girls actually 69 each other?"

He then smiled and stepped back. They looked at each other, got in position, and went at it again. This brought the room to a frenzy. Guys hooting and hollering like they had money on the outcome or something.

Then it was over. The girls slowly dressed when one of them casually asked one of the band members what time it was.

"11:45"

"Shit! I know my husband's trying to find me!" She took off down the hall.

The other girl stayed for a moment longer, enough to get teased by the stragglers. She got up and departed a different way than the first girl. Bob just smiled.

"Those two didn't even know each other. They didn't even know each other's names."

My eyebrows rose. "What?"

"Yeah. I just pulled them out of the crowd during the show." Bob grinned as he remarked on another achievement.

For this night at least, sex trumped drugs and rock 'n' roll.

CHAPTER 23 | A HERO BREAKS HIS SWORD

In America, we had Superman and Batman and the Green Hornet. In the United Kingdom, they had Captain Scarlet.

Captain Scarlet was in reality a puppet, not much more than wood and paint and strings, but he was a superhero to British kids in the late 1960s. He was the star of a science fiction show called "Captain Scarlet and the Mysterons." The short story about his character is that he possessed a strange ability to return to life after suffering a fatal injury. It made Captain Scarlet virtually indestructible. Also, he looked a little like my friend.

Our Captain Scarlet was a hero among men — one of the strangest, most entertaining self-destructive men I had ever met. He was talented. He was misunderstood. He was usually in a state of inebriation, be it through alcohol or crystal meth. He was a self-burning and branding, self-piercing, tattooed, never-washing, charming, lovable, hugely irritating, perpetually drugged-up and drunken lunatic – a typical roadie of the '80s. But most of all he subscribed to his look-a-like's mentality of invincibility.

And, despite all that he was still a hero. To me anyway.

We were sitting a room in the La Mandarin Hotel on Sunset in Hollywood one night in 1986 or '87. There were about six or seven of us in the room along with several groupies. It was the roadies for this popular punkish band and me — the truck driver. We were passing around some English bullshit beer and some assorted hard liquor. There was a big pile of blow on the table. There was pot, cigarettes and spliffs everywhere. No worries for these guys. They weren't even afraid of the cops.

I was the only American in the room and was doing my level best to defend my country. These English roadie fucks can tell you everything that's wrong with America.

"You know what's wrong with America?" That's how it always started. And it never got solved. These guys come over here to earn a living year after year with band after band. And every year it's the same for me... Oh Joy! Another English invasion! Fun for me! And the same complaints roll around year after year.

I'm sure another argument was cropping up when we heard a knock on the door. Nobody moved too fast. The drugs were everywhere. Nothing was hidden. Like I said, these guys didn't care. They figured since they're foreign roadies they can get away with this type of thing. Cops are supposed to bust the bad guys. No bad guys here, right? Just English roadies.

So one of them — Pete — saunters over to the door and opens it — doesn't check the peephole, doesn't ask who it is, just opens it — and there stood good ol' Captain Scarlet.

The Captain stands about 6'2" and wears all black – black pants stuffed into his black boots, black belt around those black pants and a black buttoned shirt, usually with the sleeves cut out. He also cut out the black shirt to exposes his nipples, mainly to show off his piercings. And on top, he wore an airline pilot's hat.

His fingernails were painted black, and he was a fan of eye shadow. His head was shaved except for a yarmulke-sized, Rastafarian-style hairdo that sprouted and came down toward his back. There were tattoos around his ears and down his neck highlighting flames like sideburns. He had dozens of piercings: eyes, ears, nose, nipples and many, many other parts.

This man attracted the best-looking women around, most of them pierced like him.

So Pete opens the door, and Captain Scarlet is standing there casually... with his dong in his hand. Not only is it in his hand, but it's also shooting out blood at an enormous rate. At this point, Scarlet announced, "O'we mates, I'e pierced me knob."

These guys who were so nonchalant before suddenly bursting into action. They dragged Scarlet into the room. Someone grabbed a white towel while blood flowed faster than a tapped keg. After a couple of minutes of chaos, it calmed down, and then we started to laugh. And we laughed and laughed and laughed. This nut job tried to drive a nail through his dick! Who would do that? Well invincible, indestructible Captain Scarlet, that's who. It was one of the weirdest things I have seen in my life.

A few days later, after a drive from Los Angeles to Salt Lake City, Scarlet got sick. He was really, really sick. He was turning all sorts of colors, so he headed to a doctor in Utah. The doctor took one look in disbelief.

"I've never in my life met anyone like you, let alone anyone with this sort of... problem," he said as he put Scarlet back together. After the SLC show, Scarlet spent the night in the bunk and hit another hospital in Denver. He stayed there for a couple of days before rejoining the tour.

It was a little dicey for a while, but Captain Scarlet really is invincible.

CHAPTER 24 | HOME AWAY FROM HOME

Any entertainer who's anybody has to go through New York City with his or her show. It's a given. In any year, I have averaged 30 to 45 days in a small town outside the city called Secaucus in New Jersey. I should have bought a home there on my first visit.

Parking for custom coaches is very limited in NYC, so after dropping off passengers at their designated city hotels, most drivers head over to Harmon Meadows Plaza in Secaucus where there is ample parking, dozens of hotels and amenities. Food, drink, laundry facilities, movie theaters and shopping are all right there within walking distance. On any given day, coaches fill the parking lots and it's a place to meet old and new friends with something in common. I have spent some memorable evenings with a bunch of buses corralled with dozens of drivers and friends cooking on grills and sharing stories of the trade.

Secaucus is a neat little town just out of the Lincoln Tunnel west of Hoboken on Route 3 at the end of the New Jersey Turnpike. I have come to know a few of the residents and established some nice friendships where we all smile when I come in the door. The little town has grown in various ways since the first time I visited in 1985. For years, there was a great laundromat where several women worked and would take a load of bus laundry in the morning and get it all done by mid-day. One year, it closed and the building became the Bagel Buffet. Not as useful as a place to do laundry, but hey, bus drivers eat bagels, too.

On the early coach models everyone who rode the bus had to have a key. After every tour new keys had to be made since most people kept theirs when they left. Generally, the key is kept on the lanyard next to your laminated backstage pass. They are equally important. Newer coach models now have coded door locks and the driver changes the code after each tour to ensure security. On Paterson Plank Road just before County Line Road in Secaucus there is a locksmith who has cut hundreds of keys for the many buses I have driven. It's always a fun time to spend a few minutes with them joking about various lifestyles. Two bus companies on County Line Road provide drivers a place to dump and clean their equipment. For many years a 24-hour diner on the intersection of Charlie's Corner and Paterson Plank was a great place to get breakfast after a long night of travel. It was also a great place to be alone or visit with other bus drivers about schedules and share road stories. After many years in business the old diner closed down and another one opened on County Line Road. It's a nice place. It's not open 24 hours. It will take some years to get use to it. A hardware store for parts is close by and Prevost Car, the bus manufacturer, had a large repair facility nearby. It's all there in Secaucus, and Secaucus is a great American town.

Secaucus is always a comfort. The other hundreds of days spent on the road have me checking in and out of hotels. Hotels are a circus. Some care about your comfort, others could care less.

I'm no hotel genius, but I've had years of over 300 nights spent in a different hotel every night. Depending on the entertainer's budget and who you're driving on a tour, you might stay at a Ritz Carlton or a Four Seasons and it may seem like you're living life as a king. Or you may end up in a run-down cheap downtown motel where prostitutes and drug dealers sell their wares. I've stayed at motels and hotels in every state and all the providences of Canada, and I will tell you they are all the same once your eyes are closed after driving 10 hours or more and spending another four or five servicing the bus and getting it ready for the next run.

Finding a place to park always takes time if it hasn't been arranged. Interior cleaning, exterior washing, generator servicing, repairing anything that may not be working, it's all part of the job – keeping the passenger comfortable at all costs.

I've told many that the only reason I'm in this business is for the endless supply of hot water. Getting rest in a bed and a hot shower and a warm meal prepares one much better for a long drive than waking up in the back of a semi-truck sleeper, pissing between the fuel tanks and wheels and driving on till you drop again. When you wake up, order room service, take a hot shower and get a ride to wherever your bus is parked, you can drive longer, be more alert and be prepared for any situation that might occur.

I've met some of the least concerning, rudest people at the front desk of hotels whose corporate policy is 3 p.m. check-in. I, and many folks I've transported, have spent hours in hotel lobbies waiting for a reserved room to rest in or to freshen up in so we could then enjoy the town, go shopping for necessities or find restaurants. Many times the corporate hotel rules don't fit into my schedule, so I've had to argue for a room to get my rest. Try stopping at a hotel near the highway and checking in at 10 a.m. after driving all night, needing some sleep before having to drive all night again, only to hear, "Sorry sir, no check-in until three." It ain't a good feeling.

Some groups and band parties I've traveled with book their rooms the night before, so when we arrive at six, seven or eight in the morning everyone can go directly to their rooms. Not every group can afford to do this but some can. Some hotel sales agents will work with the entertainment travel agents when they want the business. Most hotel employees are only concerned when they can go home. They could care less about a weary traveler thousands of miles from home. Sometimes they can't even tell you how to get to the hotel. It's always confused me when I call a hotel in a big city and realize that the person answering the phone can't tell you directions to the hotel they work in. I've always wondered how these people get to work if they can't tell someone else how to get there.

Hotels want business from entertainment groups. More rooms booked equals more people equals more resources used and more money made for the hotel. They solicit entertainment travel agents with promises that rarely are kept. I'm not the only one who just wants a hot shower and a fluffy pillow to lie on for a brief rest from the road. Roadies just want a relaxing day off to catch up with the world. Many times the promises made at the corporate level and the needs of tired travelers don't translate to a hotel's front desk person. To them, we're just another batch of faces that cause them more work.

There are ways to let your disgust known, not that I condone these actions. One night after seeing a drunken roadie lift the lid and piss on the ice inside, I realized it was probably a bad idea to get ice from a machine that wasn't sealed. Shoving a pizza between the mattresses must give a hotel a problem at some point after the roadies are long gone.

CHAPTER 25 | GET A GRIP

The year was 1995 and the family and I were having dinner at our house with the in-laws when my father-in-law, an avid tennis player, announced to me that he felt I needed to take up a sport or hobby of some sort. Burt, a California Jewish man, liked, really liked, to get his way. I'd been too busy to really take the time to do anything sporty. He explained that I probably couldn't learn how to play tennis and become good enough to enjoy the sport at my age. So he offered up a spare set of golf clubs he had and strongly suggested I give golf a try.

They were a nice set of clubs, and I took them to the driving range as he suggested. I started hitting balls and reading books and magazines. Went to the range with friends who gave me pointers. I dove into it, and the more I did it, the more I wanted to do it. The pro at the range explained that I needed to put new grips on the clubs.

Soon after taking up the game, I left the house heading to Cleveland to pick up the Aerosmith crew. I was one of about six or seven crew buses. I left home a couple of days early to give myself plenty of time to get there and have the bus and myself in order. After spending the day driving to Corinth, Mississippi, to the bus shop to get things together, it was a long day. I got out of Corinth late and made it north on Highway 45 to I-40. A few miles east from Jackson, Tennessee on I-40 is a parking area where tired truckers usually park to rest. There are no facilities or anything. I grabbed a spot out of the way of trucks. I awoke to the sound of someone beating on the side of the bus. I was on the back couch and opened the rear window and stuck my head out.

A Tennessee Department of Transportation officer, the highway police for commercial vehicles, came walking to the window.

"Sir, you have to leave. We are using this area for inspections."

I jumped right up and got out of there not wanting to have to deal with them first thing in the morning. After getting on the highway, I'd gone maybe five miles, just getting up to speed when an American Eagle Motor Home passed me going well above the speed limit. As he went by, I noticed something about grips on the side of it. I accelerated and caught him to get a closer look at what was on the side of the camper.

"Grip it and Rip it" was on the side, and in my weird way of thinking I concluded that this guy was selling golf grips, thinking he was probably following the golf tour or something. I tried to get his attention on the CB radio. No luck there and he was hogging the left lane so I moved up on his right to get the guy's attention in the jump seat. He opened his window, and we were screaming at each other out of our windows driving 70-plus miles per hour.

"Are you selling grips on the tour?" I screamed.

He yelled back, "NO! It's John Daly" and pointed at the driver. New to golf, I had heard his name but really didn't have a clue what he looked like. I was more concerned with my grip idea.

He screamed back at me "Whose bus is that?"

"Aerosmith!" I yelled back.

We're still driving 70-plus, and he started to slow down. We rode up the road a bit and pulled into a rest area. We introduce ourselves. I'm not timid with people who think they're famous. We had a minute of good conversation. Donnie, John's friend and assistant, and a third person were in the camper with John. John was on his way up to Custom Coach Corporation to see the new MCI Motor Home he was having them build.

Custom Coach was one of the premier builders of very expensive motor homes. John Madden, the football guy, used a Custom Coach for years. They built mostly on the MCI chassis. Some incredible equipment has come from their shop. I'm not a fan of MCI; I've been spoiled by the quality of a Prevost, so I made a joke and apologized when he said he was buying an MCI. We made laughs for a little while, and I invited John to ride with me for a few miles to get the feel of a Prevost.

We left the rest area with John in the jump seat and Donnie driving the camper. I enjoyed talking to him. We are both Arkies, so we had a few good laughs. I appreciated his genuine nature. After we had traveled for a while, he said he was going to be driving his own motor home and that he wouldn't hire anyone to drive it. As I drove, we discussed my opinions and differences of the MCI and the Prevost we were riding in. He got up a few times and walked through the coach as we rode on. Finally, I asked him if he wanted to drive. When he agreed, using a trucker's trick, I got out of the seat and he slid in while we traveled along at speed. He seemed to be a pretty good driver after he got the feel of it. Much different than driving the 35-foot camper he was traveling in.

In Kentucky, we slid into the McDonald's he said he had stopped at when he was racing last minute to get to the tournament in Indianapolis from Memphis. John invited me to go to the factory with him and see his coach. I was going through Columbus to get to Cleveland, so I made the stop at Custom Coach in Columbus. John and his gang went to dinner while I stayed in the lot at Custom Coach, did some cleaning and got some sleep. John's camper was parked next to mine in the Custom Coach parking lot. When everyone awoke the next morning, I went in with John and the guys to see the new bus.

The salesman who was handling John's bus had been a salesman for the Eagle Bus Corporation in its hey day. I had met him several times over the years at bus shops. He was now selling for Custom Coach. He was curious why I was there. I joked I was there to encourage John to go with a Prevost. Not a good joke to him. I went through John's bus with him and was impressed with the design and quality of work being done. I asked him why he didn't have a club bay for his clubs and shoes and other golf stuff. Not sure if that idea ever came to pass.

Several weeks after I had that encounter with John, I received a package in the mail. Several pairs of Oakley sunglasses, one of John's sponsors at the time, an autographed book by John and a complete set of golf grips with "John Daly" imprinted on them.

Thanks, John.

CHAPTER 26 | THE ROAD IS A HARSH MISTRESS

Some of the happiest times in my life have been in a crowd escaping and enjoying the music, forgetting the troubles in my life, dancing and singing with thousands of "Shiny Happy People."

Some of the lowest lows have also been at these same type of events, watching couples and families in love with one another enjoying the excitement, walking, holding hands, glowing, hugging and cheering. I see many every day. Families holding hands when they enter the event, dads chasing kids, moms trying to keep them all organized. The joy and stress of it all brings to mind my own family memories and desires. Seeing a family doing things together puts a knot in your heart when you are away from your own family trying to make wages.

Saratoga Performing Arts Center (SPAC) in upstate New York is a grand place to see a concert. I've driven into the beautiful park many times over the years with bands and crews. The venue, north of Albany, is a regular summer stop for many. The golf course next door is always fun and handy to play. The trees and woodsy feel make for a great evening under the stars when concerts are performed there. The place is the summer home of the New York Philharmonic Orchestra. The old venue built in the '60s has typical orchestra rooms behind the stage where in one room an old upright piano sits. I've noticed it a few times over the years. Folklore has it that Jonathan Cain, the keyboardist for the band Journey, wrote "Faithfully," a song about missing loved ones, on that old piano. The song describes the relationship of a "music man" on the road, the difficulties of raising and maintaining a family, two strangers having to fall in love again and staying faithful while touring. The powerful lyrics relate to many emotions felt by those in the touring industry.

Marriage and the touring business are not a good fit. Having a family waiting and depending on you at home takes comprehension of a way of life that is not always easily understood. It seems in this modern age that many have to travel more and more and be away from their families for longer periods of time. From soldiers to salesmen, many do it because they have to.

My first marriage fell apart soon after I discovered how to make a living in the transportation business. The misunderstandings of what one or the other might be doing at any given time can put questions and doubts in your mind and heart. Having never traveled or toured, my first wife didn't realize what men and women do out on the road. It's hard to believe that hard work goes on 24/7. Of course, like many, she thought it was a big party all of the time.

For me, meeting someone who worked in the business and understood the lifestyle was a lucky break. My second wife was somewhat of an entertainer. She wrestled with The Powerful Women of Wrestling. She walked through the door of my bus when I was assigned to drive The POWW tour in 1987. As a passenger, she was able to view me and my approach to the business before we had a romantic interest in each other. We became friends doing fun things as we traveled the country.

When the POWW tour was over, we kept seeing each other.

Michelle traveled to many cities to visit me and continue our fun, challenging life together. There can be lots of good times when you spend time under the umbrella of an entertainment tour. With lodging taken care of in major cities, there are occasional days off to spend with your significant other. Nothing compares to a romantic weekend exploring the sights of San Francisco, the mountains around Denver or the streets of New York City. Meeting up after a tour is over and riding home together in a half-million-plus motor home or to the next pick-up point through America on your own time is a unique opportunity. Bring the kids and it can make for an even more exciting trip. Opportunities for adventurous quality time can be rare, but they are meaningful when they happen, and the memories last forever.

In 1988, while on tour with Sting, Michelle and I were married on a bus backstage at a concert in Nashville. Funny, the Starwood Amphitheatre where we married was torn down the year we divorced. Faye Cox, a close friend in the Nashville bus business, helped arrange a license and a preacher. The crew and everyone got into the bus, and we stood in the front and said our vows. That night at the show, Sting told the crowd and sang "Be Still My Beating Heart." Michelle rode the bus with the crew and me to Chicago for a couple of days off, then she went home, and I kept working.

A Jewish girl from Los Angeles, she wanted to escape the crowds, smog and grit of L.A. to raise a family. We ended up in Arkansas where a more conservative life was possible. A beautiful girl born by the end of our first year of marriage helped grow our ideas of family. We wore out the doctors playing Sting on a portable stereo while Michelle was in labor. I went to the hospital and brought her home in a bus for fun. No matter where we were, we were always bus people. There are plumbing people and electric people and so on. "Us kids," I would tell my children, "We're bus people."

All marriages and families have their ups and downs. Imagine putting thousands of miles between the problems. We struggled with all the issues that a traveling spouse and separation can bring to a relationship. In the beginning, working 300 days a year on the road and trying to get a secure hold on the financial world was a tough journey. Missing family functions and milestones and sacrificing togetherness to provide for family wants and necessities are an industry standard. Quality time instead of the amount of time is the best approach one can have when travel separates the family.

Michelle helped us gain custody of my daughter from my first marriage whose mother fell apart at the hands of childhood abuse, the bottle and drugs. She practically adopted her and helped her to grow into a wonderful woman, who's now a loving mother herself. Our own daughter grew into a bright young woman, who developed my traveling bug, and we have a son who's going to conquer the world someday. He admires his mother's history of having wrestled in the big ring.

As our life together grew, we had good times, especially during the times of travel we did together as a family. I've been lucky that my many touring employers allow family members to occasionally travel for a few days. My daughter's traveling with me on a political awareness tour was educational enough for her to miss some school days and learn from real life experiences.

A trip to the Caribbean, Disneyland, the millennium celebration in New York City, four-star hotels in Chicago and Hollywood – our family has been everywhere together. We took spur of the moment trips to Memphis for barbecue dinners and to sleep in the railroad cars at the Chattanooga Choo Choo. Traveling and experiencing places together was our way just like sporting events or farming may be a way of life for another family.

While working on the road, nothing is more important to me than my children moving forward and having their needs met. Separation doesn't always help, and being apart for what seems like forever sometimes eventually takes its toll on future dreams. I was lucky to have found love and share a true connection with a strong woman I admired. Our family had a unique way of life. After 18 years, the good times finally were overtaken by the pitfalls of the road, and Michelle and I divorced. I think of family memories often when I see other families at concerts. Sometimes I smile and enjoy their escapades. Sometimes I just turn away.

A FEW BUS DRIVER JOKES

How many bus drivers does it take to screw in a light bulb?
One. The world revolves around them.

What's the difference between a puppy and a bus driver?
A puppy usually stops whining after six months.

Trucker on CB radio:
   That's the third time today that fancy bus has passed me.
Bus driver on CB radio:
   Yes, Mr. Trucker, ALL this luxury and you still have to stop to piss.

PART II

THE ROAD TAKEN | MY PATH TO THE DRIVER SEAT

I didn't have a plan when I was young. How could I? With an abusive upbringing and no support, I wasn't given much direction. Instead, my young life became a constant exit strategy, always looking for the next escape.

The stories between the lines are like the dotted lines on the interstate. They come and go, and I keep leaving them behind. Music has always been there for me to escape to or to enhance the atmosphere of wherever I might be and make it a better place. It can change my attitude and it can fulfill my heart, relieve my sadness and suppress my anger. From the first moments I discovered how music could lay peace on my soul, I have reached for rhythms to ease the tension. It hardly matters the genre.

Discovering the entertainment/transportation business altered a life that seemed to be heading in the direction of drugs, alcohol, jails and prison. I may have made some bad judgment calls, but overall my travels provided guidance that I missed out on as child. As a boy, I can remember envying the other children whose parents seemed to provide comfort and security. The various tours I've worked on have became little pieces of family to me, providing much comfort. Music and the people behind the music have taken me to the next town, next tour and new friends. These destinations, people and sounds are a part of my soul.

The emotions felt when a tour is ending is like leaving a family over and over. When it's the last time to tear down the stage, there is much sadness that time together is ending. There is also a feeling of anticipation of what will happen on the next tour when you build the new stage. New working companions, a different genre, differently dressed fans.

You wonder how that tour will be different, even though we will all be doing the same jobs. You may wonder if you will ever work again with the people you're working with now. Fans don't see or maybe even think about what really goes on backstage – the hard work, the dedication and the camaraderie of the team doing it.

Like a poetry scholar absorbing the carefully crafted use of words, I have found the same type of intensity in music. Music is poetry in motion to me. In 1975, lyrics from Bob Seger's song, "Beautiful Loser," pinpointed many of my desires about life. As the lyrics express, I want to live a dream, have faith, wisdom and a home base, but I also have freedom to roam.

I was a young man when the record came out, still looking for answers to life. All of that appealed to me as something to pursue. Mickey Mo Johnson, a good friend and a bus driver, used to hand out little cards for folks to remember him by. They read: "No one ever said the life of a rock 'n' roll bus driver was going to be easy." He's right. It's not an easy job.

I can't imagine doing anything else at this point of my life. Perhaps I have been traveling the original path for me all along.

My young life was an uncertain journey on an unclear path until I sat in the driver seat for the first time. Before discovering my career calling, I became a Marine after making it through troubled times as a teen, and before that, an abusive and confusing childhood. I appreciate the lessons I learned during my brief time as a Marine – the protocol, how to be organized and on time. I didn't like the in-your-face yelling because it reminded me of my abusive past, and ultimately, the military life wasn't for me. I came home, where another bad choice put me behind bars. I crossed some more bumpy roads before I figured out the best direction for me. I found success by physically getting away from my troubles, traveling to other places to escape abuse and the influences that were making me want to rebel against life. I discovered that by leaving I could be a more focused person. The map I followed while driving, all centered on the music, helped me to get a grip on life. I could have taken a different path, but my life wouldn't be what it is today.

CHAPTER 27 | A CALLING

Life is full of moments, some defining and some that pile up in our memory banks. I've had my share of defining moments. Sometimes I don't realize their impact until much later. Having had many instances that have taken me down the wrong path, I took for granted the one that actually changed my life and put me in the right direction. A chance meeting in my younger years secured me a life-long friend and mentor.

Realizing I had spent seven-plus years in "the system," where many didn't even know what the system was, struck a desire within me to never see the inside of a jail or prison again. So many of the people I wanted to be like hadn't even had a traffic ticket, much less been locked up, and I wanted to change that part of me. I wanted so much to never lose my freedom again. Life could be simple, I realized, with work and music and my new friends who didn't want or have trouble in mind. I started assuring myself that I would never allow myself to get caught up in the system again. One day I realized if I would just put as much energy into doing good as I had put into trying to be bad, that maybe life's situations would change for me.

As the drummer of a bar band, Lightfoot, my money management skills left something to be desired. A week's pay for me swirled down the drain faster than I could beat the drums. I always seemed to be broke or in debt to someone I had borrowed $20 from. During my bar band days, there were several music stores in Little Rock. Boyd Music Center offered top of the line guitars, drums, wind instruments and accessories matched by no other in town, or the state for that matter. I'd spent hours in their store daydreaming of all the possibilities with drums that I couldn't afford. I purchased my sticks and a few drumheads from them, but they were also the most expensive music store in town so my selections were limited.

Bob Boyd, the owner and one of the finest musicians in the state, was a stickler about his pricing and wouldn't consider financing someone with no credit like myself. Bob can play piano like no other. Even though he performed gigs with his band and seemed like just one of the guys, he was tough to deal with and the rejections he gave to those trying to make a go in a music-poor town were disheartening. There were several other stores in town that fit better with struggling musicians like me, such as Stonehenge in the southwest part of town and another store north across the river.

Mike Pinner, a young musician, opened Strum and Hum, a music store on the southwest side of town just up the street from Stonehenge Music Store. He had been in several (almost) successful bands. Albatross and Judas, many thought, would hit the big time, especially after they had landed opening slots with some bigger acts like Ted Nugent and Styx. David Dyer, the drummer in both bands, was one of the most amazing drummers I've ever seen to this day.

Mack, the singer in my band, worked at a liquor store just up the street from where Mike's store had opened. My drum set was in bad shape to be in a band that was playing gigs three nights a week. Mack recommended I go to Strum and Hum to check out new parts for my drum kit. When he told me about Mike having been in Judas, I was enticed.

The first day I dropped into Strum and Hum, Mike, or Bean as he was commonly referred to, was not there. Steve, his sales manager, was working, and I told him I just wanted to look around. He had a few lines, but they weren't the top lines that were being offered at Boyd's. He also had a few used items on the shelf and my eyes were immediately drawn to a five-piece set of Fibes Drums. I'd never heard or seen that brand before, but what caught my eye was the shiny chrome that made their existence possible. Everything on them, except the heads, was chrome, and as they sat in the store, they just glowed. As I wandered around the store, I kept looking their way and couldn't take my eyes off them. I learned Fibes was a start-up drum company in the '60s that made drums out of fiberglass. All the major brands of drums are made out of various types of wood like maple, birch, and now even oak, to get different tones or sounds. Fiberglass shells have a unique tone to them. You can tune them to just about any note.

The hardware on the set was really weak, one of Fibes' faults. I didn't care about the faults – I was more concerned with their shine at the time. When Steve told me the asking price, I didn't have that kind of cash and asked him about financing. He said I would have to come back and talk with the owner. He told me the time frames Bean was usually there and I said I'd come back then. I left, and by the time I made it back to the store to see Bean, I was determined to say or do just about anything to get that kit of drums.

As I entered the front door of the store, Mike, his wife and mother were standing behind the counter close to each other discussing some paperwork. Steve and Mike's stepfather were chatting on the other side of the store. Their son was on the counter in a baby seat. He was only a few weeks old. Coming through the door and seeing all of them with the baby almost caused me to stagger. I hadn't expected a family operation, I remember thinking as I headed toward the drum side of the store. Everyone smiled and seemed relieved that I wasn't going to interrupt them and went back to their discussion. When I made it back to the area of the drums, I was again infatuated with the glow from the Fibes set. I could see myself reflected in the chrome and could imagine playing them at the bar with Lightfoot. But as I turned watching the Pinner family, I was equally entranced as they simply discussed paperwork. I heard Mike's mom in a lovely tone encouraging him about what had to be done. His wife was joining in on the discussion.

Turning from a "rock star" to a businessman, Mike had recently cut his hair for a more tailored look. There were pictures of him and his long hair tied up in a ponytail in that bass guitar rock-star stance. As I stood by the drum kit I had been dreaming about, my focus was on this seemingly perfect family. Suddenly, more important than this shiny drum set before me, was the simple family portrait behind the desk. I was envious.

Watching them interact, I started admiring them all, and Mike and I hadn't even spoken yet. A family and a business centered on music. I realized then I would one day want those things, too. I couldn't even concentrate on the drums that day and left the store to come back the next day more determined to get the glowing set. Our band was becoming a hit at the bar where we played and started to draw in enough customers that the bar owner was making plans to expand the building and build a new stage. I pictured my new drum set on the new stage.

The next time I returned to the store, I spoke with Bean about the drums. Respecting musicians the way he did, he knew I had a house gig and he wanted to help, but I needed a little more cash for a down payment before he would let me take the drums. After a few weeks of saving money, I approached Bean and worked out a deal to get my drums. I had been visiting the store several times a week looking at them trying to will them into my ownership, while at the same time getting to know a little about Bean and his family. One of the first things I admired about him was his faith. He was a devout Christian and seemed to speak of God in everything he did. I listened intently to his mini-sermons about how God works in mysterious ways and observed his actions, which pretty much coincided with his views at the time.

Finally, after making a deal with Bean, the day came and I had the pleasure of taking the drums out of the store. The deal included several cymbals and stands from my other drum equipment that I was going to mix with the set to make them even bigger and expand the sounds I was trying to imitate. Included in the deal was a Ghost drum pedal like the ones Alex Van Halen, one of my heroes, was using at the time. Later in 1988, when I toured with Van Halen I gave them to Andy, Alex's drum tech. Andy scoured the world for Ghost pedals and parts after the Ghost pedal was discontinued by its maker. By '88, my playing days were over, so I offered it up to him along with several others I had collected.

I took my new drums straight to the Palace Saloon, where we did our gig on Thursdays, Fridays and Saturdays and sometimes Wednesday, set them up and played them all afternoon driving the afternoon bar customers crazy. I lived in an apartment and couldn't practice there. The new set certainly helped my attitude and confidence to attempt things I hadn't before; various roll combinations and such. And I looked so good behind that set of chrome drums. At the time, I owned a two-seat Triumph sports car. Anytime I moved my drums, I would load the British green beast down with the entire set of drums. I put them on the passenger seat, behind the seats, in the trunk and on the rack on top of the trunk and then tied them down on the trunk lid.

Mack had a van and most load-in and load-out days I would borrow it to move everybody's equipment from our practice place to the Saloon and back on Sunday or Monday depending on how much partying we had done on Saturday night. We performed at the Palace three weekends in a row and would take a weekend off.

As the band became more popular, on weekends off from the Palace, we played other gigs. We played in Russellville, Arkansas in the basketball arena for a big party and several other bars in the Little Rock area. Another late-night private club owner felt he was missing out on the Urban Cowboy craze of the day and hired us to play his Urban Cowboy night once a week. He had pop music dance bands play other nights. It was a much later gig not starting until 11 p.m. and playing until 4:30 a.m. It always made the next day's work miserable.

In Arkansas the law allowed bars to stay open until 2 a.m. through the week, and midnight Saturday night. After Sunday morning, there were no alcohol sales again until Monday morning. Lightfoot would take the stage at 7 p.m. on Thursday and Friday and play till 1:45 a.m. or close to it. Some nights we were having such a good time we wanted to continue playing. On Saturday nights we would stop performing at 11:30 p.m. to get the bar cleared at the legal time. It gave everyone a chance to hit a private club and party until 5 a.m. when they had to close.

I have been to hundreds of bars throughout the U.S. and Little Rock had some of the craziest places in America. Streamer's was a nightclub on Cantrell Road, a late-night club where even a certain future president was known to have a good time. Of course, when said future president's brother came to Streamer's he always turned heads and caused chatter. When Bill Clinton, then the governor of Arkansas, came in, his state trooper escorts would clear a section of the bar for him to sit. Many others and I were asked more than once to clear a path and a booth. Some local heavies partied there also, city and state government types, lawyers and people working in the medical profession. I, like most, knew to stay out of their way when they were there. It was a crazy party location and the place to go in town for a few years, and then it went away.

Juanita's, one of the few still open from the '80s, has hosted many national acts and continues today. The club itself supports local acts as well, including talent searches. A place north of the Arkansas River, The Checkmate Club, was a notorious place for just about anything associated with nightlife. They had some great regional bands, and I caught a few over the years that came out of Memphis, Nashville, Austin and Dallas. It was in the basement of an old church in downtown North Little Rock and could get several hundred drunken people in at 2 a.m., and during various stages, it could have been a dive bar champion. I loved the place. It was an adventure just about every time I headed that direction.

The Wine Cellar, an after hours dance (Oh my God, we thought we could dance) club, would be packed shoulder to shoulder with 300-plus drunks from midnight to 5 o'clock in the morning. When we finished our sets for the nights, some of us would escape to the Cellar. It was a big change from the mainstream country music we were doing across town on Asher Avenue. Sometimes it was much needed after grinding out five hours of country songs.

From the moment I stepped into Mike Pinner's Strum and Hum Music Store, my life took twists and turns for better and for worse. But I credit Mike and his company, Concert Staging Services, for leading me to the positive path I have traveled since our chance encounter. When I first stepped into his store, I was just beginning to realize my career path. Music and driving were at the forefront of my mind. Mike helped me grasp my life's passions and make something of them. I've been able to make a decent living and deal with personal struggles and joys. Through everything, two things have remained constant: music and driving.

CHAPTER 28 | THE STAGE IS SET

During the months of all my playing and dancing, I missed a few drum payments. The fifty dollars a night playing with Lightfoot and the few hundred I would have left from my day job after a hangover-day off or a "fuck it I don't feel like going to work I'm too busy with another life" type of day off wasn't covering the payments. One afternoon I stumbled into Strum and Hum to get some supplies and Bean called me aside to remind me of the payments I had been missing. He mentioned the word "repo" and I got pretty nervous.

Bean then asked me if I might be interested in working for him. He explained he had purchased a concert stage from someone in Louisiana and he needed someone to work on it for him. I was taken aback. I think some images of Led Zeppelin flashed through my mind and the concerts I'd seen at the local coliseum. I probably had that same starry-eyed look I notice in the eyes of people who approach me or the celebrities I drive. Me a stagehand? He assured me it was not going to be that glamorous. But he also assured me that I could work off my debt much quicker if I worked for him.

My first task was unloading a stage that had arrived on a semi-trailer from Louisiana and putting it into another trailer that Bean had purchased to transport his new stage. In order to properly pack the new trailer, the stage had to be completely unloaded onto the ground and its order reversed into the new trailer. This way when we arrived at the show destination, we could unload the trailer as we built the stage.

The stage itself consisted of wooded deck sections that mainly sat on rows of scaffolding. It had a shade roof only that couldn't hold any weight. Speakers were stacked onto the deck of the stage and Genie Lifts were used to hold the lighting tresses. The stage measured 60 x 40 feet when all parts were used. It could be built in different configurations to meet the requirements of the show and the venue wherever that might be. Bean had the trailers backed up to one another with enough room between them to set the equipment on the ground. All the work was completed behind his music store on Geyer Springs Road in Little Rock.

Todd, a teenager a few years younger than me, had also been hired by Bean to make the change over. Todd had been a troubled teen, and Bean and his wife had taken him into their home to help him make sense of the world. We became life-long friends after we got to know each other while toting walk boards and all the gear for the stage. It was a typical hot Arkansas summer and working in the back of two semi-trailers and on the ground doing the work, which normally had a dozen or more people doing, was miserable. Just like when I was working for the carnival in my teen years, though, he and I made fun out of the entire situation.

Todd is an exceptional guitar player, and at that time he was into playing licks from bands like AC/DC and Jimmy Page. Both of us were very naive about the business, and having a good time while doing our work was our main interest. On a trip to a small college in Cleveland, Mississippi, where we built a stage in the gymnasium for a Jimmy Buffett show, Todd and I had a good time working the show. We loaded in the stage the evening before and returned early to be there for the equipment load-in and show. Stage-stagehands have to be available from the time the stage is set up until it is taken down. We were given passes and milled around all day doing odd jobs to the stage. That evening at the beginning of the show, Todd had wandered over to the stage-left steps watching as the musicians went on to perform. The lights went down. Jimmy came out of the dressing rooms and stood in front of the steps waiting for his cue. The vibe was in the air with the crowd cheering.

Jimmy leaned over to Todd and said, "Think it's going to be a good show?"

Todd looked at him squarely and said, "I don't know, I don't know who he is!"

The announcer announced: "Ladies and gentlemen... Jimmy Buffett!"

Jimmy sprang up on the steps and took the stage. Todd's jaw dropped. I was so envious of Todd for getting a chance to speak to Jimmy. I loved Jimmy Buffett's songs and played many of them in our bar band. "Margaritaville," "Fins," and "Get Drunk and Screw" always were on our set list, among others. When I asked Todd, "Oh my God, what did he say?" and Todd told me, I laughed my ass off. That was the first time of many that I worked around the Jimmy Buffett organization. I've worked on many single shows, known as one-off shows, as well as several tours driving Buffett's road crew. Todd and I have always had good times working together. After stage work, Todd learned about the sound industry and worked for many big acts like Patti LaBelle and others as a monitor engineer, or a "knob-ologist."

When the changeover of the stage gear from trailer to trailer was completed and the new trailer was packed, Bean began soliciting it for rent to a promoter or a festival. When he secured a show in Birmingham, Alabama, at the Birmingham International Raceway, we prepared the stage to ship and the necessary gear to set it up. When we arrived in Birmingham, the week went well as Todd and I did everything we were told to get the stage built. We worked as a team, equally excited about our work while directing a crew of local helpers. When we returned, Bean paid me my salary. It was the biggest paycheck I had ever earned in my life. Considering the fun I had, I was impressed with its sum. I opened the envelope he gave me, and I'm sure he noticed my wide-eyed look as I shuffled through the one-hundred dollar bills. He immediately held his hand out, saying, "Time to pay for those drums." I gladly handed over the money and caught up on my drum payments.

Staging is hard work, maybe the hardest part of the entertainment business. Staging is first to arrive and the last to leave. And the hours are the longest in the entertainment industry... with the exception of driving. But it hadn't seemed hard to me at all. With people telling me several times a day what a good job I was doing it lifted my spirits even more to give more energy to the job. When it was pay time and the accolades came with the check, I knew I wanted to do it again.

It was time to get another drummer for Lightfoot to fill in for me on the weekend. After going off several more times to work the stage, my band mates cornered me at a practice with a "You going to be the drummer for Lightfoot or be a stagehand?" With a gig in the near future pending with the stage work, I politely handed in my sticks and suggested a couple of replacements. Lightfoot continued on for several years after that with the lineup changing and eventually replacing all the original band members and the style of music played by the band.

The staging company started to grow, doing regional shows in the Midsouth. While working a show at Stephen F. Austin College in Nacogdoches, Texas, I met a roadie, who was touring with the main act, Chris Cross. Chris had a hit song at the time called "Sailing" that was climbing the charts and increasing his album sales. The roadie I was working with that day had a break, so we headed out behind the arena to relax before the next duties had to be fulfilled. In our conversations, he explained he had worked with numerous acts practicing his trade. He was a guitar tech, someone who keeps the guitars in tune and maintained. He was an experienced roadie who could easily see my inexperience in the business. He said entertainers, mainly bands, would come and go but there would always be a need for the people behind the scenes to work. Become a professional at what you do, and you can make a career out of it. An entertainer may be hot for a few years, but they almost always fade away at some point or they cut your pay. Get a gig with the next one coming along and you'll be able to make a career out of being a roadie. This was a new view to me. I had always thought everyone worked for the same act forever, never considering that one could change bands.

In 1980, a local Little Rock promoter plugged The Wild Hog Boogie in War Memorial Football Stadium. The concert featured The Doobie Brothers as the main act with Molly Hatchet and 38 Special as opening acts along with a local band. The stadium is owned by the city and was managed by a tough old guy everyone referred to as "Coach." He's a great guy and a legendary figure in Little Rock. He complained about putting a concert on in the stadium telling everyone in city government it would destroy the stadium. It is mainly a shrine in the state's biggest city for the University of Arkansas Razorback football team and where central Arkansas supporters of the program have a chance to see the team several times a year. The stadium had never had a concert performed in it. Billy Graham had crusaded there but no rock concerts. Coach wasn't fully convinced that a rock concert could be held in his stadium without some kind of permanent damage to the facility.

Loads of plywood had to be laid out for the tractors moving the gear in and out on the grass field. Dozens of precautions had to be taken to prevent any damage whatsoever. Everything went well for the facility and The Wild Hog Boogie turned out to be one of the biggest concerts Little Rock had ever had. Several other gigs came my way and every one of them was a lot of work, and for me, a lot of fun. But generally, outdoor staging is a seasonal profession and in the winter months there was rarely any work.

CHAPTER 29 | A DRIVER IS BORN

In my driving career, I haven't always been behind the wheel of a bus. I started out in trucks trekking across America long enough to learn what this great country is about, learning the highways and how to find various locations, an important part of the job now.

Following my staging stint, I needed a steady paying job, and by the time I was 21, I had already driven various sizes of commercial and military trucks. I thought, "Why not give trucking a try?" When the staging company I had been working for gave me a reference at a large trucking company, they hired me right away.

ACB Trucking was a company owned by the Bruno family. I was told they were a wealthy family from the Chicago area and had many types of businesses. ACB Trucking was based out of North Little Rock, Arkansas, and when I joined was running a fleet of over 100 trucks. Their fleet of trucks was made up of cab-over International and Peterbilt trucks.

After going through the paperwork maze, which included some of my entertainment contacts giving me high recommendations, I was accepted as a driver. The regulations to drive a semi truck in 1979 were not as strict as by today's standards. Arkansas driver's licenses in those years were just a small piece of cardboard-like paper and didn't even have photos. ACB had more than 25 employees in their office and shop, which was located next door to a truck stop, and a 100-plus drivers. Once clearance was given for me to drive, they assigned me to a 1975 cab-over International Tran Star II. It had red stripes on it that wrapped around the back of the sleeper. It had a short wheelbase so it road like crap. But it was the first truck I was assigned to, and I was excited to have it.

I was then assigned a tractor and given a trailer and a dry load going to California. I spent a couple of hours getting my stuff situated just right in the truck just right. It was filthy and had the remains of the 20 or more drivers who'd driven the truck before me so cleaning it up was on my list of things to do. Once the bed was made and the unit cleaned and washed, I headed out going west on I-40.

By the time I had reached Conway, a distance of about 30 miles or so, I was hungry and stopped for food. I was feeling good, driving the truck and having a new job with a company. After eating, I drove on to the Russellville area, just 40 miles away and stopped again. Just hung around, admiring my vehicle, then I got back into the truck and drove 80 miles to Fort Smith, Arkansas. It was early evening by the time I reached Fort Smith, so I stopped again and had some dinner. Milling around not really doing anything, I finally traveled west to Sallisaw for another 25 miles.

Sallisaw is a small eastern Oklahoma town that didn't have many amenities. There is a truck stop there that is a regular stop for a lot of the "Bull Haulers" that travel from the cattle sale barns in Arkansas, Louisiana, Mississippi, Tennessee and Alabama headed to the Amarillo, Texas area where many of the large beef operations are. With the Oklahoma scales closing at night, once the truckers reach Sallisaw they are able to take on extra fuel. It's been a meeting place for years where truckers meet other truckers and head west.

Bull Haulers have to drive long and hard to reach their destinations or they have to stop mid-way and get the cows out of the trailers for a period of time per government regulations. Sometimes at night, across Oklahoma and Texas, these trucks top a hundred miles per hour with five, seven or more in a convoy. It takes a steady hand to drive 80,000 pounds at 100 or more miles per hour. They talk on the CB radio watching for police and dangers on the road. Many of the "Large Cars," as they're referred to, sometimes have hundreds of lights, and when many of them convoy it's a neat sight to witness. All these custom trucks are in a line working with each other. Hauling ass. Teamwork.

I woke up the next morning sometime after nine and went into the truck stop for breakfast. After I ordered, I called in to ACB Trucking to let them know my location, let them know all was well and so on, as required by company policy. I sat down, ordered some breakfast and then went over to the row of phones on the wall and called the 800 number on the paperwork the company gave me.

"ACB Trucking," the lady said when she answered the phone. I ask for dispatch and was transferred to the person in charge of me. There were several dispatchers in the offices and each one had a group of truckers they dealt with.

My guy finally answered the phone, and I could see the waitress delivering my breakfast to my table.

The dispatcher was a little gruff when he said, "Hello."

I identified myself, name and truck number and said I was the new guy. He laughed and said there was probably a newer guy than me by now considering the company's high turnover rate.

We banter normal details a minute then he asks, "OK where are you at this morning?"

I'm sure I had this air of accomplishment in my voice when I said, "Sallisaw, Oklahoma." I had walked across the lot to the restaurant thinking how grand life was about to become. It was a beautiful sunny day; I had a new job, new career, seeing new things and no trouble with the law.

The phone was silent long enough for me to say "HELL-LOW."

The dispatcher was shuffling paper and said, "When did you leave?"

"Two o'clock yesterday." Twenty hours had passed.

Today, with more than 25 years' experience, I can get behind the wheel and drive a thousand miles in less than 24 hours if it is required. On my first day on the job for "Al Capone Brothers," as they were called on the CB radio, I had driven less than 200 miles. And was so proud of my accomplishment.

The dispatcher started screaming at me and calling me names. Suddenly, I didn't know how to respond.

"Shit. What if he fired me?" I thought to myself. But I kept my mouth shut and tried to listen as he bashed me with criticism. I assumed he had been a Marine Corps drill sergeant the way he was digging into me.

He had me get my pen and paper and told me never come to a phone to do trucking business without a pen and paper. He called me the slowest trucker on the earth, and that offended me greatly. Not sure why, I started to talk back, and he told me to "shut-up."

He told me to get a CB radio, hook it up and "FUCKING LISTEN TO IT." He told me I'd better be in Los Angels, 1,500 miles, by the next night. After a few more minutes of chewing my ass out, he hung up on me.

I was so frazzled from the call I didn't know what to do for a second. I wasn't hungry anymore. That's for sure. Now that he had hung up, I wanted to kick his ass. I was angry, then got to thinking about being "the slowest trucker on the earth," and my anger started to subside. It became more of an attitude thing. So I got busy.

When I reached Amarillo, I got a CB radio from a CB shop by a truck stop and paid them to put it in and tune it to the truck. Suddenly, there was a whole new world before me. A world I had never known about. Underground sub-cultures in our culture of cultures.

Truckers have long used CBs to communicate about speed traps, accidents, bad road conditions and their location. On long rides, truckers convoy with one another talking on their CBs watching out for each other helping to keep each other alert. It has long been a tool for good and bad. Prostitutes use the CB in the truck stops and rest areas, drug dealers sell their wares on the CB and thieves sell their loot at or near the truck stops. You can hear social commentary about any subject in the world, and you can join anytime you want, all you have to do is speak into the microphone, hold the button and ask it a question or make a comment. There is almost always an answer.

So I'm back in the truck in Amarillo with my new CB, and I started trying to make this deadline I had been given. I drove the rest of the day and all night into the morning and made it to Flagstaff, Arizona, before I called the office. I got another ass chewing and drove on west toward L.A. Going west out of Flagstaff, there are several mountain ranges that have to be crossed. They can be dangerous, especially to the inexperienced driver or while driving a truck that's not equipped accordingly. ACB trucks weren't equipped with jake brakes or retarders, devices that help slow a truck. Some of the downgrades are five, seven or more miles long. Brakes can heat up fast on a downgrade and become useless if not used properly. Learning to drive in the mountains using gears to keep at safe speed was a big help in learning to drive altogether.

When the delivery was made, I called and got another ass chewing and then dispatched to pick up a load going east. And so it went for months. No matter how far and fast I drove, I got an ass chewing every time I called that dispatcher at ACB. At first it inspired me to do better, to learn more and more, but after a few months it became ridiculous.

After many loads learning the trucking business with ACB, I happened onto another driver who helped me move to a company that had long-nose trucks, generally referred to as "conventionals" by truck manufacturing companies. Conventional trucks ride differently and are smoother than the cab-over models. With a longer wheelbase and with the driver not sitting directly over the front wheel, the ride is much better. The longer wheelbase trucks aren't as easy to back up in tight situations, and during the '70s and '80s, length laws were very strict in states like Missouri, Illinois, Arkansas and others. One just learned what to do when those situations arose.

The more I learned about the trucking industry, the more of a benefit I became to my production friends at home in Little Rock.

Several local guys in my hometown had entered the production business, and, with Bean's help, I was able to start doing some production work for them. The Calhoun Brothers had started a sound company, CalBro Sound Company, and Byl, founded Bylites. Bean assisted with getting my foot in the door with those guys. They always needed gofers to load and unload equipment from the trailers – pull cables, stacking speakers and whatever needed to be done at shows. I went on several runs with them doing gigs with Air Supply, Mickey Gilley, Johnnie Lee and the Urban Cowboy Band, and quite a few R&B and funk acts.

One night on an off day, Todd and I and some others were all staying in the Houston area between some shows we were working with Mickey Gilley. We were invited over to Gilley's Club in Pasadena. I was standing at the bar in front of the dance floor with Todd and several other guys on our crew when David Allen Coe walked up. Just about everyone into country music in Texas can identify him. Our band Lightfoot had covered several of his songs that I liked. His ball cap said "DAC Himself" on it so that helped recognize him, too. DAC is a big man and had a bit of the biker look to him with long braided hair.

He spoke to one of the guys I was with, and he turned to the rest of us and said, "Let's go out back and burn one."

DAC took off across the dance floor and stepped right up on the stage where a local band was playing. He stepped up onto the stage beside the lead singer while he was singing, walked around him and between the guitar amps and went out a back door that led off the stage. All four of us followed him step for step and when out back, several joints were lit and passed around. When everyone was done, we followed DAC back through the door across the stage and back to the bar to order drinks. DAC had spent a lot of time around Gilley's and the local band playing knew who he was and never said a word to any of us.

It was nice to be working on the road with people from my hometown. Today, as a driver switching from group to group, it is rare that you work with anyone from home. If you work on a sound crew or lighting crew the chances are you can work with people from your hometown, but drivers rarely get that chance.

Between entertainment gigs, I would drive semi trucks to various points in America. Grab a load of processed chickens and take them to San Francisco from Arkansas. Drop them at a warehouse somewhere in the Bay area and drive empty to Salinas, California, the vegetable basket of our country and get a load of produce going to Hunts Point Market located in the Bronx area in New York City. Unload in the Bronx and head south to Delaware and pick up liquid fiberglass from a factory located beside the Delaware Memorial Bridge and head for Houston, Texas. Depending on the time of year, after unloading in Houston you might make the long drive empty to the Texas Valley and pick up more fruits or vegetables from the McAllen and Pharr area. Take that load to Ohio and pick up some newsprint to return to the Arkansas area. Take a break and do another turn starting with rice from Stuttgart, Arkansas, headed to a distributor in lower Manhattan's Chinatown area. It's not that easy to drive a 65-foot or longer semi truck in lower Manhattan, but I took many loads into the city and did my best each time, never having any real problems. Traffic in New York City is very predictable.

Driving a semi in NYC can be a real pain. After driving across the country one of the few ways for an 18-wheeler to reach lower Manhattan is to cross the George Washington Bridge, the GWB as locals refer to it, exit at 178th Street and go south down Broadway. It is a slow process stopping at every fourth or fifth stop light, pulling away and shifting the transmission half a dozen or more times, stopping again and starting over. After going through more than 250 stop lights, you reach your unloading point, only to figure a way to park close to the customer's door. The best times to get into the city is in the middle of the night so the entire trip across country has to be timed for that. Boston's Chelsea produce markets can be just as demanding to get to as are many of the northeast markets and customers accepting fresh produce from the California farms.

The small streets in the French Quarter of New Orleans are as tight as anywhere in America as you try to get to the produce markets along the river. Once on a trip to Pittsburgh's Consumers Market in the Strip District, the trailer I was pulling had a thermometer problem with the refrigerated unit on the trailer. When I arrived the front half of the load had frozen. Frozen lettuce was unacceptable so the receiver of the shipment refused it. After sitting for two days figuring out what to do with a load of bad lettuce, the trucking company, very angry with me, sent me to Hunts Point Market where I sat for four more days while the load was auctioned off in small amounts to various venders. Hunts Point is an area of the Bronx with hookers and drug dealers walking the streets just outside the market area. No place to eat other than the roach coaches that work the area and the few services inside of the market. I was really glad when all that mess came to an end.

Between driving the hundreds of loads of freight and food loads, I tried to time my schedules to get back to work for the production companies in my hometown. Entertainment production was my main interest. The trucking business can be a brutal way to make wages. Somewhere in this time frame, CalBro Sound Company sold itself to Mike Pope from Nashville, Arkansas. Mike renamed the company M.P. Productions. The two Mikes, Mike Pope and Mike Pinner, approached Barbara Mandrell's management team about providing production logistics and equipment for her tour.

Once a deal was secured, M.P. expanded their equipment, teamed with Bylites and Bean's company, Concert Staging Services, and started touring with the

Mandrell show. M.P. Productions had gotten the job by impressing Irby Mandrell, I had been told. With my trucking experience and connections, I started driving the trucks that hauled sound and lighting gear for M.P. Productions and thus the Mandrell show.

Irby was well known in the Nashville area, as not only the father of the Mandrell sisters, but also as a very thrifty man-about-Nashville when negotiating contracts for production. It was also rumored that his bunk on the bus he rode had a speedometer in it, and his driver was never to top 55 mph. I never saw it but heard a lot from his driver about it. I once approached him in the catering tent at one of the shows and thanked him for a tour jacket we had been given.

He turned toward me frowning, "If it had been up to me the money wouldn't have been spent on jackets for everyone."

I was grateful nonetheless and always admired his approach to the business and his story to success.

During that time, I had driven several very nice trucks hauling freight. Having a comfortable truck can make the miles a little easier. M.P. was renting older model cab-over International trucks that had hundreds of thousands of miles on them and had had a slew of non-caring drivers who had driven them. The trucks would be nasty inside and it was a crapshoot every time we picked one up from the rental agency.

CHAPTER 30 | TRUCKING TYCOON

Having driven numerous trucks by this time, I understood the difference between a crappy truck and a nice one. One day, I confronted M.P. with the idea of me buying my own truck and using me exclusively to pull their gear. Mike agreed and gave me a letter of intent to use me if I obtained a truck. I went to work writing a business proposal, day dreaming about how I wanted to start with one truck and turning it into a large trucking company specializing in transporting entertainment gear. For several months, my every waking moment was spent reading books about how to write a business proposal, and trying to get someone interested in it. I succeeded in finding a capital investor who was interested in investing in the small business that I named Complete Entertainment Transport.

With M.P.'s letter of intent to use me if I had my own equipment, I found an investor. His only catch was that I start with a brand new truck instead of the used truck I was dreaming of owning so that he could take advantage of all tax incentives. I had been going to the Kenworth Truck dealer on a daily basis wearing out a salesman over a beautiful, gunmetal grey used truck that they had on the lot. It was in great mechanical shape having been an owner-operator's truck. Never smoked in and pristine inside and out. Every day I went to the dealership and would sit and pray they wouldn't sell it before I got the deal organized. I attended classes offered by the Small Business Administration learning how to manage the business of business.

In 1984, when I was trying to accomplish all of this, the interest rates to borrow money were over 21%. It's surprising that anyone during that time would have wanted to risk finances with a brand new truck when a used truck half the price could have done the job just as well and was all ready to go. I ended up getting pretty close to the truck of my dreams with a 1984 Kenworth conventional that was loaded with amenities every trucker wants. A very comfortable, VIP interior with a sit-down bunk. It had a brand-new electronic fuel injected 400 HP Caterpillar motor. A 15-speed transmission with the last two gears turned around – that's trucker talk for "it will go fast and pull strong."

M.P. had purchased a specially made drop deck electronics van designed to haul sound and lights for the Mandrell show. It had polished aluminum all the way around and it looked great behind my maroon Kenworth that had silver stripes down the side of the hood up over the sleeper cab.

On its first trip, it was impressive sitting next to the Barbra Mandrell rig. Things were rolling along. The first show I showed up to in my new truck someone made mention of it to Barbara, and she came over and climbed up into it and told me how beautiful it was. I was so proud to have an opportunity to show it to her. She congratulated me on getting it and said how good it looked beside her own truck.

At the time Barbara Mandrell's husband was involved with the Nashville Peterbilt dealership. They had built for Barbara a cab-over Peterbilt, which at the time was the longest cab-over ever built for on-the-road use. Modern trailers these days can be up to 53 feet long but the cab of the Mandrell Peterbuilt was so long it could only pull a 38-foot trailer to stay within the length-laws for trucks. It had a special Double Eagle sleeper built and put behind the cab. The sleeper was designed like a bus interior with bunks, with the original plan for crew members to ride in. It was a beautiful truck and trailer combination with a matching paint scheme. After a few rides in it, the crew guys complained that the ride was too rough, compromising their rest. The crew eventually went back to riding in buses.

It was kind of rare at the time for production being provided to a Nashville act by someone other than a Nashville company. Most acts used local Nashville companies for sound, lights and stage gear or at least used a Tennessee company. I was pretty happy being able to tour with my hometown friends. We would go out on the road for a few days at a time, rarely more than a couple of weeks at a time, do a series of shows and return home. Most of the Nashville acts operate this way with acts heading out and doing two or three shows a week and returning to Nashville for a few days off and doing it again. Most rock and pop tours go out for months at a time touring against an album, not returning home until the tour is over.

Working with Barbara Mandrell, I learned a lot about Nashville and the Nashville scene during that time. I think anyone who lives in that town can tell you that there are so many tour buses leaving that city on Wednesday and Thursday nights that you could get run over by one. Many pick up their passengers at shopping center parking lots around metro Nashville and hit the road by midnight. Leaving Nashville on a Wednesday night for a show in Lincoln, Nebraska, on Thursday, a show in Wisconsin on Friday and a show in Ohio on Saturday night and returning to Nashville Sunday would be a typical weekend for the Weekend Warriors. The next weekend may take you to Texas, Louisiana and Georgia and back. An endless tour or just a job, whichever way you want to look at it.

A couple of times, when we were out for a few days and there was a day off, the crew and band did some things together. A picnic in a park had Barbara cooking on the grill for everyone. She was so genuine with everyone who worked around her and of course the fans. She was very popular during the early and mid-'80s and was selling out just about everywhere she did a show. Many acts from Nashville opened for her during that time, and I got to see a variety of some of Nashville's up and comers.

In 1984, a tour package was put together with Lee Greenwood as opening act for the Mandrell show. Barbara and Lee had recorded together and had a hit on the radio. The tour did well everywhere we went. The Greenwood band and crew was a fun bunch to be around, and as we traveled we played tricks on each other, creating good memories.

On September 11, 1984, Barbara had a serious automobile accident. The Little

Rock production team was gearing up to do a series of shows in Wichita, Kansas and throughout the Midwest. Barbara almost lost her life, and her children were also injured. Everyone on the Little Rock production team was devastated. I was disappointed that all the relationships I had made with the Mandrell team, her band and crew would be put on hold during her recovery.

The Mandrell show was basically the Little Rock production crew's only source of revenue. We were all left with no way to pay the bills. I grabbed a refrigerated trailer from a truck broker in Arkansas and started trying to make ends meet hauling exempt commodities, chickens and produce and the like. I had been running as a private carrier and had no authority from the government to haul anything else. Eventually, the talk turned to Barbara making a big comeback when she recovered and everyone on the Little Rock crew had their hopes set high.

When the time came for the comeback, another production team was hired and everyone in Little Rock was left out. We all went into scramble mode trying to make ends meet right after the accident. Leasing my truck to a large carrier wouldn't have allowed me to grow into the trucking operation I dreamed of, so I tried to do it on my own. One thing I quickly learned about the trucking business is you either have to be a driver or an office person taking care of the accounts, finding the loads and doing the mandatory government paperwork. Generally, you can't do both. At least I couldn't.

In '84 and '85, the interest rate for loans was around the 21% range. To make the revenue to make those payments, driving was all there was time for. With the majority of the speed limits at 55, it made it hard to have the time to do much else. I had had a great deal with M.P.'s production company making $1.25 per hub mile. In general, it was costing me less than 60 cents per mile to operate the new truck. When I started to haul exempt commodities the rates were much lower, paying the truck on book miles, which always seemed short. The rates were generally in the 70-90 cents per mile range for the freight going west and a little higher for loads going to the east from California, which meant I had to cover a lot more miles to make enough revenue to make the payments. The loads were much heavier, thus wearing on the truck more.

In entertainment transportation, drivers usually have more opportunity for rest time. When the truck is unloaded in the morning it is not until late into the night before you're reloaded to move to the next town. That leaves the day to sleep and get your paperwork done. Hauling general freight you go, go, go, find another load and go, go, go again. M.P. started getting a few shows commonly referred to as "One-offs" with artist like Patti Labelle, The Bar-Kays, Stephanie Mills and a few festivals. Whenever possible I would make my freight match to a location so I could get back to haul their gear, which is not always an easy task.

Eventually, in order to keep up with the pace, I turned to drugs to keep me awake and on schedule. Speed could be found at just about any truck stop in America in the mid-'80s. For instance, you could drive into the old Chevron Truck Stop in El Paso, Texas, and before you could get parked someone would be by your truck giving the hand signals for drugs. Uppers, bennies, whatever you needed, it was available there. A yell on the CB radio in West Memphis,

Arkansas, can get you just about any type of drug you want or an array of stolen goods that top a Wal-Mart. Listening even today to the CB as you pass there, it's business as usual.

"Make a deal with Lucille." "Fulfill your need for chicken feed" – all CB slang for drugs. In the '80s stopping at just about any major truck stop in America could get you anything you wanted, just ask the CB.

CHAPTER 31 | JEREMY

The life I chose may not be a recipe for home life happiness. I've had my ups and downs with relationships, but I knew that it would be tough to maintain a relationship and a family when I got into the transportation business. Along the way, I've had my share of drama and bodies left in my wake. I still had my share of drama and bodies left in my wake. I was one of those bodies in another's wake as well.

When I had gotten out of prison I returned to Little Rock to start fresh. After I was out for a few months, my parole officer started giving me some leeway to set up a new life. My younger brother and I moved into an old house on John Barrow Road in the west part of town. It was a place to live, frat house style of living and mostly a place to party. The old house had been built in the 1940s, and it was a real dump. Our living in it didn't help. We were no housekeepers. We were more like doormen. There was always an endless number of people coming and going.

A block away on Barrow Road was The Electric Cowboy, a place where teenagers hung out playing pool, foosball and video games. The man who owned it had four or five of them located throughout the county. They opened in the afternoons after school, and kids migrated to them every day. Further north up the street was Parkview High School, and in the afternoons, many of the kids stopped by our place, smoked pot, hung out a little and then made it over to the Cowboy. Many afternoons, girls would stop by, and my brother and I would get lucky with some of them. Some days, we had parties well into the night. Who knows how many people would stay over.

And you never knew who might show up at the door. One day a young girl came over with a child on her hip. She joined in the partying along with everybody else. More than one person knew her and thought it was perfectly fine that she brought her son to the party. She had placed the kid on the floor, sat down and took a bong hit. I was more than a little concerned with a barely walking baby being around while everyone was drinking and getting high. She wasn't as concerned.

"Listen, this is the way I do things," she said. "I'll keep an eye on him."

After a couple of days of coming and going, she ended up in my bed. We went at it for several times over several days, but one day when she came over, I was with another girl. She got mad, threw a fit and left. She came back a few days later and we went at it again, several times over several days. Then another girl came along. When she showed up, the fireworks started up again. I told her not to come back.

The parties continued, and I was starting to get a set of drums together, jamming with some kids from a different part of town. A five-piece band with drums, bass, two guitars and a lead singer that we all thought we sounded pretty good, at least in our practice room. For the most part, the kids that were into music didn't hang out too much with the kids that were always in trouble. I was finding my music friends to be a better crowd, less stressful and more encouraging of positive things.

Life was just bumping along when one morning, the girl knocked on my door again. I had been working the night shift, running a metal lathe cutting forklift parts and had just gone to bed. I hadn't seen her in a few weeks, and I wasn't in the mood to deal with her drama. On top of that, I was just grumpy. I opened the door, and she marched right in with her son on her hip walking at an angle to support him. She turned around looked me in the eye and said those wonderful words every young man wants to hear.

"I'm pregnant and it's your kid."

She was a full foot shorter than I am, and as I looked down to her I said the first thing that came to my mind.

"You're fucking crazy." That didn't go over well.

We argued about her getting it "taken care of" because I had no feelings for her, I hadn't even given her a ride in my car. Hell, I witnessed her having sex with two other guys at my house. The argument continued.

"Fuck you! I am going to have the kid and I don't care what you think. Don't worry. You won't have any ties to it," she said and left in a huff. I honestly believed she didn't know who the father was. I didn't think it was me.

Eight months later she had a little boy and named him Jeremy.

By the time he was born, I was dating my first wife, Tammy Sue. It was definitely a sore subject with her, the thought of this other woman about to have my baby. Tammy Sue worked in the records department at the children's hospital where Jeremy was born a few weeks early, and she called me the day he was born.

"He is sick, and he could die," she told me. "If you ever want to see him, you should come now."

For Christ's sake, I didn't want to get involved, I thought, but went to the hospital right away and saw him. I hadn't had children at that point, but I know that the confusing feelings I felt for Jeremy that day were not from feeling that this child was mine. I held him and touched him, and I didn't feel any connection whatsoever. Actually, that was wrong. I started feeling anger toward Jeremy's mother and the mess she was creating, bringing another child in the world with no way to care for him. Most importantly, he wouldn't have a father. She had one child already that wasn't being cared for and nurtured. Those thoughts stayed with me as I walked out of the hospital.

Jeremy's mom called me a few months later, and I could tell she was stoned and being a smartass.

"I just wanted to tell you, you have nothing to worry about," she started in. "I am not going to chase you for money or try to make you be a dad to Jeremy."

"I really think you should give him up for adoption to a secure family that can give him a chance at a decent life," I shot back. She wasn't going to have any part of that. She was a young woman with no education, no job and living with her mother.

Years passed, and I had no contact with her or Jeremy. I got married, had another child, got divorced, met the girl of my dreams, you know, "the one who got away." Met another girl, fell in love and got married again. We had our first child together. When I met my second wife and we were dating, she started talking marriage. I told Michelle every detail about my past. I was trying to talk my way out of it, but it didn't seem to work. She assured me that my past had nothing to do with my future anymore. She loved me, and I could put those things behind me and use them to grow on. We could have a good life.

She knew I drove buses for a living since we met more than a year earlier when she walked through the door of my coach. Michelle was from Los Angeles, and I was almost embarrassed when she wanted to set up shop in Arkansas. The nightmares of my life had started in Arkansas, and I surely didn't want to start over again in the place I referred to as my "Hillbilly Nightmare World." She was tired of the L.A. scene, the crowds, the traffic and the smog. She wanted to start a family and raise children in a more serene environment, so we ended up back in Arkansas. Eventually, Michelle became the apartment manager of the complex we lived in. Coming back here seemed to be a good idea after all as life started to grow.

Sometime during one of the years I was traveling for work, Jeremy's mother had shown up at my mother's house with Jeremy in tow. She knocked on the door and made her usual announcement with bravado.

"Thought you might like to meet your grandson," she said to my mother.

I can't imagine what my mother said, but I know she struck up a relationship with them to the point that she started including his birthdays and Christmases and extra time in her schedule. This was all hidden from me. I didn't know anything about it. I don't think my wife knew about it until Jeremy was reintroduced back into my life. His mom met a good man, married, and they grew a family. She became a Christian and changed her partying ways. We ended up living close to each other in the southwest part of town. I actually passed their house several times. I didn't know they were there until someone told me. I then started going a different route.

One afternoon I was somewhere in America on tour when I made one of my daily calls home.

"You're not going to believe who walked into my office today," Michelle said.

By this time it seemed like my wife had become the mother hen to many of the people in the apartment complex. Everyone there had problems in their lives, and when you manage an apartment complex, you seem to get included in it all. So I didn't have a clue who she was talking about.

She explained that Jeremy's older brother, the kid who had been on the floor years ago while his mom and my other friends were smoking pot and having sex, came into the apartment office. His father had killed himself with a shotgun when he was still a baby. I had known his father, had socialized with him only a couple of times, but I ran with a different crowd.

It wasn't hard for Jeremy's older brother to figure out who and where I was. We lived close to each other, and when I was home, I parked a bus on the street in front of the apartments. He just walked into my wife's office one day.

"Hi, I'm your husband's son's big brother."

Michelle knew who he was from the stories I had told her. She looked at him.

"So what do you want with me?"

He told her some tale about Jeremy being upset, and he said he wanted to know his father. Jeremy's mother later told me that Jeremy's brother was mad at her, and it was his way of rebelling against getting at her.

After a lot of discussion with Michelle, we decided to atone my behavior toward Jeremy and try to make a difference in his life. I figured it was something in my past that I had to face and straighten out. So we made plans on how to incorporate him into our world. When I came home from a tour, I reached out to him, and we tried to get to know each other. Eventually, Michelle and I included him in our Christmas and welcomed him during family meals together and a couple of short family trips. The way I had felt trapped in my childhood, Jeremy also was trapped in the confusion of life. He was a teenager by this time, and he was getting in a lot of trouble. He didn't live with us, and he didn't share have my last name, but we tried to treat him as part of the family.

It didn't work. I tried to work on his attitude and his life choices, but after a while, we concluded he wasn't going to go along with our family plan or values. I sat him down and told him the facts.

"If you don't want to do it our way, then we can't participate in your life," I told him. "I think it's best if you don't come around here for a while."

Michelle and I were trying to build our own family, and he was making detours in our plans. I had gained custody of my daughter from my first marriage, and she had felt she had gained a brother, so it was an issue for her when we sent him away.

A few years later after Jeremy was in his early 20s, I called home, and Michelle told me Jeremy was suing me for 18 years of child support. He had hired my first ex-wife's attorney at her encouragement, the one who lost her case in the custody fight over my daughter. Jeremy thought I was going to give him $25,000 or more when he won his case, a sum that seemed liked all the answers to his lack of money skills.

My lawyer countered right away and challenged his claim of me being his father. After decades, we would finally find out if I was actually Jeremy's father. We went to take a paternity test. I was on tour at the time and headed to a hospital in Chicago, where they drew my blood.

It took a couple of months for the results to come back, but when it did, Jeremy's lawyer called me.

"OK, you're not the father," he said. "You're off the hook, we're dropping the suit. Jeremy hasn't been told yet, so don't contact him until we do."

At the moment, I wasn't planning on it. I was angry about the whole situation. Then I became very sad. I felt bad for Jeremy, a confused young man who would be even more confused now. I talked to Michelle about it, but her coldness shocked me.

"Do you feel bad enough to send a get well soon card and $500?" Michelle was angrier about this situation than I was. She really thought we were taken advantage of.

Jeremy contacted me again after some time had passed. He explained how he had his life in order. He was learning a good trade in heating and air and had a girlfriend he loved. I wished him luck, but I had no desire to get close to him. I just wanted to let bygones be bygones. I figured time would eventually sort out the emotions.

One night I ran into him at a bar, and we chatted for a minute. I wished him luck and went to another bar. It was hard to face him again unsure of his intentions. We shared many of the same problems that life had dealt us, but I couldn't bring myself to look into his eyes with what I had felt was the disrespect he had shown.

On May 27, 2007, a Sunday evening, I was at my home with my children enjoying a few days together before I was about to head out on a five-month summer tour. The phone rang with the news that Jeremy had put a shotgun to his head and pulled the trigger, killing himself instantly. Jeremy had been living in the northern part of the county with his girlfriend.

The news took the wind out of me. For a moment I couldn't breathe. Equally disturbing was the additional news that his mother had also killed herself. His mom had been living alone in a house in the southwest part of the county more than 20 miles away from Jeremy's home. She had shot herself in the heart with a pistol.

I never sought after the entire details of the incident nor have I ever wanted to. Rumors circulated that he had killed his mother and then went to his home and killed himself. Others said they had done it together while talking on the phone. No one knows except those two and God. The situation and the entire way our lives intertwined has weighed heavy on my heart. I will always regret not being able to make a real difference in his life.

I felt like him once, or at least how I imagine he felt, when I was younger and so sick of what life was giving me. I later realized it was what I was giving life that was hurting me so badly.

I was once where Jeremy was, and I came close to the edge. Standing up on the guard rail on the I-430 bridge where it crosses the Arkansas River, I had the choice to quit this bullshit life that I had been dealt. Standing in the cool evening summer breeze with my arms stretched out and my eyes closed, the feelings, emotions, adrenaline rushed through me, knowing that leaning forward a couple of inches was certain death.

Or there was the other way. Stepping down to face more of an unhappy certainty, a desire to start over and the impossible challenge of making it happen. Fuck it. Lean forward and make it all go away. Give up on trying to figure it out. That's the way I felt.

I can't even explain where I was inside my mind. The rushing thoughts were so loud that as the occasional car passed, I didn't even hear it. I certainly didn't hear the policeman the first time he yelled at me to get down. The second time he yelled, he snapped me out of my trance. My attention turned to him pointing his pistol at me. By that point in my life, I had already had pistols pointed at me by several other cops, so it didn't scare me at all. Suddenly the decision I was contemplating wasn't mine; someone else was making it for me.

As soon as I stepped down, the officer handcuffed me right away and placed me in the back of his car. I sobbed uncontrollably on the ride to the jail and for several hours while sitting in a cell. All I could think of was the value of being alive, which shut out any other emotions I had about jumping.

Talking to my beautiful daughter many years later and telling her of my decision and how close I came, she made comments relating to her existence. Her sobering words brought home how different the world would be without me in it. I'm grateful the policeman broke that trance. I'm glad to be alive to see what the world is like with my daughter and my other children in it.

Many get dealt a strange hand when we're born. Fate is kind to some, harsh to others. Sometimes all you can do is make the best of the hand you're dealt. Since the time I almost gave up on playing the hand I was dealt, I've learned that if you really want to change your situation, you can. It's up to you.

CHAPTER 32 | A BROKEN FAMILY TREE

I've known parents who stay together for the children and others who sacrifice the tight-knit family life for their own happiness. I'm not advocating one way or another. I do believe that during these complex situations consideration of the immediate and long-term effects divorce can have on a child often is left out in the cold. Divorce affects different people in different ways, and it is impossible to apply one cure to the problem. You definitely don't get the same results.

In my case, I don't think my mother and father ever gave a second thought to what would happen to my brother, sister and me while they were tangled in the war between themselves. The anger they shared for each other was palpable. They were so caught up in the heat of their debates, they forgot often about our needs.

The world around me seems consumed with the epidemic of divorce. As an adult having gone through my own divorce, I have come to understand a lot of things about myself. I also now understand more about my parents and how their approach to life had been handed to them from their parents and the parents before them. This cycle had been placed at the doorstep of every generation, and they handed it to me. Their emotions and actions were the results of what grandparents and great-grandparents had taught them.

My father, Harold Fitzpatrick, didn't have a relationship with his father or his grandfather. Rumor had it that on the day my grandmother gave birth to her 11th child, my grandfather was at another woman's house, "shacking it up." Dad once explained to me that my grandfather had dozens of children with various women throughout Kentucky where they had settled. I don't remember ever meeting my grandfather, and I have wondered many times just who he was and what it was that I got from his gene pool. Do I have any of his traits or habits? Would I journey down his road?

My grandmother, Lida, eventually moved to Dayton. Some of my uncles had made their way to the northern Cincinnati area and settled around Dayton and Germantown, Ohio, looking for a better life. Many of them jumped into business with the National Cash Register Company. NCR had an enormous factory and grounds in Dayton and was a major employer in town. The company even owned a large park for its employees. I remember going to a few family reunions there. My uncles would all brag about what a great company it was to work for, but in the mid-1960s, most of them began to lose their jobs when the company began to go electronic. The old dependable cash registers were not being made anymore, and these men in my life and family were all out of work. Several of them fell on hard times and became bitter. Perhaps their stories deterred me from ever seeking to join a company or a union where my job was not safe. It's better to care for oneself, I came to believe.

Lida was a small woman who always wore dresses and skirts. She had long hair that she never cut. She worshipped at a Pentecostal church and was very strict with her opinions. In her religion, women didn't wear pants or cut their hair. Nor did men grow their hair long. My grandmother and other people of her faith followed these rules based on biblical scripture found in Deuteronomy and Corinthians. Guess I have some explaining to do to the Corinthians. Once I visited Grandmother with my future first wife. The fashion of the day had me growing my hair long, and my girl had trimmed hair wearing hip hugger blue jeans. Grandmother allowed us into the front room of her house but wouldn't let us go much farther and wouldn't let us spend the night. It was the last time I saw her before she passed away.

When my father was old enough, he joined the Air Force to escape the hardships of the Kentucky backwoods. After he went through boot camp, he was sent to the Little Rock Air Force Base in Jacksonville, Arkansas, just north of Little Rock. Like most servicemen, they hit the local towns surrounding the bases chasing girls and drinking at the bars when the workday was done. On an outing to downtown Little Rock, my father was at a hamburger drive-in when he met my mother, Marion Louise Davis. Even today, having known the two, I can't imagine what the attraction was for each other. They must have met while arguing or something.

When my mother was a young girl, her father was killed. William Boydston "Boss" Davis, from whom I got my middle name, was described to me as an incredibly good-looking man who would fight anyone at the drop of a hat. He loved his beer, and he loved his women. One of my mom's brothers once said, "Dad had 40 and 11 girlfriends, even after he married Mom." That's Southern slang for a married man stepping out on his wife.

Boss worked the railroad and was killed in a train accident while in the switching yards in St. Louis, Missouri, when my mother was only three or four years old. My grandmother, Rosie Bell, was devastated by the event, and she was forced to raise my mother and two older boys alone. Rosie Bell had been a stay-at-home mom and had few job skills. The insurance wasn't much, so it wasn't too long before she was cleaning houses to make ends meet.

She met and married John Sawyer, an older gentleman, and our family became connected with the Sawyer clan. John had children from his first marriage. His wife had died. Upon remarrying my grandmother, he helped raise my mom. But despite his influence, my mom was a Davis through and through. Many of the Davis clan had migrated from the Paducah, Kentucky area where they had been firefighters. They were there during the creation of the fire department in the late 1800s. When the Davis family made it to Arkansas, many of them naturally navigated toward the firehouses for work. My mother was so proud to be part of the Davis clan and spoke of them all as heroes.

As children, my brother, sister and I were kept aware of Mom's linage as a Davis since they were regularly featured in the newspapers. Jack Davis became the Little

Rock fire chief, and many of the family were high ranking in the department. Photographs of the Davis men fighting fires were featured in the newspaper at least several times a month. They were shown wearing their protective gear with the Davis name on their backs like football jerseys. Mom retrieved the Arkansas Gazette newspaper every morning and always looked for a Davis. She would always remind us of our connection, and although I admire them, for me it is from a distance.

Rosie Bell's way of keeping kids in line was with physical force. For whatever reason, as the kids got older, the spankings became brutal beat downs. The boys got older and bigger, so things weren't as bad for them, but my mother endured years of this kind of abuse. An aunt once told me she had discovered my grandmother beating my mother with a chair for a childhood infraction. She came to my mother's rescue and threatened Rosie Bell with the police. It slowed her down some, but it continued behind closed doors.

My mother was a bit of a racist. She cursed like a sailor and smoked like a chimney. She would take no grief from any man. She could handle her liquor pretty well when she drank. She didn't like beer much, but there always seemed to be a bottle of Old Charter Whiskey around our house. She drank when she hit the bars for a night of dancing, but she didn't drink every day. She did smoke all the time, however. There must be a picture of her somewhere breastfeeding me with a cigarette hanging out of her mouth. It may be why I have found it so hard to fight the habit of nicotine. She attended Little Rock Central High School and graduated in 1956, just before the infamous situation of the National Guard escorting nine black students to school. I remember her talking about it. She had gone with others down to the school when all that was happening and screamed obscenities at the students and the Guardmen.

When I was a child, my mother and many around me laid blame for every problem in our community and the world to the black man. "They're taking all the jobs, going to our schools, eating in our restaurants," I would hear from her and some of her friends. It was confusing in elementary school to be in the same class as black children since I'd been told how bad they were as people. All of us kids played the same during recess. Some of the black kids I had befriended explained that their parents were equally racist toward the white man. They were just as confused.

When she graduated from high school, Mom started working at Colonial Bread and Bakery making cupcakes. She also hung out at a hamburger stand on Main Street, where she met my dad.

Harold and Louise met, got married and had me in the span of a year or so. They separated by the time I was four years old. Dad was an enlisted Air Force man, and Mom wouldn't leave the state to live with him at a different Air Force base in another state or country when he was transferred. Mom wouldn't move away from her mother as her brothers had. They fought about it as my dad tried to force the situation. Mom wouldn't budge, and soon the fights were over infidelity and money and anything else they could think of. I can't ever remember my parents not fighting. Even after the divorce, they never talked civilly to one another. A brother a year and a half younger and a sister just being born made up the short-lived Fitzpatrick marriage. Mom was pregnant with my sister when they divorced. Before and after the divorce, Dad was stationed at various bases around the world. He would drive to Arkansas from wherever he was stationed in the country and pick up my brother and me and take us back to the base. My first trips out of Arkansas were to places like Nebraska, Michigan, Florida and Texas. Much of it was traveled on two-lane highways in the back seat of a station wagon.

My earliest memory of my father was that of a hero. I must have been about four. We were lying on a blanket, my mother, my father and me. They were arguing, as usual, and my little brother, still in diapers, was sitting on a child's riding tractor. It was kind of like a tricycle except it looked like a tractor. Our yard at the time had a slight hill going away from us from where we relaxed on the blanket. My brother started to roll backward, slowly at first then picking up speed. At the property line there was about a three- to four-foot drop over a stone wall into the neighbor's yard. My mother spoke up.

"Grab Mark, Harold!" Dad must have been a bit slower than Mom liked so she raised her voice. "HAROLD! HAROLD!"

Dad, in his Air Force uniform, jumped up and got to my brother just as the tractor was about to go over the wall. My mother was yelling and screaming through the entire incident. My brother started to cry as my father brought him back over to the blanket, all the while Dad smiling and saying it was all right. We all laid back down for a minute, and Mom and Dad started right back into their argument. Dad then got up and left, drove over the hill, and I didn't see him for quite some time. When he did return, the divorce was final and Dad had remarried. Arrangements had been made as to what would be best for the kids: 30 days or so in the summers with Dad, winters with Mom.

During those days, the Cold War was cranking up. Cuba was over, but Russia was the enemy. The United States was gearing up to fight the Communists in Vietnam, and American military men and women were constantly on some kind of alert status. Dad was always busy someplace, and I never saw him. He was out saving the country, as were thousands of others. Father, son and family sacrifices were just a way of life. What other way can one look at it?

At a young age, I came to realize that my mother was abusing me. I don't think I realized what the word meant, but I did know that just about every day of my life, my mother hit me, slapped me, kicked me, pulled my hair, yelled at me and put me down. I must have been seven or eight years old when I started to object. I realized that most of the parents in the neighborhood weren't hitting their kids. Most of the kids didn't seem to be afraid of their parents like my siblings and I were.

My mother never inspired me to do anything, instead choosing to tell me what an underachiever I was and would be all my life. I was a chubby kid, and she called me "Fat Ass" and "Round Ass" and other names. My dad wasn't around to stop it. My mother remarried soon after the divorce. She met Ray Adams at the bakery where they both worked. Ray was from Bigelow, a small country town about 50 miles from Little Rock. After graduating from high school, Ray got a job at the bakery and ran a bread line machine. Apparently, they met on a break and started dating. I admire Ray to this day. He was a great man to take on a young woman in her 20s with three children. He was a hard worker who never missed a day of work.

Ray and Mom were able to buy a brand new three-bedroom house in a subdivision that sprang up west of the downtown area. Meadowlark was surrounded by many other subdivisions with hundreds of homes of mainly white families. I remember going to visit the house as it was being built and walking between the framework and other areas. Those walk-throughs brought comfort to me. I enjoyed bouncing around through the house to the smell of the wood and figuring out which room would be mine. When we moved in, my younger sister had a room, and I shared a room with my brother. We started the typical family routine with work, school and play with neighborhood kids. It seemed to be a better life.

CHAPTER 33 | SEEING THE FUTURE THROUGH TELEVISION

As a child, I was a big dreamer with thoughts of flying jets and driving racecars and playing baseball. I was also into Army games at an early age.

Somewhere around the age of eight or nine, I remember a group of neighborhood kids were in a park close to our neighborhood. We would go up on a small bluff overlooking the park, about 20-30 feet from the road, and we would run through the park with our fake rifles and pistols hiding behind trees, jumping creeks, making shooting sounds and screaming, "Grenade!" We would drive the enemy back through the woods across the road and up the hill. We would wait out the traffic... or enemy tanks... and cross the street to the hill. At the edge of the road, a steep incline to the top scattered with loose rocks and slate became an army test. It was a good climb, not too hard, not too easy. We would get to the top, secure the ground, sit around and yap. One day one of us showed up with an egg. The egg became a de facto grenade. It got thrown from the hill, and of course it hit a passing car. We all "shit our pants" and took off running. As we ran away we heard a woman yelling but couldn't make out what she was saying. We then started walking and laughing. We joked it up for a while and went home to supper.

The next day, of course we all showed up with our own "grenade." We made it through the park and up the hill with all our eggs and started planning a major bombing of a high-ranking enemy official that would be coming down the road any minute. From the angle we had, we could see the tops of the cars as they passed but not inside. There were no sunroofs on cars then. There was a stop sign where the traffic pulled up and then turned left on the main thoroughfare through the park. From the top of our little hill, we could hear the cars pull away from the stop sign and see them for three or four seconds as they passed under our position and traveled on to the park exit. As one of the passing cars pulled up to the stop sign, we all got ready to launch our grenades.

Pretty soon, we found our prey. We all stood up and launched our eggs in perfect timing.

"SPLAT!... SPLAT! SPLAT! SPLAT! SPLAT!"

We took off running. About 30 yards later, a man climbed to the top of the hill and came at us in a full sprint screaming the whole way. We all froze, and when he got to us, he had on military fatigues and boots, and a lieutenant's silver bar on his collar. He hit the hill so fast that we had no time to get away. He had left his car door open and engine running, and someone pulled up behind his car and started honking the horn. He was crazy mad and threatened to kill us, but then he took off for his car. I had never been so afraid in my life. Just some crazy kid crap that happened. I have no idea where the idea came from to act that way.

Back at home, my mother and stepfather had an old black and white television set in the living room that stood on old, skinny, spindly legs. There were several shows that we watched each week like *Bonanza* and *Dragnet*. *Sky King* was one of my favorites, and so was *The Rifleman* with Chuck Connors. Each week someone would die in the name of honesty. I got a replica of the Winchesters the star used on the show. It had a curved lever different from a regular rifle, so he could cock it fast when he was in a shootout. It was pretty cool, and I learned a lesson at the same time. If you're not honest, you'll get caught. Unfortunately, it took me well into adulthood before I adopted that lesson.

One thing that was always on each night was the 10 o'clock news. Each night the sound of an old-style typewriter clicking signaled the start of the kids' baths. It got to a point where when we heard that typewriter we went into action getting the bath thing over with. By the time the news was over, we had better be done and in the bed before the last note of Doc Serverson's musical intro to the *Tonight Show*. When that trumpet was blaring, clear the hall because kids were scrambling. What a nostalgic moment it was the first time I visited the *Tonight Show* stage as a driver with a musical act. I didn't make it there during the Johnny Carson era, but I have visited the Jay Leno set several different times. Each time I have watched Jay drive to his parking spot in a really neat car. He's a collector of automobiles, and he drives something different each trip it seems.

Depending on the size of the band, the group you're driving usually goes to one of the late shows to perform and promote their latest project. Because of that, I have visited the sets of Leno and David Letterman several times. They are unique in their own right, and I have had good times observing the production on both coasts. In Burbank, you park your bus close to the building; the set is on a lot surrounded by various studios. In New York, you have to get a permit to park close to the entrance door on 52nd Street. In Burbank, you get to eat in the NBC cafeteria. In New York, next door is the closest food, but there's no free pass.

I had arrived at the Letterman show with Bruce Hornsby sometime in 1993. They tape the show in the late afternoon. Just before the show was about to start, I entered a side door and went looking for the stage. I wound up on the stage side of the green room door. The green room is a holding cell area where the guest stays during the show when they aren't on stage. I stood by the door and heard all the noise, and I figured the show was about to start, when David Letterman came around a corner and stopped right in front of me. He wasn't facing me. Someone had his jacket, and someone was powdering his face, and someone was telling him something, and a strange looking little man with bifocal glasses at the end of his nose and a clipboard suddenly noticed me. Guys with clipboards always think they're in charge.

He was looking at me from around Dave while all this other stuff was going on and suddenly bolted for me. He got right in my face.

"Who are you?"

"I'm with the band."

He opened the green room door quickly and said, "You can watch from here."

He gave me a shove and closed the door.

I sat down on a couch when another door opened and a man and a woman entered the room. The room was relatively small so I had to move a little for them to get through. They sat across from me at such an angle that they were in my line of sight when I watched the monitor in the ceiling's corner. I had nodded to them as they entered and went on watching the television. The woman was incredibly beautiful. It was so hard to keep from staring. After a few minutes of trying to avoid another look, I started to notice the guy. He was looking more and more familiar, and each time I exchanged looks their way he would look back at me and smile.

"You sure look familiar to me," I finally gave in. "I am Bruce Hornsby's bus driver. Do I know you?"

We reached for each other's hands to shake. "I'm Jeff Gordon, and I don't believe we know each other."

I was floored to have not recognized him. After all, he was wearing his racing jacket, but I hadn't paid much attention to that. I kept thinking... Tom Cruise or someone. In 1993, Jeff Gordon was just moving up through the ranks to become the driver he is today. We chatted for a few minutes, and then I went out to the bus to get ready for the drive out of NYC. I've met many racecar drivers who are fans of live entertainment. Many are as star-struck of their favorite rock star as rock stars are of them.

CHAPTER 34 | TESTING THE LIMITS

Cars, motorcycles, things with fancy chrome and things that went "VROOM" caught my attention at a young age. A lot of the neighborhood kids had mini bikes and small 100cc motorcycles, and a guy who lived across the street from me had a race car, a 1967 Chevelle SS396 square back. He spent many hours working on it in his carport, and I would go over to watch and hang out with him and a couple of his buddies. I would hand him tools while the grownups made fun of me. They were good sports, usually drinking beer, and could see I loved hot rods, so at least they treated me like a person.

The car was white, had mag wheels and slicks on it that he used for drag racing. It had an incredible big-block engine in it that he ran straight exhaust headers on. When he started the car, anything not nailed to the walls in my house across the street would rattle. I'm sure they did at the neighbors' houses too. Sometimes folks would complain but not that much.

One day he announced he was going to bolt a new Dodge transmission to the 396 Chevy motor. Since they weren't made to go together, he had to do much rearranging and buy lots of separate parts to make it work. I helped him every day, handing him the tools and bothering him because I was so impressed with the car. It took several weeks to get the transmission in, because he was a working man and couldn't devote many daytime hours to his hobby. When he finished, he fired up the car and offered me a ride in it. He pulled it out on the street and did a few burnouts. I thought it was the greatest race car in the world. When it all checked out, he said he was taking it to the Carlisle Drag Strip to race it on Sunday. He invited me to go and be on his pit crew. I couldn't believe he was asking, and he went with me to get approval from my mom. Somehow, she said okay, and on Sunday morning I was up early helping to get everything in order. He painted the side of the car "CHEVODGE", a combined word for the Chevy engine and the Dodge. Seemed cool at the time.

Carlisle is a small town 30 minutes east of Little Rock. Through the racing season they would have races a couple of weekends a month. The radio advertised it all the time with the same words at the end of each spot. "BE THERE... SUNNNN-DAY!" It was a fun day and an escape from home life. I came home so excited and talked about it with such inspiration until my mother eventually tired of the topic and told me to quit talking about it. After that I collected magazines and models and became a bigger fan of drag race cars.

Life continued to press forward, and at the age of 11, I got a route delivering the Arkansas Gazette, the state newspaper. My mother insisted that I get a job of some sort to make some money for the things I said I wanted: skateboards, bicycles and hip clothes. I wanted to follow the longhair fad of the time, but Mom refused that fashion in our house.

The newspaper had a statewide competition to sell subscriptions, and I won in my area. I sold enough papers to double my route and won a trip to Washington D.C. with other winners from around the state. When the time came to make our trip, we traveled by bus through the night to the Oak Ridge National Laboratory in Oak Ridge, Tennessee, where we went to the American Museum of Science and Energy. We traveled through the night again and spent three days exploring as much as possible. We went to the Air and Science Museum along with the White House and FBI building. It was a great time and another chance to escape the abusive family life. It was a time when I started realizing that I could get away from my troubles at home and make independent decisions on my own.

When I returned from the D.C. trip, I continued delivering papers getting up at 3 a.m. to meet the paper truck and finishing my route by 5:30. Between it all was a constant barrage of physical abuse. There were weeks when my mother beat me and my brother and sister every day. She would put us across a chair and tell us to grab the legs. Then she would whip us brutally with a belt. Many times I was told I was getting whipped for an infraction that I had already been beaten for the day before. Mom would come in from work angry or upset with her day, look at me and say, "Get me the belt." It got to where I feared her coming home.

I generally walked my route with a paper-delivery bag strapped over my shoulders. I could carry over a hundred papers through the week, but I would have to make two or more trips on Sunday because of the size of the paper and the additional Sunday-only customers.

One morning while I was on my paper route, I was walking through the yards dropping the papers on front porches. As I dropped a paper on one particular porch, I walked by the carport. There was a Suzuki 125 motorcycle sitting at the edge of the carport. Being into motorcycles at the time, I stopped and admired it for a minute. Then I noticed the key was in the ignition. I freaked out. I thought I should knock on the door at 4 a.m. and let them know they had forgotten their key. After a moment of debate with myself, I walked on and finished my route. The next morning I looked to see if the key was in the bike again. The bike was in the same place and the key was right there in the ignition. After several more mornings of passing the bike, I started to think that's how the guy did it every day. He just rode the motorcycle to work and then parked it in his carport without removing the key.

One morning, instead of going to my paper pickup point, I went directly to the house where the motorcycle was. I quietly pushed it away from the house. There was a slight hill on his street so I jumped on it and coasted down the street. When I thought I was far enough away from the house while still rolling, I reached up, turned on the key, put the bike in second gear and released the clutch. The motor fired right up, and I took off into the night riding the bike through the neighborhood. I went to where my paper pick up was, rolled my papers and took off fast, tossing the papers from the bike. When I finished, I rode for a few more minutes and then took the motorcycle back to the guy's house. As I topped the hill from the opposite direction, I shut off the motor, coasted into his carport, parked the bike like it had been sitting and took off for home to get ready for school.

I had so much fun that I went and did it again and again and again. Every morning I was getting the motorcycle, doing my thing, taking it back, and there was no one to stop me or warn me. One morning I fooled around a bit too much and the sun came up over the horizon. I lost track of time playing around. I freaked out and didn't know what to do so I took the motorcycle to the woods by my house, and hid it in the weeds of the woods. I was nervous and disappointed with myself for not keeping track of time.

I went to school, and the rest of the day I was worried about what kind of beating I would get from my mother. When school was over, I checked on the bike to make sure it was still there. The next morning when I got up to do my route, I got the bike, did my route fast and under the cover of darkness returned the motorcycle to the carport. The next morning, I did my route and as I came up to the house that had the motorcycle I noticed it was parked in a different part of the carport. The key was not in the ignition and the bike was lodged between the car and the wall. Too hard to get that thing out now. I felt like I had gotten away with something, but I wasn't sure what.

CHAPTER 35 | THE DEPARTURE OF DAD

My dad made his obligatory trips to Little Rock during the summers. I looked forward to the time away from my mother, and each year I would hold out hope that Dad would listen to my stories and rescue me from her. The first couple of summers when my brother and I traveled to my dad's home, we had great times. Dad was sensitive and soft spoken, and during our time time together when he took his leave of duty, he seemed very dedicated to my brother and me. My sister didn't travel with us those years. My mother claimed she was too young.

In 1967, we spent our time with dad in Omaha, Nebraska. After being stationed in Little Rock, Dad had transferred to Offutt Air Force Base, just outside of Omaha. As the Air Force headquarters, I remember the base being really large. By this time, I loved planes so much that all I talked about was flying them, riding in them and working on them. There was a museum outside the base that had a bunch of World War II aircraft, and Dad took us there several times. We played baseball together – Dad was a big baseball fan – and we did a lot of fishing. Dad loved to fish freshwater rivers and lakes for bass and catfish. Good times spent together. I didn't matter the activity, really, I just enjoyed being with him.

I'm not sure how it came to be. Perhaps I was trying to get a glimpse of my dad because I thought he was so important in the Air Force, but I started watching the news. John Sawyer, the grandfather I got to know, was diligent in his news. Every day he read the paper, and in the evenings he watched the nightly news. I spent many days watching him watch the news, and many times he was making comments to the television in response. He taught me how to watch it. I remember when President Kennedy was assassinated because we watched all the coverage right up to the funeral. I took an even more keen interest since there seemed to be a lot of stories about our military build-up in Vietnam, the war and the people starting to protest against it. Walter Cronkite was telling me what was going on in the world several times a week when I was younger, and I watched intently hoping to see my dad somewhere.

When the summer was over in 1967, my dad explained to me that he was going to Vietnam a few months after he dropped my brother and me back with my mom. While he explained it in the car, I didn't completely understand his words. He knew I watched the news, and even though I didn't fully know what they were saying, I did understand what a war was. To me, it meant my dad, the hero, was going to save the country again, and it meant I wouldn't be seeing him for a long time. I was so proud to have a dad like him, and I knew the other neighborhood fathers wouldn't be going to war, so I thought I would have something to brag about – my father.

By the time Dad got to my mother's house, I got that sick feeling of transferring back to a different way of life. Just about any child of angry divorced parents knows that feeling. My dad hugged me at the end of the driveway and drove off down the street. I stood there and watched him disappear, standing and staring for a long time watching the empty street. He had dropped my brother and me off as the sun was setting. I was occupied by a million things: knowing my dad was going to war, praying my mother had changed during our trip, and having a lonely feeling so deep it was hurting my chest. I eventually sat down and cried, staying there until well after dark. There was a gas light in our front yard, and I was leaning against it when my mother came out to look for me. The driveway had a steep incline, and she came out of the carport door and stood beside the car to call my name. When I answered she could tell I was crying. She walked down next to me.

"What is wrong with you?"

I looked up at this woman who terrified me so.

"Dad is going to war," I started to cry even more.

She pulled me up and escorted me into the house.

"Your dad is going to be just fine," she said.

When we got into the house, the table was set for dinner, but I couldn't stop crying. Mom sent me to bed, and I cried myself to sleep while praying for my dad. I watched the news just about every day after that time. The newspapers I picked up after Mom discarded them were showing more and more about the war and the protest against America's involvement. I learned to read the newspaper, and I did okay in school, especially in social studies as well as geography and history. In the late 1960s and early 1970s, war was on the front pages every day and the evening news always led with something about Vietnam.

I watched Walter Cronkite often and always was interested when Dan Rather was in the jungles giving reports on our servicemen. My mother and a few others explained that I shouldn't be so consumed with the news of the war and protests. None of that was going on in Arkansas. Things seemed to be falling into the same abusive routine with my mother as the winter progressed. She hadn't changed at all.

CHAPTER 36 | PLANNING AN ESCAPE

When I reached the fifth grade, I started attending Southwest Junior High in Little Rock. Mom would drop me off and go to work. Since I arrived early before school, I would stand in the parking lot and watch kids arrive on their bicycles and motorcycles. There was a fenced compound where all the kids parked their transportation. Every morning, kids would turn off the street and drive about 150 yards or so, go through a gate and park their rides.

Two kids named Rocky and Tommy were the show offs of the school and could ride on one wheel forever. Each morning they arrived about the same time, turned the corner onto school property, pulled a wheelie and rode it across the parking lot and right through the gate. Every morning dozens and dozens of kids would hang out just to watch these two ride in. They never missed the gate. They were the "Fonzies" of the school. Everyone wanted to be like them. I got to know Tommy later on in life when we ended up being neighbors for a short time, but many kids – myself included – thought they were the shit when we were young.

I had a good friend, Ronnie, who was squared away compared to all the goofiness I pulled, but he still hung out with me nonetheless. Ronnie had a small motorcycle that he rode around the neighborhood. Close to his house was a large empty lot where many of the kids met and rode their bikes, mini bikes, and motorcycles over mounds of dirt and small hills. Sometimes it would get pretty crowded with kids trying to learn to do wheelies and jumping over things, racing each other and having a good time. Boys being boys, I guess. There weren't many girls riding with us.

Ronnie's motorcycle wasn't licensed for the street, and I believe he was still too young to have a license at all. One day he was returning home when he popped a wheelie and lost control of the bike. He ended up crashed under a parked car, and he died from his injuries. As word spread through the neighborhood of what had happened, I went to the scene of the accident. Everyone had already gone except a few kids. I sat down by the accident scene and had my first real thoughts about death. I hadn't really been confronted with death at that point in my life. There were a couple of relatives who had passed away, but it wasn't like I knew them like I'd known Ronnie. I have carried occasional thoughts of Ronnie with me over the years. He was a good kid. His death made me think of the way people rode their bikes and motorcycles, and it put fear into me about riding that way for a long time. Stretching the limit with stunts and speed suddenly wasn't so appealing to me.

Many mornings my mother woke me for school by yelling obscenities at me. More than once she grabbed me by my legs and pulled me onto the floor while I was asleep, my body hitting the floor with a crash. After waking up to screaming, yelling, cursing, shoving, hitting and punching, it would be very hard to get into a groove at school. Other kids and people, it seemed, weren't going through this sort of thing, and I came to realize that I didn't want to put up with it anymore. One day after a particularly bad beat down from my mother, I decided it was time to get away from her. I had made up my mind that I wasn't going to be a punching bag for her or anyone else. I devised a plan to make an escape.

The first time I took off, I didn't go far. I made my way under our house with a sleeping bag and set it up in a corner away from the door that led under the house. When no one was looking, I slipped under the house and sat and listened to my mother when she came home and started to look for me. I heard her cussing that she was going to beat the shit out of me when I got home. The first night went okay. I wasn't afraid of anything, and I could hear the conversations upstairs. The next morning, I came out and went into the house, ate and goofed off while everyone was at work and school. I missed school but wasn't thinking about that, only of keeping away from the beatings. On the third day, I was in the house eating when my mother drove up and quickly came through the door. I think someone had called her and said they had seen me. As soon as she came through the door, she grabbed me and started punching me. She hit me in the face and bloodied my nose. She hit me so hard that I fell down. Then she started kicking me. I was yelling and screaming, trying to get away, but I couldn't do it. She beat me until she was tired and then held me down while she caught her breath. Mom grabbed the belt and put me over the chair and beat me with it for a few more minutes. She then led me to my room and shut the door.

The next day when I had to get up for school, my face was bruised and cut, and I had a black eye. Bruises were on my back and butt, and I was really sore. Not one person in authority asked me what had happened. Not one person could identify with what I was going through, and I felt really trapped in a situation I couldn't get out of. I made another plan to escape and it wasn't going to be under the house this time.

CHAPTER 37 | MUSIC MAKES AN ENTRANCE

When I was 12, my mother got me a job as a bus boy and dish washer at the Golden Dragon Chinese restaurant on Asher Avenue in Little Rock. She had been working for the Lee family, doing their books several nights a week and hanging out at the bar in the restaurant. On the first night I went to work, the grill cook walked out, and Francis, the older son working in the kitchen, put me on the grill preparing ribs and meats and deep frying won tons and egg rolls.

I admired Francis right away. I often wondered why a guy in his early 20s wasn't out partying like most other people his age. Francis worked really hard and made an impression on me that hard work paid off. He was in charge of the kitchen with a man we called Uncle Billy. Uncle Billy was an Asian man who had been a family friend of the Lees for years. Mr. Lee had been a Little Rock restaurateur for a while, and Uncle Billy had worked for him most of that time. A few years later, Uncle Billy opened his own place, Hong Kong Restaurant. It was located in the Old Cantrell part of Little Rock and was a hit for years. They kept the kitchen in order, working like a clock. Francis' easy manner was a hit with me, and he taught me how to do most of the things on and around the grill. When I took a break, I would get some fresh steamed rice, cover it with butter and put sugar on top of that. Uncle Billy teased me every time about how fat I would become.

"Oh, you get so fat," he would say to me with his Asian accent. I would just smile and enjoy the perfectly cooked rice.

Most of the money I made, my mother said was going into the bank. I wasn't making much, just minimum wage, something like $2.75 an hour. I figured it was about $40 a week with the hours I was getting. It was fun, and it was a way to avoid my mother even though she would be in the next room doing the books. She left me alone and rarely came back to the kitchen. She never hit me or yelled at me when other people were around. When she did come into the kitchen, Francis and Uncle Billy would give her glowing reports about my job performance, and she would make comments about what a good kid I was. But when we were at home the abuse continued.

For a few months, throwing papers, working part time in a Chinese restaurant and going to school kept me so busy that I didn't have any real time to enjoy being a kid.

My mother and stepfather were avid bowlers. Monday nights they bowled with a team, and on Tuesday and Wednesday they competed in individual events. On Saturday mornings, when we were old enough, Mom would get up early and take us to the bowling alley for the kid sessions. Then she would go back home and sleep until it was time to come get us. I learned to bowl well. I didn't set any records, but I was pretty consistent at it. I tried to impress my mother, but that seemed impossible. I don't think we ever bowled a game together. I still enjoy bowling, and I have had several outings with crews and band folks that were very memorable times.

When school was out for the summer, some of my workload eased, and I looked for ways to plan my moving on. I didn't think of my plan as running away. It seemed more important than that. By the summer of my 12th year, I felt that I knew what life was all about, and I wasn't finding it in Little Rock. As with most kids, I did not recognize the value of my hometown or state. The media promote so many life choices that it's very easy not to see the value around you. Arkansas is a beautiful state with fresh air and fresh water. From the northern border to the southern one, the typography of the state changes from Ozark Mountains to the Delta with swamps. With forests everywhere, it is referred to as the Natural State for those reasons and others. The people here are as genuine as you can find anywhere in America. But when you're young, you don't consider those values as important to life. Most young folks want to move away and find a life that is different. Head for the glitz and glam.

With the scars already imbedded, I couldn't see the value of anything in Arkansas. When my dad picked me up for the summer months and took me somewhere else where there was no abuse and only fun, I knew there was a better life than what my mother was providing in Arkansas. It was a place I wanted to get far away from and have a normal life, whatever that was.

I had quit making newspaper deliveries and had taken on the Chinese restaurant job full time. My grades in school were average. I did well in history and geography, just okay with my science and downright bad in my math and English studies. My mother bought me a cornet, and I joined the school band. I got no encouragement from her to play and wasn't allowed to practice at home. After a few months in the band, I wanted to switch to the drums and that caused a problem with my mother. I wanted to grow my hair long like the fashions that were sweeping the country, and that too caused her grief.

Boyle Park, only a couple of blocks away from our home, had become a place that I escaped to more and more. A large city park with more than 100 acres of woods and streams, I would ride my bike for hours there. I knew all the trails from one end to another. Three large pavilions stood at a crossroads in the park where occasionally bands would set up and play music. Mom and my stepdad had warned us not to go down there when the bands were playing. They were all a bunch of drugged out hippies, they would say. They made it sound like zombies eating kids – crap like that.

I was discovering music and after hearing it in the park I was drawn to it. From our house we could hear the thumping and a few high notes once in a while depending on how the wind was blowing but couldn't really make out the songs that were being played. I rode down one Saturday afternoon and all three pavilions had bands in each one. The pavilions were three different sizes with the largest one being a massive thing put together with large trees made into logs. A very large fireplace was at one end, and the steps leading up into it were all rock. In the summer it was a beautiful place nestled into the hillside with greenery all around. Several hundred people could get inside it. The band was set up in front of the fireplace with the drummer centered in front of it. I remembered they were playing protest songs about the war. I know I objected to the war from my own viewpoint because it had taken my dad away from me, but I felt compelled to defend my dad and others who were there fighting it. I was taken by the music just the same and mesmerized by the guys playing it. They seemed to be in another world.

About that same time, there was a dance downtown at a place where the Masons met for the DeMolay kids. My uncles and cousins were all a part of it, so I was encouraged to join DeMolay as well. The Saint Frances Group, a popular local band at the time, was playing our dance. They had lights and sound and several guys running it all. It was a big production for a local band, and it seemed like a really big event to me at 12 years old. Some of these same guys playing in the band and working the lights and sound I would meet later in life and they assisted me in my start in the touring business.

There was a guy in my neighborhood who was a drummer at the time, and he played in another local band that seemed to be the talk of the town. Linc lived only a few blocks away, and I saw him coming and going a lot. I thought he was even cooler because he had the same name as Linc on the popular TV show, *The Mod Squad*. He never let me hang out with him. I'm sure he thought I was a weird, little fat kid, but I admired his cool demeanor and the fact that he played drums for a band named Reminiscence who, in our little world, was as big as The Beatles. I went to the fairgrounds one day to see Reminiscence play. Many neighborhood kids couldn't wait to go the show because of Linc's connection. The band wore matching outfits. Fred Moorhead, a young black man who fronted the band, had a good singing voice. How unique that, during that time, a black man was lead singer of an otherwise all-white Arkansas band playing rock music.

Another kid, Brooks Brown, who was an incredible guitar player, sat in with Reminiscence that day. When I was older, I met Brooks. He grew to become a well-known musician in the area who later was in several other local bands. One of them was called Fifth Cliff. I really enjoyed their music and took a couple of demo tapes to several record company offices in New York City when I became a driver. We never played together, but when I went on tour with Eddie Murphy in 1988, I called Brooks at the last minute, and he got into a small rental truck and followed the tour carrying Eddie's entourage's luggage. We had a great time traveling the country together, staying in some of the finest hotels in America, doing all kinds of things in the various cities and hitting the bars. I was so shocked and let down when a few months after the tour was over that Brooks ended his life with a shotgun in a local hotel room. I don't think anyone saw that one coming.

CHAPTER 38 | PRIVATE LESSONS

My desires to get away from my abusive mother sent me running away and into endless amount of trouble. I had been arrested numerous times by the time I turned 13, and she had enough. She called my dad and made arrangements for me to go live with him in the upper peninsula of Michigan at the Air Force Base where he was stationed. Dad returned from his second tour of Vietnam and had been sent to the 46th Air Refueling Squadron where he worked with the KC-135 Stratotanker. He picked me up in Arkansas during Christmas break from school, and we drove back to the base in the freezing weather. The snow was already knee deep when we arrived at K.I Sawyer Air Force Base. I remember thinking I would never have to go to school. For a southern boy growing up in Arkansas, snow meant no school. The state and cities have small budgets for winter weather, and when snow falls, most everything shuts down until it melts.

Life goes on in the northern states no matter the weather. Base kids attended school in a small town named Gwinn. The elementary, middle and high school campuses were all within walking distance of each other. When school resumed after the holiday break, I was a little shy of my surroundings in the middle school. I was teased some for my southern accent, but I was a pretty big kid, so no real hassles came my way in the beginning. Jokes about how I talked came from the locals more than the base kids. They were more traveled and understanding of the world outside of Gwinn.

Within a couple of weeks, I started to become friends with a few of the base kids and some of the locals, but there was something between the base and the local kids that kept them from befriending each other. Occasionally, there would be a fight or shoving match between the two groups. "Big Mike Shaw," a local, was a giant compared to his comrades. He was the bully who tried to keep the base kids in line while I was there. We had a couple of run-ins but nothing major because I knew to stay away from him. Some years later I was working a show in Atlanta, Georgia, and I ran into him. He was working as a stagehand. We had some good laughs about Gwinn. Small world we live in.

Gwinn was a unique American small town that survived mainly in the shadows of the base. Federal money helped the town with schools and other things. I met the school bus in the mornings at the corner of Voodoo and Dart streets. I lived on Dart, which was named after the fighter jets that were stationed at the base. (The 106 Delta Dart Aircraft are no longer in use.) Those bus drivers made their pickups every morning no matter what the weather was doing. Some mornings it would be snowing so much you wouldn't see the bus until it pulled right up to you.

Tucked on a corner about a half-mile from school was Gemma's Sub Shop, a popular lunch spot. In my first year there, Gemma's moved down across the street from the high school, and we made trails there several times a week. In the early '70s, there were no sub shops in the South, or at least not in Arkansas. Gemma's had more than 50 different kinds of sandwich combinations, even a peanut butter and jelly one. I loved eating there.

I discovered that the cool kids would head over to an old bar called The Gwinn Inn during lunch. Kids would gather around and play the pool tables in the back. The bartender would sell and heat prepackaged hamburgers and chips. Around noon only a couple of the locals would be there drinking, and no one seemed to mind the kids being there. The jukebox only had a couple of pop songs on it with the rest being polkas and country. Every day when the lunch crew got to the bar, the pop songs were loaded into the lineup. It must have driven the bartender crazy to hear the same songs over and over. Rod Stewart's "Maggie May," "Reason to Believe" and "Mandolin Wind" were on that jukebox, and they became some of my first anthems.

An old bowling alley was around the corner, and Forchini's Grocery Store was across the main street that went through Gwinn. One of the Forchini daughters was in my grade. I had such a crush on her. She was friendly to me, but she knew that like most base kids, I wouldn't be around long term. I could never get her attention. I eventually started liking a girl named Kathy, a base kid like me. Dad had never given me "the talk," and one day after some heavy petting in my bedroom, she said something to my dad on the way out.

"You need to have a talk with your son," she said. Pretty fucking embarrassing, huh?

One night just before my 14th birthday, Dad came home with a tall, slender black man named J.T. with a younger white woman in her early- to mid-twenties. At the time, I thought the girl was J.T.'s girlfriend. While dad and J.T. were talking in the living room, the girl looked at me.

"Why don't you show me your room?" she said.

I thought she was bored with the men's conversations, so I took her upstairs to show her my model cars. Before too long while we were sitting on my bed talking about various things, she leaned over and kissed me. The unexpected kiss scared the crap out of me. My first thought was that J.T., who was two ranks above my dad, would beat my ass. She assured me it was all right, and we continued. As she continued to kiss me, she undid her shirt and unhooked her bra. Her breasts seemed huge and like nothing I had ever seen or touched. She guided me to kiss her nipples, and I was overwhelmed with excitement and confusion. I was still nervous, but after a few minutes or so, I started thinking she liked me more than ol' J.T. with some of the things she was saying.

I was too apprehensive and nothing else happened, so she finally went downstairs, and she and J.T. left.

The next night she returned with J.T. and came up to my room again. As she closed the door, she turned toward me and removed her shirt. She quickly undressed me, led me to the bed and started giving me a blowjob. I will never forget that first one. I was so scared J.T. was going to come up to the room, but he never did. As she undressed me, she teased me and played with me throughout the entire encounter. She was so patient with me and did all the things boys dream of, even a few things a boy couldn't imagine. This girl knew how to "honk a bobo."

After she finished with me, we got dressed. As we were leaving the room she explained that my dad and J.T. didn't have to know what we had done. I felt weird as we walked downstairs. I couldn't look at J.T., but he and my dad were grinning from ear to ear making little comments. They knew.

Some years later, I confronted my dad about what had happened that night, and all he would say was "Happy Birthday." He did say it was an expensive present, but he felt it was money well spent. After that, I didn't have too many problems with girls.

CHAPTER 39 | THE NOT SO GREAT ESCAPE

My dad was sent overseas on what the Air Force calls TDY, Temporary Duty, for four to six months in Germany. That left me with my stepmother, who I was not getting along with very well, even when Dad was around. After several months of staying with her, it was obvious she had no parenting skills.

I had befriended a kid my age whose father was a civilian employee of the base. For some reason, Bobby had started losing his hair at 14 years of age, and he made as much fun of himself as the other kids did. He was funny with his jokes about baldness, calling himself "Chrome Dome." Bobby and I hung out just about every day talking about chicks, the turbulent times in our society and mostly how we hated the cold weather.

One day during lunch, he invited me to go with him and a few others behind Gemma's to a wooded area with several other kids we knew. When we got into the woods, someone pulled a joint of weed out and lit it up.

I had never smoked marijuana at that point, but I knew all about it from the fear factor that was being tossed around. Still, I didn't hesitate when the joint was handed to me. The weed was simple compared to some of today's varieties, and I was so nervous, I don't think I actually got high. Bobby knew someone from Marquette, Michigan, who had access to it, so it became almost a regular trip behind Gemma's at lunch hour each day. As winter progressed our conversations varied about girls, weed and how we hated being stuck in Gwinn.

Sometime after my 14th birthday, my dad bought me a car, an old Plymouth Valiant that was black. The day we went to look at the car, I was surprised that Dad had a car for me on his mind. He had been teaching me to drive for years. I had actually been driving my Dad's car since I was 12. He found it in the paper, and when we went to look at it, I was just thinking it was going to be for him. The Valiant had a red interior with a six-cylinder motor and a push button transmission on the dash. It had several mechanical problems, nothing too serious, that my dad said we would fix together. Little did I know at the time that there was a different lesson in store for me with that car.

One night when Dad came in from work, I was standing in the hall. "Dad, some n****r stopped by here to see you a few minutes ago."

In the blink of an eye, he grabbed me by the throat and threw me to the floor. He landed on top of me with his knee on my chest. His entire weight was on me, which seemed a lot even though I was slightly taller than him by that age. He slapped me a couple of times and got down into my face so I could feel his breath.

Living in the South, that word is frequently spoken, and I heard it a lot in my mother's house. The history of that word and what it means to so many people was lost on me until my dad drove the point home with his knee.

"If you ever say that word again, I won't stop beating your ass!" He didn't stop there. He punched me a few more times and sent me to my room.

He was very angry with me, and I could see spit coming out of his mouth as he dispatched me to my room and I ran up the stairs.

A little while later, Dad appeared in my room calm as ever. I was lying on the bed still hurting and whimpering when my dad started to explain why he became upset when I uttered that word.

"The fair meaning of a person isn't his color but who he is. When you start to realize that, son, all people will become more important to you. I was in Vietnam with everyone of all races dodging bullets and hiding in bomb bunkers. We all lived with sniper and mortar threats. Everyone shared the same fear. We are all the same! We're all the same, no matter the color of our skin. Our family is not racist."

Many of his Air Force work friends who came to our house were of a different race. I didn't speak that word anymore, and I gave new consideration to the entire subject.

One of the things I took from that night was how my dad had just lunged at me at the drop of a syllable and assaulted me. It was very close to how my mother would react when she attacked me. I thought that I had gotten away from that, and it would never happen again. I was very disappointed about it. Now I started developing ideas about escaping before the abuse became daily ritual. Bobby and I were talking about it, and I had all but decided to leave in my new car. We talked about heading out to California. He said he wanted to get away from his problems too, and we made a plan.

When the time came, I snuck my things into my car after Dad had gone to work. At dark, I headed down to Johnson Lake near Gwinn to pick up Bobby, and our plans were to head west. Bobby chickened out. It became a weird scene, me trying to convince him to go. It really threw a kink in my plans. I had already left, and it wouldn't be long before it was discovered, so I decided to go it alone.

With my car loaded down, I drove up to Marquette to catch the highway west toward Minnesota. But on Highway 28 close to Michigamme, Michigan, my car broke down. The drive shaft fell out of it and started dragging on the ground. I got it off the road when a Michigan State trooper came upon me. Busted! No license and all my shit in the car. He took me to Michigamme and called my dad. They didn't lock me up, but we waited for hours to pass until my dad arrived.

I was very nervous that a beat down was about to occur, but it never came. I lost the car of course, and I was assigned to years of restriction, but there was no beat down. Of course doing the restriction time was kicking my ass. Just spending time in my room after school, doing chores and putting up with the grief of my stepmother was torture. Bobby and I were still friends, but it seemed we were on a different level. The winter kept us indoors a lot, and one day while grabbing a sandwich at Gemma's, Bobby once again brought up the subject of leaving. I told him since he had abandoned our plans at the last second, I didn't believe he was serious this time. He assured me he was ready, and with much reservation, we started to plan another escape. I was determined that I wouldn't be caught this time. While making plans, we decided we would head to Florida.

In the '70s, many small-town car dealers would put the keys to the cars in the ignition each morning so customers could start them and check them out. I don't know when I had discovered this, but it seemed to be a common practice of most dealers. After a lot of discussion and making plans, we set a date, and Bobby assured me he was in this time.

On the day we were going to put our plan into action, I skipped school and hitched into Marquette to find a car. I ended up at the Ford dealership, and where the used cars were parked, I spotted a black 1971 Mustang. The car was loaded with all the options one could get including a 351 Cleveland engine with a four-barrel carburetor and automatic transmission. It even had an eight-track tape player in the dash. As I read the specs, I knew this was the car that would take us to Florida. I removed the keys, and no one at the dealership even noticed my presence. I pocketed them, hitchhiked back to Gwinn and went to school, telling everyone I had overslept. When I saw Bobby and showed him the keys, he got excited and assured that he was still in.

My dad was out of the country on some temporary flying assignment. A few days before he left we had a run in. My bicycle had fallen off the porch, and my stepmother had told me to pick it up while I was out shoveling snow off the sidewalks. I had come in and forgotten. When my dad got home, my stepmother started screaming about my insubordination. My dad responded by punching me in the face with his fist, bloodying my nose and blackening my eyes. He had kicked me when I went down and was screaming various profanities at me. I didn't think twice about leaving after that.

When it got dark, I grabbed a bunch of belongings I figured I couldn't live without and I hitchhiked into Marquette again. It was close to 10 p.m. when I got dropped off by the Ford dealership. I walked down the street in front of the sales lot, saw the car, jumped in and fired it up. After a few seconds, I put it in gear and turned out of the lot with no one around or seeing what I was doing.

I called Bobby from a payphone in Marquette, and he said he would be at our pick-up point. His parents seemed a little annoyed when I asked to speak to him. They complained that it was way too late. When I pulled up, Bobby jumped over the snow bank with a bag of his stuff and got in. We headed east on Highways 94 and 28 to 77 and then on to Highway 2 to the Mackinaw Bridge and into the lower portion of Michigan. We had planned on going to Petoskey, Michigan, where Bobby had a girl cousin with a girlfriend. Both were to be Florida-bound with us. We pulled up in front of her mom's house around 4 a.m. Her mom was out of town, and the girls were up and came out to greet us. They freaked over the car and were giggling about how much fun we were going to have. I hit it off with his cousin right away, making her laugh with my jokes.

We went into the house with plans to rest. We would head out when we woke up. Bobby was sweet on his cousin's friend, and as soon as we got into the house they took off for the bedroom. I sat on the couch with his cousin and before long we were kissing and petting each other. Daylight was dawning and the TV was just coming on as the stations generally went off the air at night. The volume was low, and as I kissed her on the couch, I heard a police radio come through the TV speaker. I jumped up in a flash.

"Shit! The cops are outside!"

Sure enough, I saw a Michigan state trooper sitting behind the Mustang when I peeked out from behind the curtains. I grabbed my coat and was heading out the back door when a local Petoskey policeman came up the steps toward me with his gun drawn. He yelled, and I turned to run the other way as the trooper entered the front door. Busted again!

The trooper had noticed the car had no plates and started investigating. When he called it in, I heard his powerful radio bleed over into the TV. We all were taken to the Petoskey jail and locked up. Apparently, the night watchman at the dealership had noticed the tracks in the snow not long after I left and had called it in as well. Bobby's parents had noticed him missing and had called the police. So the perfect plan was not so perfect after all.

In the late afternoon, a policeman came to my holding cell.

"I talked to your dad, and you're not going home."

"What?"

"You're going to be sent to a juvenile detention facility. He said he is giving up on you because you cannot screw up his career in the Air Force."

Shit.

I was trying to escape my parents, and I did. But it was not what I had planned. Not at all.

CHAPTER 40 | ANOTHER HOME WRECKED

If there was any link to the life I lead now and the one I had when I was a teenager, I couldn't think of a better one than my days at a Michigan youth home and my attempt to escape and see the country. Throughout that time, music kept me stable and the potential of travel kept me excited.

Toward the end of 1972, I had been placed in The Harbor House, a facility for youth who were not exactly welcome at home. This was in Muskegon, Michigan, just a small trip from the Upper Peninsula where I had been shipped from and a long way from Arkansas.

I had basically worn out my welcome everywhere I had been before being placed at Harbor House — running away, stealing cars, screwing up every potential foster home and even another youth home — before I got shipped there. I was still clinging to my Southern accent, and it made me stand out... really stand out. It could cause trouble, but it also was a blessing at times. People wanted to help this kid out. Go figure.

During that time, I had discovered — along with millions of other people around the country — the AM radio sensation known as Beaker Street Beaker Theater. Broadcasting from Little Rock, this late night rock show from megawatt station KAAY 1090 was a gateway for all of middle America into more of the cutting edge music of the day. The host was Clyde Clifford (his real name was Dale Seidenschwarz, but come on... Seidenschwarz?) and because the show broadcasted late at night and on a 50,000-watt station, people from Mexico to Canada could tune in. I joined the crowd from the Upper Peninsula. Knowing it was coming from home base made it that much more of an attraction.

Back then I got so much help and understanding from people who wanted me to get on the right track. I just didn't get the message at the time. Before I was sent to Harbor House, I was staying with the LaFleurs, a family in Gladstone, Michigan, who acted as a transit family for troubled kids who needed a more permanent place to live. They were a great family, and they provided a great atmosphere. They even had kids of their own. Although the place was like Grand Central Station with kids being shuffled in and out — and the house did sit next to the railroad tracks — I was there for nearly four months. But when I left there, it was to go to a stricter program. I couldn't resist being the troubled person that was inside of me.

Maybe a problem with having a house filled with troubled teens is that we could be a bad influence on each other. Until that time my drug choices had only been marijuana. Wasn't it just my luck that another kid there had a pretty good education with all kinds of drugs. Before long, we slipped into a drug store and took some over-the-counter stuff. Problem was, I had no idea what they were for. I only knew they were "downers."

This other kid told me not to worry and took a handful. Not to be outdone, I took several handfuls, much more than I should. All night long I was puking and spinning, and my ears rang for about a week before it was over. I scratched downers off my "to do" list after that.

Other than that, what got me sent to Harbor House was a lot of little things. I broke about half a dozen house rules from jumping cars for a trip down the street to jumping trains for a trip to the next town, usually Escanaba. Jumping cars was easy. In the winter, there were enormous amounts of snow from the lake in Gladstone. With that came ice. Like any other kid, we would go out and play, but our games concerned grabbing the bumper of a passing car and letting it drag us down the street as our feet slid on the ice and snow. Since people got so mad at that, I guess the trick was not to get caught. Sooner or later, the LaFleurs and counselor assigned to me had had enough.

CHAPTER 41 | THE CRIMES CONTINUE

Harbor House was an old-style three-story home that had been renovated into a youth home. It was located in downtown Muskegon, just a few blocks from the arena. The lakeshore was beyond the arena. An old ship sitting in the harbor once ran to Chicago daily, almost straight west across Lake Michigan, with cars and passengers. The lakefront was a great place to escape to and think when it was warm enough.

When I arrived at Harbor House, I was given a number as we all were. When you first checked in you were designated a number four. Do well, follow the rules, for a few weeks, and you move up to a three and get some privileges. Keep acting right, and move up to a two and just about all the privileges that could be had were at your disposal as a reward for being responsible and following the rules. There was only one 1 in the house. You really had to have your shit together to be a one.

When I got there, the other kids, already set in their routines, gave me funny looks. It took me the whole weekend to become acclimated. That Saturday night one of the other kids overdosed on downers and alcohol. He stumbled in late and collapsed on the floor right in the doorway of his room.

Then his heart stopped.

The on-duty counselor in charge of the youth home that evening applied CPR until emergency medical personnel rushed in, took over and saved the kid who had just died in front of me. I, and others, stood watching the entire scene from the hall as they applied the defibrillators and somehow revived him. This tall, lanky kid with his enormous limbs flopping around each time he got a charge — I will never forget. Someone died and came back to life. I saw it, and at the time I didn't even know his name.

As the new kid, I was first assigned to the kitchen where every kid starts. In a group setting, everyone has a job to keep themselves, as well as the house, in order. Not taking care of chores meant not getting privileges. As a newbie, I didn't have any privileges and would have to earn them. Working in the kitchen mostly meant helping Mary, a black lady who was in charge of the kitchen. She was a wonderful person who genuinely cared for the kids in the home, but she was able to put fear in our eyes with her approach. She gave the youth home a sense of home.

The house was unlike anything I had been involved with. There were a dozen other kids, ranging from 14 to 18 years old. Each had his own problems, some self-inflicted and some by whatever chaos parents had caused. Two times a week we had group therapy. We would all bring our pillows, and if we thought someone wasn't being honest, we would hit that person... with our pillows. Sometimes it got rough. We sat on the floor because there was no furniture in the room. We covered some pretty serious things about ourselves, and it got pretty emotional. It was a time that I started to understand why I was who I was. But I was still a young confused person.

The kid who died? After he came back to life and returned from the hospital, he was punished. He was now the new four, I got bumped up to a three and was assigned another chore right away.

Pete Stall was the director of Harbor House. He was a loud man with a baritone voice. He sang in a gospel group that had recorded several albums. I admired him instantly when he showed me one. The group had on matching red jackets, black ties and white pants. There was Pete right in there with the lineup. How impressive he looked on the album cover. I told him how I had already played coronet in the school band as well as drums and he encouraged me to keep on learning. Pete had lots of contacts in town because of his position with social services, so he secured various jobs throughout the town with businesses for the youths who lived at the house. He secured me a stocking position at a department store in the downtown area. Pete explained how important the job was and how hard it was for him to secure it. I started working a couple of days later. My job consisted of collecting trash from all the sales counters, stocking items in the store, sweeping the floors and generally doing what anyone told me to do. Everyone was nice enough at the store, and I was nice enough back. Of course with my Southern accent, it wasn't hard for me to make friends and influence people. Everyone seemed to know who I was within a few days. There was a part of the store that had a music department. It was there I started migrating every day I came to work. I wasn't interested in much else.

I would arrive at the store just after the guard unlocked the back doors each morning. I would hit the second floor, looking for new music, studying the records arranged in a dozen rows. Everything. All types. But rock was the best. About this time a rock band named Black Oak Arkansas was bursting onto the scene. Naturally, with the Arkansas connection, I was becoming a fan and was learning everything about them. Rumor had it that they had stolen their high school PA system to do shows with and of course everyone thought that was the most rebel rock 'n' roll thing in the world to do. Their music was edgy, and I liked it. Their first album had a map of the state of Arkansas on it, so I stole one of them. I grabbed a few others while I was at it. I just came in early, picked out what I wanted and put them in a bag by the exit door that I took to go home. It was all too easy.

I started to get a collection stacked up under my bed. Didn't even have a record player. I just wanted the albums. I had my eye on a player but didn't get that far because of Pete. I came into the house one afternoon, and as I was hitting the staircase Pete's voice echoed.

"JERRY, MY FRIEND! COME INTO MY OFFICE, AND LET'S TALK."

As I topped the stairs to drop off my coat and new records, from the hall I could see my bed, and I noticed that the blanket had been lifted up and all the albums were missing. As I entered my room, I freaked out and knew immediately I was busted.

"Crap! Crap! Crap!" I danced around nervously before finally heading downstairs. Pete had a loud voice but rarely threatening. He always had a smile no matter the subject. As I rounded the corner to his office, the stack of records was on his desk. "Crap," I muttered.

"Jerry, my son, let's talk."

It was simple. Big disappointment, major restrictions, back to the kitchen and writing a lot of forgiveness letters. Maybe some begging to avoid prosecution. I took the records back to the store manager. That was that.

So I was the low guy on the list at the house ... again. I couldn't leave. I was pretty bummed with myself, mainly for getting caught, I guess, but I had let a lot of people down, and it hadn't taken me long to do it. I didn't have any music, and I sat in my room just waiting for time to pass. I also got the shit beat out of me at the next group session.

By the second weekend, I was allowed to watch TV and move about the house, but I couldn't go outside. It was winter and the wind from the lake made it seem even colder. At least there was heat in the kitchen. Muskegon gets its share of lake-effect snow, so staying in and staying warm was okay with me. Many of the kids in the home were on furloughs through the holidays, but I didn't really have a place to furlough to that year. One Saturday night, I was downstairs in the main living room area watching *The Midnight Special* hosted by Wolf Man Jack. He introduced a band named KISS. I hadn't paid too much attention to them because they wore makeup. I even giggled when they came on, but when they started rocking, I sat on the edge of my seat. Before they were finished, I was up jumping around and screaming whatever lyrics I had just learned from the songs "Firehouse" and "Cold Gin Time." They blew me away with their stage show, and it started me on a whole new adventure in my quest for music.

I hadn't listened to many glam-style bands. It was a bit nostalgic for me when later in life I toured in the late '90s on the Pyscho Circus tour with KISS. Before I was 15, I had attended several concerts on the glam side, but I hadn't been in the front row. Muskegon had a small arena that the hockey club played in, and they had concerts there. I saw Ted Nugent and the Amboy Dukes about every month in that arena. Each time, it seemed Ted and the opening act's guitar players had the guitar battle of the century. Ted had these huge stuffed animals on top of the amps and acted like a wild man. I saw Brownsville Station in that arena. Their hit "Smoking in the Boys Room" was on the radio, and I remember the drummer doing a flip over his set at the end of the show. He wore these black silk looking pants with silver chains on the legs. He would do a perfect flip, land on his feet and wave to the crowd. I don't think I have seen anyone do something like that since. I was into what they were doing. Bob Seger played there a couple of times. He was a huge hit in Michigan, but my friends in Arkansas had never heard of him.

I eventually got another job working at an Elias Brothers (known as Shoney's in the South), a 24-hour restaurant. They had different names around the country, but they all had the Big Boy out front. I was a bus boy and dishwasher. The winters in Muskegon are cold… very cold. When the northwest winds blow across the lake, the wind chill is brutal. After a couple of years being in Michigan I was longing for the warmer climate I had been used to in the South. I had spent most of that winter inside as much as possible. Working in a kitchen helped keep me warm, so I put in extra hours to keep myself warmer. When spring was starting to creep into Muskegon, I wanted to get outside more to embrace the warmer weather.

After working there a few days, the cook started having me help him when the morning rush started — about 5 a.m. or so. At first I would bring him ingredients and he would show me how everything went together. I was getting pretty busy in the kitchen after a couple weeks of informal lessons. The cook would go out back several times during his shift to smoke. If we weren't that busy, he would smoke a joint. One night he came back in after smoking. "Fuck all this! I quit!"

He left two waitresses and me with the place. We made it until the manager came in. He made me the cook. Gave me a raise and hired another bus boy. I was movin' up.

CHAPTER 42 | A CARNIE'S LIFE FOR ME

One spring day at Harbor House, one of the guys said he was going to do some work at the carnival that was coming to town. As a building helper, he would work for three to four days setting up the rides and booths and then tear them all down when it was over, he explained. He claimed he was going to make a few hundred bucks doing it, so I wanted in on some of that action. Big bucks to a kid in the mid 1970s.

World of Pleasure Shows was based in Coldwater, Michigan. They were just starting their season as a medium sized carnival company that would grow in size as it moved around the country. As vendors joined en route, the fairs got bigger and bigger until they were state fairs in the southern states. More rides, game booths and food vendors joined the parade as the carnival moved south. Working mainly in towns in the upper eastern and southern Midwest – Michigan, Ohio, Indiana, Kentucky, Tennessee, Alabama and Louisiana. When the trucks started arriving into Muskegon, we went right to work. One minute we were standing around, and then the next, we were busy unloading blocks of wood for the rides to be set up. Measurements had to be made, and various amounts of blocks had to be placed wherever a ride part touched the ground. In order for the rides to get their certificates of operation, everything had to be level.

It seemed like it took forever to set the rides, but once everything was laid out things started moving pretty fast. We worked several more days of twelve hours or more. It was hurry-up-then-wait kind of work — nothing to do for an hour or so then rush, rush, rush, to get something done. But it seemed kind of fun to me. Each accomplishment got me a pat on the back and a "Come with me, we got something else to do over here." Within a couple of days most of the rides were in place, and the work slowed.

One of the guys in charge of me turned me over to a guy who had five Crazy-ball games on the midway. He needed help setting up the tents and booths. His name was Mack Truck. No kidding. Mack had a contract with the carnival. He provided the games, he ran them, and he got his supply of merchandise from them at a discount. The guy who turned me over to him told me to look him up when the teardown started at the end of the week. Mack had a dually pick-up truck and a trailer that transported the tents, and he had an attractive girlfriend named Wendy.

We assembled the roofs first. The whole process only took a few minutes. Compared to the rides, tent building was easy. Once the tent was up, we built the counters and set up the Crazy Board – a square table set in the middle of the tent area. It was topped with holes cut out of it about the size of drink holders. A clear plastic ring was around the board. Toss a ball into the ring. Win a prize. Keep playing and your prize got bigger every time you won. Simple. We had the booths all up, including the lights, by the end of the day. Mack told me he wished he had someone like me to work for him every day. He asked if I would be interested in working one of the booths we had just set up while the carnival spent the week in Muskegon. I explained I would be very interested. I was just trying to impress him, for what reason I had no idea. I told him I was staying at a youth home up the street and had some strict hours. But they would give me some slack since the carnival was around, and I would be working.

So for that ten-day period, I went to work at Elias Brothers at 11 p.m., worked until 7 a.m. I went to the Harbor House and slept a few hours. By one o'clock I was headed back down to the fairgrounds to work until it was time to go back to work at the restaurant. A pretty grueling schedule for a 16-year-old, but at the time, it didn't affect me much. I was excited to be doing something a little different. I was making lots of money and stashing it away. The Harbor House had me putting it all into an account. I was allowed a few dollars of each week's pay to run on, but the majority of it went into an account and was managed closely by the House staff. I was putting $100-$150 a week into the account all winter. After I'd paid for all my mistakes from the record stealing idea, I was starting to accumulate a nice savings. The carnival was paying me at the end of each day – $50 to $75 a day with Friday and Saturday nights paying me over $100. The house staff knew this and met me at the door each night and collected my earnings.

Working my ass off for the money was not the reason for me being there. Something else was driving me to work hard. The pats on the back inspired me. I never had much desire to be the richest person on the block. My parents weren't wealthy, and neither one of them taught me the value of money, how to manage it or what to do with it. One thing that had been constant in my life, however, was a strong work ethic. Many in my family, and outsiders who had an influence on my life, had been hard workers. Missing a day of work never entered their minds. Always doing extra, always working a little harder or longer seemed to be the way things were done. As a young person, I tried many ways to get out of work, but when I did work, I gave 100 percent.

The week flew by, and on Saturday, Mack approached me with an idea. He explained I was the best help he had ever had. He wished I could work with him for the summer traveling from town to town. Since I was a ward of the state of Michigan and living in a group home, traveling with the carnival was not an option. He didn't suggest I actually run away, but when I graduated from the Harbor House program, all I had to do was find him, and I would have a job for life.

Wow. At the time, that offer looked very appealing to me.

I had banked almost $500 that week. I couldn't even count the cute girls I met. A little stuffed animal seemed an easy intro. I made a bunch of friends with the carnival workers, many from the South who realized I talked almost like they did. Living in the North for a few years had taken some of the twang out of my voice but not that much. It had been an incredible week of work, and I didn't want it to end.

When the last tent was loaded into Mack's trailer, he settled with me for all the work and then gave me a $100 bonus. His beautiful hippie-like girlfriend hugged me and then they drove out of the park while I started to walk back to the Harbor House. It was about five to six blocks back to the house, but it was one of the longest walks I had ever made. I was on the verge of crying. I was so depressed. I didn't even separate the bonus money I had been paid by Mack. When I came in the door, the staff member on duty looked at me.

"What's the matter?"

"I just don't feel that good."

"You look like crap. I can't believe the hours you've been working."

He took my money and I retired upstairs. I had been working so hard that I hadn't even noticed the new guy who had moved in to my room. A new guy, another freak like me, I guess. I passed out and didn't wake until late the next afternoon. When I wandered down stairs it was between lunch and dinner so nothing for me to eat. Mary saw me. She knew I had been working long hours, as she hadn't seen me at any meals all week. About the time she was telling me she would give me a snack, Pete, the House director, came around the corner and it was the same banter. I look like crap, blah, blah, blah.

"Come into my office when you're done."

I'm double-checking what rules I might have broken and thinking of excuses. I couldn't think of any major ones. Well, I did smoke a few joints at the fair, but there weren't any drug tests to prove that. When I entered his office I sat in "The Chair," the one you don't want to be in. Pete always tried to imitate hillbilly slang when I was around.

"You've come a long way, boy," he said. "You're a couple of months away from your one-year anniversary. Most kids don't stay past 18 months."

I knew this already. Kids graduate and go on to the next program, go on their own or they go to a lock-up facility somewhere. Sometimes both. But I had never considered the day I would leave the place. Up until the time the carnival came things were pretty routine for me. I had worked my way up from being a four to being a two in the house discipline/privilege program. Pete explained that he was going to start looking to get me into the next program.

Following our talk, I went upstairs to try and sleep but couldn't. I felt I needed to already be at work at the carnival. I kept imagining what I would be doing if I were there. I could hear the sounds and smell the smells in my mind. I felt like I was missing the world. After a couple of days of falling into my normal routine, I had made up my mind that I was going to hit the road — run away like I had done a dozen times before. I thought I had found my calling at 16, and I made a plan of escape to get to it.

It was all very simple. I threw a few things I thought valuable in a bag with some clothes and dropped it off down the fire escape. I said goodnight to the night staff at the Harbor House as I checked out to go to work at the restaurant. My heart wasn't even beating fast. I knew I was meant to do this. I went around the house, grabbed my bag and walked to the highway and stuck out my thumb. I had a map and by then understood how to read them pretty well. I had had a few lessons from my dad when we had made trips together. Having already been a champ at running away, I learned to keep a map handy. I knew I was heading to the Jackson, Michigan area where the carnival was spending its next week, and it was only 150 or so miles away. It wasn't long before I caught a ride with a couple that took me to Grand Rapids. They dropped me at a truck stop, and I caught another ride from there and another after that. By morning I was walking into the fairgrounds. It was just getting to be daylight, and there were very few people stirring yet. I found Mack's truck and put my bag beside it. Knowing he would be sleeping in, I headed to a food trailer to get some breakfast. When the older couple working the trailer saw me they gave me a look.

"Hey! Ain't you?"

"Yep. I'm gonna travel with the show."

The woman guaranteed that I would be fed every day. She made me breakfast, and I ate while people started getting up from where they had been sleeping in their campers and under rides and tents as the smell of bacon, eggs and coffee floated throughout the area. Several recognized me and sat with me and engaged in normal morning carnival banter. Just like I was supposed to be there. I was finished eating and was just sitting there yapping with someone when Mack and his girlfriend walked up. He was getting his coffee when his girlfriend saw me and came over to me. She gave me a hug and seemed surprised I was there. I smiled and was saying something when Mack walked over.

"Holy shit! What are you doing here?"

"I want to work here. I'm 16. I can leave."

Mack had a troubled look on his face, his eyebrows lowered and his head cocked to one side.

"I am not going to get in trouble over this. As long as no cops are around, we're cool," he said, looking more confident.

I was crazy happy and headed to my tent to get it organized. I got everything in its proper place, doing little things and chatting with Kathy, the new girl Mack had hired. She was 18 and seemed like a cool person. She lived in Jackson and was heading to college in the fall. She was going to work odd jobs all summer saving money for school. She hadn't graduated from high school yet but only had a few weeks to go. She was attractive in her own way and seemed a little tomboyish to me. We got along well as soon as we met. She smoked marijuana and shared her stash with me. The weed in the '70s got you high but was nothing like the strands that are available today. It was a simple laugh-inducing type of weed compared to today's standards that really get you stoned.

We got a giggle from the weed and did the things we had to do to finish out the tent and get it ready for the opening. She was new to the job. I led our tasks, showing her things like the proper way to hang stuffed animals in the tent so that we could get the most bang for the buck. Bigger animals went up top to grab fair-goers' attention, smaller ones under the counter, usually the ones they went home with. But much money was made as people tried to win those big bears and lions. It felt good having a responsibility and being the leader. We hung out most of the day, then she went home to her parents' house, and I spent the night hanging out with the carnies around the rides.

There was a campfire and more than a dozen people had gathered around drinking and telling stories. I hadn't really taken up drinking yet, so I just hung out and listened to the stories and jokes. Occasionally, someone would talk directly to me, but for the most part I listened. I slept in the Crazy Ball tent. Mack had an army-style cot that he gave me to set up in the tent. The sides of the tent rolled down and were tied off from the inside so there was a bit of privacy. I was living my dream, I remember thinking as I fell asleep that night under the tent.

The next day the carnival opened. The Crazy Ball operator had a microphone and speakers to draw the crowds. Kathy and I went to work, she collecting the quarters and handing out the prizes, and I barking the chants trying to lure people over to play and working the ball.

"Twenty-five cents to play—TWENTY-FIVE CENTS TO WIN!"

"Come on DAD! Win the kid a prize!"

Late the first night Kathy had gone up to another tent to exchange something with Mack. When she returned, she said the cops were at Mack's tent questioning him about me. I freaked out, pacing not knowing where to turn. She said Mack wasn't giving me up but I had better get scarce for a while. I exited the tent and wandered down the midway. As I got close to Mack's truck with its camper shell up, I saw him getting something out of the back. We talked for a minute. He was assuring me all was okay, but as we walked away, he said again he wouldn't go to jail for me.

Without a photo of me, the cops really didn't know who they were looking for at the time. I made it through my stay in Jackson, made a few dollars and was feeling like my life was secure. Then during the teardown of the carnival, Mack came to me and explained he wasn't going to work me anymore. I felt like a truck had hit me. I had seen him and his girlfriend arguing for the last couple of days and could tell the tension between them was getting thick. I didn't realize it was about me. I saw them coming to breakfast, not really walking together, like tempers had flared that morning. They got their breakfast and came over and sat next to me.

Looking at me squarely, "I can't do this anymore. We're going to Ohio, and I don't want to be involved with you traveling over state lines," Mack said. "I got thousands of dollars in this stuff. Maybe you can go work one of the rides."

He gave me the name of a guy who was operating the Flying Bobs. Apparently, he had a guy that he was about to fire and had told Mack he would take a look at me. After breakfast I went to the Flying Bobs ride, where there was a crew of four working. A couple of them gave me a curious look as I stepped over the chain.

"What's up?"

"I'm looking for Bill," I replied.

"Around back," someone pointed.

The Flying Bobs is a ride with swinging cars riding on a circle track. Loud music plays and various color lights blink as the ride moves forward and backward with a DJ screaming, "You wanna go FASTER?" The ride doesn't go that fast but the ups and downs and the cars swinging back and forth make it seem like you're really hauling ass. As I walked around the ride, I could see the artwork on the ride of polar bears and snow-capped mountains. This would be a different world than the Crazy Ball tent.

I saw Bill. He had grease up to his elbows and a wrench in his hand and a short cigar stub hanging out of his mouth when he noticed me. He was a stalky man with Popeye sailor type arms.

"You the little fucker Mack told me about?" he grunted with the cigar stub in his mouth. I said yeah, and he started telling me the rules. He barked out a half a dozen things about what not to do and a dozen about what to do. I listened and responded to his grunts. After he was finished, he told me to come back after Mack was done with me that night. I got the job.

I headed back to the Crazy Ball tent to get organized for the day, my last. I was happy to still have a job with the carnival but wasn't happy about not working with Mack and the Crazy Ball games. The day seemed to drag, even with thousands of people there for the last day of the carnival. Kathy and I were busy from the moment the gates opened, but the day was so long it seemed nightfall would never come. I told Kathy I was going to become a ride jock, and it was the subject of our morning chat, but the conversation waned as the day got busier.

When the carnival closed that night we went about taking down everything and storing it in the trailers and then hooking the trailers up to the pickups. When the task was done we gathered around one of the trucks, and Mack handed out pay to Kathy and me. With the week's work and a nice tip from Mack, I had over $700 in my pocket. Money to blow for a 16-year-old who had no bills or responsibilities. But I wasn't that concerned about how much money I had or was making or spending. At that point I wasn't there for the money. I was there to live, have fun and get away from all the troubles I had created up to that point in my life. I might have worked for free believing that this was where I was supposed to be.

We passed a joint, said our goodbyes, and I headed over to the Flying Bobs to start my new position. The midway was chaotic with people running everywhere. Rides were coming down and folded up to be placed on trucks. Yells and mechanical sounds echoed throughout the park. Bill saw me and didn't hesitate to holler at me to grab this and tote that. Curse words flew out of his mouth, just because he could. The night's work turned into day's work before everything was put in its place and ready for the ride down to Ohio. About halfway through the night I turned to hear Bill reaming one of the helpers for being a lazy no-good whatever. Finally he screamed, "Get your shit and get outta here before I kick your ass!"

Bill walked past me.

"You better work out better than that lazy fuck."

Bill had three helpers and he had just fired number three. I slipped in, knowing I wasn't a lazy fuck, and just got busy doing whatever I was told. James and Lenny were the other two guys who worked the ride and drove the trucks for Bill. James was a pretty solid guy who had worked for Bill more than five years. Lenny was in his second year with Bill. Lenny was a shaky kind of guy who drank a lot. The guy who Bill fired was from Muskegon and had only made it two weeks. I was hoping to make it a little longer and was working my ass off doing whatever I was told as fast as I could. The last things to be picked up were the blocks of wood that had been placed for the ride to sit on to make it level. As the sun came up we were just about finished when Bill approached and said to find a place to sleep and that we would be pulling out of there at noon. I hadn't noticed how nasty I had gotten through the night. Setting up and tearing down tents and Crazy Ball games wasn't nearly as oily and greasy as setting up and tearing down rides. It's a good feeling when the job is done and an even better feeling to get clean when it's all done. But there is no place to clean up when everything is torn down at the carnival.

I found a place to sleep on the ground close to the trucks and let my heavy eyes lead me to some much-anticipated rest. I woke up to the sound of trucks roaring. I felt like shit, was nasty as I had ever been in my life and didn't have a good mindset when Bill came by me.

"Get it together, kid!" I frowned back at him.

"You're going to be in the cab with me, so get your ass moving!"

We were shuffling around getting into our seats when he released the brake and started to back up. My window was rolled down, and as I put my arm on the door, it swung back open. The truck was really old and a mega piece of crap. It probably shouldn't have been on the road. I grabbed the door and slammed it really hard to get it closed as Bill started to move the truck backward. The sound of the door echoed and probably sounded like the truck shattered a concrete wall. Bill slammed on the brakes.

"WHAT THE FUCK ARE YOU DOING?"

Bill was a short stocky man in his late 50s. He looked rough with years of hard-work wrinkles in his face. He was missing a couple of teeth, and he had tattoos on both his forearms from the Army. He smelled bad all the time, and I think he slept with that cigar butt in his mouth. If he slept at all. At night when the carnival closed he got drunk until he passed out. But he woke up each morning like nothing had ever happened. No hangover, just his bad attitude. He was one of the meanest motherfuckers I ever met. I was a pretty big kid for my age. There was no doubt in my mind he could kick my ass and throw me out of the truck.

Some of the wrenches he had been working on the truck with were laying on the cowling of the truck, also known as the doghouse. I grabbed the big crescent wrench, pulled it back a little and looked him square in the eye.

"FUCK YOU OLD MAN!"

I must have looked pretty ridiculous, a 16-year-old kid threatening badass Bill. He started laughing out loud. The first time I had seen him laugh. He made a comment about liking my spunk. He didn't bother me the rest of the trip except when I had to piss, and then he yelled at me the entire time I stood on the side of the road relieving myself.

When we arrived at our destination, I was still feeling dirty, beaten and worn out. As soon as Bill got the ride location, we pulled over and got the trucks situated. Like clockwork, Bill started barking orders. He was screaming for me to start getting so many types of blocks. The setup was going to be on a pretty level surface so not as many blocks were needed as was used in the last stop. James and Lenny knew the drill, but Bill was yelling out orders, because that was his style. Maybe in his dreams he was a drill sergeant. James and Lenny were always talking back to Bill but not to his face. James was a big athletic type of a guy with a gentle nature about him. Lenny was a skinny hippie type. They would say all kinds of weird and funny things about Bill when he wasn't within earshot.

We worked through the night. Most of the local help was late arriving so the four that made up our team had worked together getting things set for the ride. I slept on the ride in my sleeping bag and rose early to find the breakfast trailer. We worked through the morning and afternoon getting the ride ready for the opening the following day. I learned a lot about how the ride went together and how it operated. I learned the things I would be doing when the crowds were around and what would be expected of me when they weren't. I set my bedroll under the ride when we finished. Bill slept in the truck, James slept in a tent next to his truck, and Lenny and I slept under the ride. There was headroom enough to hang up some blankets and make a private area almost like a room comfortable to relax and sleep in. Lenny had a hammock that he slept in on his side under the ride. I had just found some merchandise boxes and put them over the grass and put my bedroll over it. I hung some blankets, made a stool to sit on, and I was happy to have a home once again.

Once everything was in place and had been tested, Bill called us over and gave us some wages. The best part – he directed us to the showers in the small cattle arena that was on the property. It had been several days since I had bathed. We cleaned up and went into town to find some good food. Everyone seemed to migrate to a little dive bar that was between the fairgrounds and the food area of town. Ride jocks congregate together and the games and food vendors seem to hang together. Everyone in the show is friendly, but not too much time is spent together partying. A carnie told me that if someone was giving me grief and if I was ever in any danger to yell, "HEY RUBE!" and anyone who was a carnie within earshot would come to my defense.

When the gates opened on the first day, I started working taking tickets and putting people in their seats. The music was loud and a crowd of people started gathering around our ride. We got busy, and the fun began. Lenny was running the ride and talking all kinds of crap on the microphone, attracting the patrons our ride. James and I got a rhythm going with taking the tickets and getting people in and out of the buckets they had to ride in. Everything went smoothly the first day. I kept noticing a girl hanging around the ride and we started talking. She was attractive. She was only 15, but she ended up spending the night with me under the ride. We hung out together for the week, and then I never saw her again.

The next few weeks were pretty routine with several moves going well. Bill didn't disappoint. Every day, there was yelling, screaming, cursing at people and bitching about something. As for me, I simply did the job and enjoyed meeting a girl – or several – in each town, hanging out with the carnies and feeling like this was my life. Bill had taken the time to show me some of the basics to driving a truck and some of the maintenance. The ride itself was a constant chore to keep in order. It was a dangerous ride so upkeep was top priority.

It seemed no one was looking for me anymore, and I settled into a routine of fun and hard work. By the time a couple of months had passed, we had worked our way south through Ohio, Indiana, Illinois and into Kentucky. I had learned the job pretty well and had gotten to know just about everyone who was traveling with the carnival. I had discovered what the best jobs were on the midway and was quickly discovering that just about everyone was tired of Bill's constant pissing, moaning and threatening. He was causing arguments everywhere.

I had started hanging out with the guys who were running the Sky Wheel. Our ride had been set up next to them in one city, so we became familiar with one another. They were more in tune with the times, embracing the hippie movement, which was a refreshing break from Bill's military style. When one of them dropped out one day they invited me to come work for them. The turnover with people working the carnival is pretty quick. A lot of people come and go.

I was considering it the next day when Bill lit into me over some silly bullshit.

"Fuck you!" I was done with Bill.

I grabbed my stuff and headed over to the Sky Wheel. It took me several days to get the money he owed me, but he finally paid me after many arguments and confrontations. Even people like other vendors and breakfast cooks stood up for me. The lady who said I'd always be fed on the first day of my carnie life told Bill if he didn't pay me, she was going to piss in his oats.

I will give Bill credit for teaching me mechanical aspects of the rides on the midway, which made my move over to the Sky Wheel go off without a hitch. Setting up carnival rides was like building Legos. All the parts have their place and learning where they all went and why and how they worked was always a fascination to me. Today, I see that fascination in the setup and tear down of a rock show. After a couple of setups and teardowns, I became comfortable working the machine. The Sky Wheel was a cleaner ride to work on and operate. Tom, the guy in charge, was into cleanliness so we spent a lot of time cleaning the ride and ourselves. What a long way from Bill's standards. The ride was bright yellow with white buckets and lots of lights. Each day we could spend an hour or more keeping things in order. On warm days we carried numerous water hoses with us to wash the ride. After we were done cleaning the ride in the morning, we would stretch the hoses out and fill them with water and let them bake in the sun for a while and then set up makeshift showers with the hot water that had been heated up by the sun.

It was about that time that I was learning to drive the small truck and trailer. A Ford 9000 Super Duty truck pulled the small 35-foot trailer. It was a single axel gas powered conventional style truck with an eight-gear shifter. Shift it four times, pull an air valve and shift it four more times. The trailer had a single axel and was steel plated. It was heavy. The entire unit loaded weighed in a little less than 30,000 pounds. Once I made the first move with it from one town to another, I got a raise. Drivers made a few extra bucks for the skill.

It was late August as we traveled farther and farther into the South. I had worked almost five months traveling with the carnival. I had several thousand dollars in my pocket stashed away. Life was looking up. The carnival had moved into Jackson, Mississippi, and things were seemingly normal throughout the week. As we were tearing the ride down in Jackson, I was on top of the trailer securing some beams when I slipped and fell about 12 feet to the ground, landing square on my back.

The fall took the wind out of me, and I was paralyzed for a few minutes. A lot of folks gathered around and commented, but no emergency people were called. At daylight they helped me get into the truck and I drove it to Alexandria, Louisiana, convoying and following Tom's lead. When we arrived I was very sore and could barely move. When the guys started the setup all I had the capacity and energy to do was tell the local guys what to do. I hadn't been to a doctor and thus had no medication for the pain. A few of the carnies had various pills that I refused. I didn't like to take pills.

I realized I had to save myself. I reasoned that since there was Barksdale Air Force Base north of Alexandria and Fort Polk, an Army base to the west, I could call my dad to arrange for me to get some medical attention at one of their facilities. As an Air Force dependent, I had an ID card that would allow me to be treated. As soon as I made contact with my father, he blew up. Another failed plan on my part.

"Where the hell are you? You have screwed up this time! I won't be able to help you." It hadn't occurred to me what I might have been doing to him or my mother, for that matter, while I had been gone traveling with the carnival for the past four to five months.

I gave him some details about my accident and about which bases I was near. He said to call him back the next day and he would see what he could do. I got high and drank some whiskey someone had offered up and passed out.

I awoke to a Rapides Parish sheriff's deputy shaking the cot I was sleeping on. I moaned because of the pain.

"Boy, get up. We got people looking for you!"

He allowed me to get some things together and say goodbye to a couple of people. He wouldn't let me wait to get the money I was owed.

He took me to the parish jail and then to see a doctor. I was telling them about my travels, and they seemed pretty interested that I had gotten so far without being arrested somewhere else.

After getting checked out by the doctors, I was taken to the Alexandria Youth Services facility somewhere on the outskirts of town. Tired and sore, I was given a room where I slept for two days. When I woke up on the second day, I learned that the Michigan Department of Child Services was sending someone down to pick me up. It was going to be a few more days before they arrived. If I obeyed the rules, I was promised no lockdown. I was too tired and sore to run and didn't have a clue where I would go even if I did.

A few days turned into a week before someone arrived to take me away. I spent my time hanging with several of the kids there. Some had gotten into some mischief but nothing too serious. They were there because their parents were screw-ups or in jail. Most were teenagers, and I hit it off with several by sharing my stories of running away and traveling with the carnival. The facility had a couple of horses that we rode in the afternoons. I connected with a girl there and we snuck out a couple of nights and held each other talking about the world and the future. I didn't have a clue what mine would be once I landed in Michigan again. I thought I would be sent to prison when I got back. She didn't have a clue what was going to happen to her either. But for a few days, we found security in each other.

When Frank arrived at the facility to take me back to Michigan, I was depressed about being trapped back in the system. I had lived a free life, and the routines of being in an institutional setting following authoritative rules and regulations saddened my frame of mind. Frank was a young guy in his mid-20s with medium length hair and a big smile. A bit of a football player build like a linebacker. He was easy going enough. When he arrived some people from the facility showed him around giving him the low-down on the place. They were impressed that he was from Michigan. Michigan's approach to troubled youth was unique in the '70s. They seemed to really care and were trying to make a difference in young people's lives.

We met in one of the concrete rooms and he explained the plan of return to Michigan. He wasn't going to cuff me, although he had a set of cuffs on his belt under his sports coat. He said if I tried to run he would take me down and use them and be a really big asshole to me so there was no point in attempting an escape. I assured him he would have no trouble out of me and that I was ready to go back. We were on a late flight to Detroit then into Grand Rapids. From there we would drive the rest of the way to Muskegon and back to the Harbor House. I was ready to go back and face my punishment.

It was a three-hour ride back to the New Orleans airport, and Frank announced that we were going to go to Bourbon Street in New Orleans to kill a couple of hours before the flight. I agreed. I assured him I would stay close and out of trouble. We had been talking on the ride to New Orleans and I was comfortable because he listened to my adventures and troubles and commented with some good advice. He didn't know what was going to happen to me, if I was going to go to jail, stay at Harbor House again or what. I certainly hadn't a clue.

After finding a place to park, we walked down Canal Street to Bourbon and strolled by the Bourbon Street bars. He drank several shots at the street bars as we walked along and then he darted into Pat O'Brien's and got a Hurricane. The memories from that trip and many others have makes New Orleans my favorite town in America.

By the time we made it back to the car, Frank was pretty tipsy. We argued a minute about me driving. Crap, I had been driving tractor-trailer trucks all summer, I explained He caved, and I got us to the airport. We stumbled onto the plane and flew all night to Detroit. Frank slept the whole way. We switched planes in Detroit and flew to Grand Rapids. Frank freshened up at the airport, and we made the hour or so ride to Harbor House.

When we arrived, the staff gave me the cold shoulder. There was only a couple of kids still around that I knew. Everything had changed. When Pete finally came in he expressed his deepest disappointment in me. I was doing so well, he said. I assured him that I had done well in my travels also. I tried to make him understand that being a carnie was my destination. He laughed so hard and encouraged me to strive for so much more, but I wouldn't listen. I had to get back to that carnival, I thought.

Pete explained that since I had run away from Harbor House I could no longer be in their program. Since I was over 16, I was going to be released to the custody of my dad, to whom he had already spoken. He gave me a place to sleep until my dad arrived the next day. By the time my dad came for me, it had turned into a sad farewell for the staff and me. I learned a lot about life and myself during my short time at Harbor House. I had discovered pent-up feelings of anger that probably led me to my troubles. I often wonder about the people who passed through my life at Harbor House.

The drive north to the Upper Peninsula was long, and when we arrived I could feel the changing seasons in the air.

My dad didn't know what to do with me. I had changed from the kid I was who had run away in the Mustang. Not long after we arrived back at the base he had to go to temporary duty to another base, "TDY," the Air Force called it. I sat at home and didn't do much of anything. I played many hours bouncing a baseball of the side of a wall that would produce pop flies I would catch. My friend Chris and I started hanging out as the winter weather started getting cooler and cooler. He had an older brother named Chuck who had joined the Marine Corps while I was away.

Chuck had been somewhat of a troublemaker like me, and when he was caught for the who-knows-how-many-times, he was given the choice of jail or military by a judge who had come to know his name pretty well. Chuck chose the Marine Corps. I had been home a few weeks, not doing much except bumming around when Chuck graduated from his boot camp in San Diego and came home on leave before he was headed to his duty station. It was a big day when he arrived at the airport with people holding welcome signs and balloons. A few folks were waiting at the house for his arrival. I went down the street to their house, about two blocks away, for the homecoming and cake. Chuck was wearing his dress uniform with a blue coat and white pants. His expert marksman's badge shined on his chest and his shoes were spotless. A very sharp looking Marine by any standard. He had longer hair than me when he left for boot camp and now he was bald and clean-shaven. He was in better physical shape, easily noticed by the way he wore his uniform.

After the hoopla over his coming home, Chris and I were in the basement getting high when Chuck joined us. We had a ton of laughs going over all the crap he went through in boot camp and the stories he told mocking the drill instructors. It was tough as hell and the way he poked at the toughness of it all made me laugh.

People were looking at Chuck differently. I noticed they all had that "what a great guy Chuck turned out to be" kind of look about them. I started thinking I could clean up my act and follow in the footsteps of my father. I wanted to pursue the path Chuck had taken. With my 17th birthday approaching, I started making plans to become a United States Marine.

CHAPTER 43 | SOME FUN NOW

In October of 1974, I was approaching the age where it would be legal to join the military. I was thinking if I could stay out of trouble, I could bypass everyone's bullshit and be my own man. I believed that on the day I turned 17, as long as I stayed out of trouble, I would be a free adult. No one would be able to tell me what to do with my life, and I was going back to the carnival to live happily ever after until I heard Chuck's stories.

I had returned to the Upper Peninsula of Michigan to K. I. Sawyer Air Force Base where my dad was stationed. I was just trying to bide my time until December. The Vietnam War was still going strong, and the images of it were being plastered on the news and in the papers. The protesters were getting louder and louder. The separation the military had caused my family was something I had never seriously thought about. After spending a couple of days with Chuck, who had just returned from Marine Corps boot camp, I changed my mind and began to chart a different future.

I came home from my friend's house late one night, and my dad had just gotten in from working out on the flight line at the base. Winter was coming, and it was a terrible time to repair K.C.135 Tankers in wide-open spaces. I had been looking forward to hitchhiking my way out of there before the snow got waist deep.

Dad was sitting in his chair eating when I came in and sat beside him. We really hadn't spoken much about anything. He didn't ask me too much about my life or what I had been through the last year when I was with the carnival. So I just blurted out my newfound intentions.

"Dad," I said. "I want to join the Marine Corps."

He looked at me and smiled.

"You don't want to do that." He kept that grin on his face.

"Oh yes I do." I launched into a thousand reasons why I thought it was the perfect path for me. I knew that this was the best thing in the world.

Dad had returned from his second yearlong tour in Vietnam just a few years earlier. Many of the memories of the conflict were still fresh in his mind. It was still being plastered in the news of our kids dying, and the protests were stronger and bigger.

"Listen, everyone in our family has been in the Air Force or Army Air Corps," he told me. "The Marines are just a different type of service." He didn't say much else. He must have felt he didn't have to. To him, the subject was moot. I didn't let up for several weeks. I had explained that I went to the Air Force first, but the recruiter told me my age and not having a high school diploma would slow me down. I didn't want to wait. I was ready to go now.

I had hitchhiked to the Marine recruiter office in Marquette and talked to a recruiter. He gave me a ride back to the base when we were done, and he checked on me every week. During one of our visits, I told him I wanted to be in the Air Wing of the Marine Corps. He had said that wasn't going to be a problem. I just had to keep working on my dad to sign the papers. With a parent's signature, a youth could join the military. A few days before my birthday, Dad was tired of me nagging him, and he agreed to sign the paperwork.

I was ecstatic, and I headed to the recruiter's office the next day. The young corporal had befriended me, and he had my trust. I thought so much of him. He had a Vietnam Service ribbon on his shirt along with several others. He called my dad while I was sitting in front of him. He talked to my dad the way I always thought I wanted to.

"Master Sergeant Fitzpatrick, sir: I have Jerry here in front of me, and he is telling me you have agreed to sign the paperwork necessary for him to enter the Marine Corps, sir."

They talked for a couple of minutes. He was being so respectful to my father, and maybe something like that was all it took. When he hung up, he smiled.

"Congratulations. You're going to become a Marine."

From a carnie to a Marine. At least I wasn't boring.

He took me in a room and explained that to start the process I would have to take a written test and pass it. Then we would take the next step. It took me several hours to complete the entire book. When I had finished, he brought me into an office and started giving me details on what I would have to do next. They loaded my hands with documents to be filled out and signed. They gave me copies of everything in that entire office, and at the end of the day, he returned me back to the base. It took several days, but when everything was in order, I was told I would go to MEPS (Military Entrance Processing Station) in Milwaukee, Wisconsin after Christmas. Only a few more weeks and I would be changing my life for good.

Dad approached me differently during those weeks and opened up to me like he had never before. He started to explain some of the things he had witnessed in Vietnam on his two tours. He felt that if I were going to be in the Corps, I would probably end up over there. Dad had been on a forward base where planes would come to and from supplying the war. He saw everything that came and went, from ammunition to body bags. He had assisted with loading Agent Orange onto the planes that sprayed the jungles. He had seen probably more than he cared to.

The bases in Vietnam he had been on had mortar attacks, and he told me how scared everyone would get when the Viet Cong shelled their facilities or when the Vietnamese snipers were firing at them, all the time running to find cover. I finally could see a side of my father that I had never seen before. This man was a serious man, and the time he spent over there had left impressions that changed him forever. He had changed from the father that had rescued me in the summers before he went to Vietnam.

There were hundreds of kids on our base. Many of their fathers went to

Vietnam, and Dad talking about it made me realize what it meant for all of these kids. I was one of them, but I never realized it until then.

Christmas time came and went. The house was peaceful for the most part. I had to wait a few extra days before I could get into the processing group at MEPS. The recruiters came to the house and picked me up one morning to take me to the bus station for the trip to Milwaukee. Dad had bid me farewell that morning and had gone to work. I had a couple of changes of clothes in a small bag. I was wearing bell-bottoms and military style boots. My hair had grown down to the middle of my back, and I had a pierced ear with a dangling cross in it. The Marines who put me on the bus knew I was about to go through a transformation. Let the teasing commence. I didn't even consider their humor or advice. All I could think about was the fact that I was getting away. I was going to be my own person, a Marine; no one was going to fuck with me. I would manage my life the way I saw fit, and there wasn't going to be anymore physical abuse from my dad and certainly not from my mother whom I had little contact with since I left home.

I wasn't afraid to be going to Milwaukee by myself, and I was actually excited about going to San Diego. Finally, a place that was warm! The bus ride to Milwaukee was uneventful, as it traveled down Highway 41 to Gladstone, stopping to let passengers on and off. I didn't have any time to visit the people I had known, so I hung out at the bus station until it left again. Traveling on south through Escanaba and through Green Bay to Milwaukee, the trip took about eight hours to cover the little more than 300 miles with all the stops along the way.

When I arrived at the bus station, I was instructed to walk a few blocks to a hotel where they had a room for me. As I entered the hotel, the bar was jumping with all kinds of people. I went to my room for a minute, felt alone and headed back to the bar. I wasn't old enough to drink, but someone bought me a beer. Just about everyone was there to be processed into all branches of the service the next day. That kind of sat with me for a while. There were people joining all branches of the service.

Everyone was whooping it up. "Our last night of freedom!" I struck up a conversation with a young girl who was going into the Navy. We got drunk, went back to my room and spent the night. She was a beautiful girl with long straight hair. She confided in me some of her life's story, and I told her mine.

The next morning, we were up early, and I headed over to the processing building. Line after line after line. All day long filling out paperwork, disrobing, getting poked and prodded on all parts of our bodies. It was damn cold standing in the room with 80 or 90 other naked men. After the first day, I spent the night again with the same girl. I had a good time hanging out with her. We shared the same ideas about life. She related to my troubles, having endured similar hard times, and maybe it was why we connected. Maybe it was the fact that we might not ever see each other again.

The next morning we were up early again and back for more paperwork, medical records and all the other required crap one goes through to join the military. This included raising our right hands and taking our oaths. When we had finished the processing, I was put on a bus, taken to the airport and sent to

San Diego. It was around three or four in the afternoon when the jet took off. I was excited about what the future had in store for me and was feeling a bit like a big wig.

When the plane landed, I was walking through the airport taking my time, telling myself I better enjoy my last few moments. I sat down on a bench and lit a cigarette. I kept hearing a man yell every couple of minutes or so at the end of the hall, but he was far enough away that I couldn't understand what he was saying. I finished, got up and as I rounded a corner, a Marine was standing in the middle of the foyer. Just when I looked up and noticed him, he screamed at me to hit the door and get in the bus. How did he know to scream at me? When I got on the bus, I realized that most of the people already there looked like me: young, most having long hair, and we all had this scared look on our faces.

It was around 10 p.m. when I entered the bus. A Marine was in the driver's seat and a corporal was sitting in the first seat with a ton of paper work beside him. I gave him mine, and then he yelled at me to sit down. We sat there for over an hour as people straggled into the bus just like I had done. It was just about full when the first guy who had yelled at me entered the bus.

"Welcome, ladies!"

I smiled. This is the way Chuck and the recruiter had told me they would refer to us in the first few days. The drill instructor told the driver to drive, and he started giving us a speech about what life was about to become. The distance was short from the San Diego Airport to Marine Corps Recruit Depot (MCRD) and he didn't stop screaming the entire time. He walked up and down the aisle lecturing and yelling until we pulled through the gate and up to a building with yellow lines on the ground leading inside. By this time, the instructor had worked his way to the back of the bus, and when it stopped he was starting in again.

"Get off ladies! Get off my bus!"

He was grabbing people by the arms and necks, pushing them toward the door, telling everyone to follow a line. Several other instructors joined in yelling and screaming and telling us what to do. It seemed ridiculous at the time, all the confusion they were stirring.

I was hustled into a room where everyone was standing in a line to go through a door to get their hair cut. Everyone was dead silent, and I waited my turn. The line was moving fast with the three or four barber chairs filling up as soon as someone got up. Everyone was in the chair and out in a matter of a couple of minutes each. I made it to the chair and felt the razor skin my head in about four or five swipes, and as I started to get up, a black drill instructor grabbed me by the arm. As he swung me up against the wall, he grabbed my earring that was dangling from my ear lobe.

"Come here, faggot!" He screamed for everyone to hear.

He put his forearm against my throat, lifting me up slightly with the pressure he was putting. He started cutting off my air. At the same time he was pulling down on the earring and screaming only a couple of inches away from my face. I could see inside his mouth he was so close. He pulled down on the earring so hard that it started to bleed. He just laughed.

"You're the first faggot in this group to bleed!" He screamed and spit at me.

I couldn't breathe, and I certainly couldn't speak, but that didn't stop him. He was firing off question after question about why I was wearing an earring. I couldn't think of a reason at that time. It looked cool maybe? I don't think he would have appreciated that response. Maybe it was better that I couldn't breathe.

Just when I started thinking I was going to jail or something, he screamed, "You better get this damn thing out of your ear before I yank it out!"

I couldn't reach up to touch it. The pressure on my throat and my ear was almost unbearable, and when he finally let me go, I fell to the floor gasping for air. I immediately removed the earring and tossed it in a trashcan in the corner. I got up with his kick to my tail, and that was it. Problem solved.

I was sent to the next room where everyone was sitting in front of red bins being filled up with military clothes and boots and supplies that would be used in boot camp. We were instructed to sit cross-legged in front of these red boxes while we went through the night getting gear and fulfilling all the requirements. Everything went into a large green duffel bag similar to the dozens my dad had at home. Around four in the morning, the instructors put us in a barracks with rows of bunk beds where we hung our bags and went to sleep. I couldn't sleep. On first impression, this crap wasn't as fun as Chuck had made it out to be.

CHAPTER 44 | GETTING IT TOGETHER

I was in a state between sleep and awake at 5:30 a.m. when a bunch of new drill instructors barged in grabbing empty waste cans, tossing them between the bunks, kicking them and screaming just like everyone before.

"GET UP LADIES! GET UP LADIES! GET THE FUCK UP!"

Right on time. I'm thanking Chuck as I hit the floor and attempt to stand at attention at the end of my bunk. We were given a bunch of shit to do including push-ups because a few guys were slow in getting up. When one doesn't do well, we all paid the price, one of the drill instructors yelled. I dropped and started my punishment with the others.

Out the door bopping and hopping in a group to the mess hall in four unorganized lines, we crossed the parade deck. Right away I noticed the other platoon ranks. Dozens of platoons were around us. They were around us coming and going in different directions, and I saw how polished some of them were right away. Their legs and arms were all swinging in the same motion, and there was one distinctive clump on the ground from their boots as they went along. I thought it was neat as shit with the yells of the drill instructors echoing throughout the area singing Cadence just after daylight. Our group didn't look like that at all.

We were heading to breakfast and as we got closer to the mess hall, one of the platoons marching to the chow hall had turned and marched right into our group like we weren't even there. I was a quarter of the way down the line, but as soon as they entered our group, they started to shove and push our guys and after only a few had gone to the ground, our platoon – or whatever you wanted to call it – started to fight back. Yelling and screaming ensued, and guys were shoving and pushing. The drill instructors separated everyone and got everybody in their proper lines. The other platoon went on, and our instructor chewed our asses out.

"NO ONE!" He paused for effect. "NO ONE PASSES THROUGH OUR RANKS! If anybody ever does that again, and you pussies let them, I will kill each and every one of you!"

We were a mess, a sloppy group of misfits, street thugs and farm boys from all backgrounds. It's a grueling process the drill instructors put you through to make you a lean, mean, killing, marching machine.

Over the next 11 weeks, we were put through the camp, and after only a couple of weeks, I could see the changes being made to every individual in the platoon, including myself. There were a few guys who didn't make it. They seemed to just disappear, and by the fifth week, the platoon had settled into a groove. Of course there were the daily fuck-ups, and I got yelled at more than once, but for the most part, I made progress and learned the skills required of Marines.

I was chosen to march on the color guard at our graduation. Marching was something I could do. I enjoyed it and always thought it was cool when we marched or ran as a group and sang songs. I had a problem with keeping my head up when I was first learning to march. These guys in the Marines were sticklers about marching. Staff Sergeant Black, our lead drill instructor, had a passion to sing out Cadence during marches, and he did it like no other. A couple of times he yelled at me as we were marching to keep my head up.

"A left, right-ta left, right-ta left. Fitzpatrick get that head up! Right-ta left," he would chant. I always focused straight ahead as required, but my chin would eventually drop almost to my chest as I concentrated.

One day we were marching on the parade deck when Black stopped. "Hippity hop mob stop," he yelled.

I could see him coming toward the area where I stood. I was doing everything right, I thought, and I wasn't thinking he was coming for me. As he got into my face, he grabbed me by the throat and then the stock on my rifle resting on my right shoulder. He then walloped me with it on the right side of my head. Hard! I almost fell down and as he screamed at me a couple of inches away from my face he kept hitting me with the rifle. I don't think I ever dropped my head after that. At least I didn't get caught doing it.

When we had first arrived, the drill instructors explained that if we tried to run away, we would be caught and placed in Leavenworth Prison in Kansas. We were told a story of a recruit who one winter ran off and jumped the fence at the San Diego airport next door. Apparently, he had climbed into the wheel well of a departing airplane. When the plane arrived at its destination, the recruit had frozen to death, and when the landing gear doors had opened, he fell out. DOA.

I hadn't planned on running away, not from this anyway. By the fourth or fifth day, I told myself that I was going to do my best in the Marines. I was going to be as squared away Marine as I could be. One my dad would be proud of. After 11 weeks our platoon, Platoon 1009, graduated on 11 April 1975. I was so proud of my accomplishments, and I was telling myself that I was going to make it at something finally and leave much of my personal failure behind. I was so proud to be a Marine. My admiration for the drill instructors and all Marines has stayed with me forever.

My mother had flown to San Diego and attended my graduation. This would be the first day I had seen my mom since my dad came to get me to live in Michigan with him. After I had received my orders, I had a couple of weeks of leave so I flew home with her for the time off. I had a good time seeing old friends and seeing the shock on their faces when they saw me in my uniform. My mother made it a point to get me over to a Davis clan function, and I saw many friends from the neighborhood before I flew back out to California and on to my first duty station. The ten days at home were good... different... but they mainly reminded me of the many things I was trying to forget in my life.

CHAPTER 45 | FUBAR IN HAWAII

When I, a proud new Marine, arrived at Camp Pendleton and was sent to a transit barracks to await final orders and travel papers, I was a little disappointed. The fact was I wouldn't be working in the Air Wing of the Corps. My recruiter had all but guaranteed that I would be working on jets, but when I received my military occupational title it was 0811-Field Artillery Cannoneer. My desired skill had been something to do with airframe maintenance or engineering. I talked to my instructor who sent me to a career counselor. He explained that if I wanted Air Wing I would have to be regular Corps first, improve my education and work my way in. When he went over what I would be doing as a cannoneer, he made it sound interesting, and he mentioned that once I was in the regular Corps, I could put in for a different occupational skill. I committed to doing well and trying to be a good Marine.

Air Wing ground training would have been in Memphis, Tennessee, so I was a little disappointed that I was on my way to a base in the middle of the Pacific Ocean, Kaneohe, Hawaii. I was going to be trapped on a rock in the middle of the ocean, and that wasn't appealing to me at all. While awaiting my orders, I was placed in a transit barracks at Camp Pendleton and ordered to march the perimeter around a tent city that had been set up on base where Vietnamese people were being brought to America as South Vietnam was collapsing into the hands of Communists. Since I was a private, I got the late shifts between midnight and 7 a.m. I marched around the perimeter and never had to give a "HALT! Who goes there?" to anyone. I think they were just happy to have cots to sleep on and three hot meals a day. It was the first time I carried live ammunition while on duty in the Corps. I was 17 and didn't understand what the war in Vietnam was all about. Even through all my troubles, I remained loyal to following the news of the day. I remember feeling compassion for these people being brought to America but also feeling some concern at other times that they were relocating to our country.

After nearly two weeks at Camp Pendleton, I was put on a flight to Hawaii, heading to my final destination – Marine Corps Air Station Kaneohe. After a week of orientation, I was assigned to the 3rd Marine Division, 1st Battalion, 12th Marines, Kilo Battery. A 155 Howitzer unit, our job was to back up the 105mm guns that were backing the grunts in the field. The 175mm guns and so on backed us. The 1st Battalion, 12th Marines had a long history since being commissioned 1942. They're known for their valiant efforts in several campaigns around the world, including the battles of Guam and Iwo Jima. Kilo was a new unit that was forming when I arrived, and many of the men that were being placed in the unit had seen service in Vietnam. There were many quality Marines coming into the unit and quite a few young Marines who had just gotten out of Boot Camp in San Diego and Camp Lajune, North Carolina.

There also were a few of the guys that didn't have that Marine Corps spit and polish attitude that had been instilled in us at boot camp. "Slackers," they were being called. "Shitbirds" by many. Some were just waiting on their rotation to get out and go home, so they didn't care much about anything. Their experiences in Vietnam had affected their attitudes about life, and a few were just downright crazy. Unfortunately, a small number were stone cold drug addicts hooked on heroin. Some were alcoholics and many had depression issues from the war. There were the casual drug users since there were no piss tests during those times. I lived on the second floor of an open barracks with 50 or more other men. Tall lockers were used to separate the barracks into cubicles for minimum privacy. Almost all of the squared away Marines had spots in the front of the barracks where you entered the floor and close to the bathroom that everyone shared.

As you walked through the barracks, the further you went toward the back of the large room, the more people's attitude about being a Marine was less exciting, and most of the bad Marines were all the way in the back of the room. My area was in the middle of the room, and I fixed it up like a kid might do with a stereo, lots of music tapes and posters.

In order to operate military equipment, you have to get a license for each vehicle you drive. I got mine to drive a Jeep then stepped up to a deuce and a half, then a five-ton license. A five-ton truck was used to pull a howitzer. I was assigned to Sergeant Williams' howitzer, and in training I learned every job on the weapon. I went to school to learn all the aspects of the weapon and made plans to get nuclear clearance since a 155 howitzer was the smallest gun to shoot a nuclear shell at the time.

I also started taking courses on airframe maintenance to start preparing for my future transfer to the Air Wing. Sergeant Williams had been in Vietnam working with 105s and told me some gruesome stories. He also told me he had been busted in rank and sent to this unit for telling some jerk-off officer to fuck himself. I found that honorable in some weird way and admired him all the more.

I bought a Yamaha 650 Motorcycle from another Marine that had been transferred and had to leave his bike behind. I started riding it throughout the island, visiting the north shore on weekends and hitting Waikiki or the Keys, as everyone referred to the area, at night. Staying out late in the Keys would make morning runs with the unit tough. It sucks to wake up and hit the door for a five-mile run with boots on when you're nursing a hangover. My body just did it.

I went into downtown Honolulu one night in October when I had heard Rod Stewart was performing at the HIC Arena. In order to get to Honolulu and Waikiki, I rode over the Pali Mountains. The drive over the mountains has some of the best views in America. Driving up and through the tunnel to reach the other side of the island, you could look back over your shoulder and see green valley and endless sea. Looking up as you head toward the tunnels your eyes were greeted with tops of the mountains, a breath-taking scene. Riding a motorcycle was the best way to view it. Many days it would rain in the mountains, so you would get wet going over. The warm air usually had me dry by the time I reached my destination.

When I arrived, the show wasn't sold out, so I got my ticket. I was excited to see Stewart perform. I was such a fan, and a couple of his songs were anthems for me. Of course "Maggie May" was a favorite, but "Reason to Believe" and "Mandolin Wind" were favorites of one of the first albums that I ever owned.

When the opening act went on stage, I had never heard of Peter Frampton. By the time he finished his set, I didn't want him to quit. He played most of the songs that were released on his "Frampton Comes Alive" album. I was so entranced by Frampton's show that I didn't stay long for Rod Stewart's show. I left within the first 30 minutes and went looking for a ticket for the next night's performance. I came back again the next night and was blown away again by Frampton. And again, I didn't stay long for Rod Stewart's show. I couldn't get Frampton's tunes out of my head. A month or two after "Frampton Comes Alive" hit the stores, I bought one of the first copies I could get my hands on. I played that album so much the guys in the barracks complained to me to give it a break.

When I had the time, I'd ride over to the Keys, park my bike by Fort Derussy, the Army depot, and walk to the beach, and from there down Kalakaua Avenue. Across the street from the International Market Place were some rock planters that I would sit on and watch people go by. Tourists came from all over the world. Have a beer, get a buzz and sit and watch the sunburned travelers – a good time for me. Up the street was a bar called the Crows Nest where I went many nights. They had a couple of musicians playing songs and telling jokes. Late one night, I was sitting in the booth right next to the stage with another Marine who had gotten so drunk he fell asleep. The place was jumping when one of the singers looked over and saw him asleep. He put his hands in the air and stopped the entire show. There were about 60 patrons in the place. Quiet filled the room.

My buddy was slumped over with his chin on his chest, and now he was snoring. The musician put the microphone next to my buddy's head where everyone could hear. The place burst out in laughter. He looked over at me. I had a good buzz going on, but I wasn't passing out. He put his finger over his lips telling me not to disturb him. It had been dead quiet and when everyone laughed, my drunken friend snorted and woke up. He was looking around with this blank look on his face when the musician leaned over in his face

"Do we bore you, sir?"

How embarrassing!

Crows Nest was a fun place. It was always full of military people from all branches. Most were grouped by their branch, Navy guys in one part of the room, Air Force in another and Marines in another area. Occasionally, there would be a scuffle, but nothing too out of sorts. I met a couple of guys who were in the Navy one night, one of them from Cabot, Arkansas, just a few miles north of where I started life. He had a license to drive a submarine, and I thought that was pretty cool. We partied together often when they were in town. Their sub was actually ported out of Guam, The USS Abraham Lincoln, and during their down time they came to Pearl Harbor.

I got an apartment with them in the Keys, but that didn't take long to screw up. The first or second morning, I was late getting over to the other side of the island to the base for duty. I was called in and warned. The third or fourth time it happened, I was told that I couldn't live off base. Drinking from "beer thirty" in the afternoon till 2 a.m. sometimes made it hard to make that five-mile run three hours later. I had gotten to know many of the people in my unit by the first year and had ended up spending more time with the "Slackers" and "Shitbirds" as the year went on. I still had a couple of friends that were squared-away Marines, but the more I drank and took drugs, the less they had to do with me. Several people took me aside and warned me I should straighten up, but I didn't seem to heed their warnings.

One day a first lieutenant smarted off to me over some silly bullshit. I immediately threw it back at him and told him to kiss my ass. I'm sure I had a hangover, and I let my mouth overload my ass. Of course first lieutenants need people to push around, and it was my lucky day. I had gotten along okay with him before that, but he had to write me up. I got busted a rank, docked some pay and restricted to the barracks for a few days. Perhaps it slowed me down for a few weeks, maybe a month, but I got right back into the groove of chasing music at bars.

Some of the best weed in the world is grown and sold in Hawaii. Kona Gold and Maui Wowi were unlike anything I had smoked in Michigan. It was available in large quantities and inexpensive. Other varieties were available like Tai, which came wrapped on a stick, and several nice California varieties. In Hawaii in the mid-'70s, smoking weed, shooting heroin and dropping acid were what most of the drug crowd was into. There wasn't much cocaine around. I had tripped on acid with several people when I was at the Harbor House, mainly at my own curiosity.

I hung out with some people in Hawaii who were dropping acid every day, and I did a few weekend trips. They were at a beach one day, and were tripping, and the next thing I knew I was invited to a party and eventually many others. One particular weekend, I tripped like I had never in my life, seeing things and trails from lights. After that, I didn't do any more acid. I thought I had reached my limit, so I didn't need anymore.

Drinking booze and smoking weed seemed to be a good way to relax, and I kept the pace with them for some time. I could drink late into the night, get up the next morning without a headache, open a beer and start my day. I could hit a couple at lunch with a burger and get a six-pack in the evening and start another night. The head took it well at that age. But my actions didn't, and the many stupid things I did eventually caught up with me enough that the commanding officer pegged me for a discharge a few months before my three-year obligation was up. I was sent to Treasure Island in San Francisco Bay under the Oakland Bay Bridge and processed out of the Corps with an honorable discharge. While I was on the island going through the processing, I met another Marine who was getting out in a similar situation. With the Vietnam War ending, all military branches were downsizing. Troublemakers were the first to go. He was from North Carolina, and we both were looking at ways to get home. We both had two and a half years of gear to transport and endless days on a Greyhound bus going across country didn't seem too appealing. How I would laugh at that thought later in life.

In the San Francisco Chronicle, want ads were placed for a drive-away car service. People who wanted their car sent across country but didn't want to drive them hired this company, and they used a lot of military people getting out of the service to drive cars to various locations in the U.S. We made contact, and within a few days, they gave us a car to drive to Dallas. There, we had to wait a day for another car, but we found one going on east to D.C. I was dropped off in Arkansas and the car went on. I didn't have any idea where else to go. I may not have realized it at the time, but the walls were closing in on my desperate attempt at a normal life.

CHAPTER 46 | A MATCH MADE IN MUSIC

It's a long way from Hawaii to Little Rock. It's an even longer way from having a course set for yourself and having no idea where to go next. But that's where I was when I was 20 years old, just out of the Marine Corps and feeling stuck back in the town that I vowed to leave so many years ago.

I had technical school available to me, so I signed up for a welding school, wanting to become an underwater welder for the oil companies on offshore rigs. That lasted several months and seemed to possibly be something I could get interested in. But one stupid move nixed it altogether. I went with a childhood friend to rob a convenience store. I'm not sure now why I even thought about it, but being the getaway driver was my new job, and apparently I sucked at it. When he ran out of the store, I drove the van away, but we weren't the best of criminals. I was busted for armed robbery, caught another charge of burglary and sent by the Arkansas Department of Correction to a prison farm in south Arkansas.

Cummins Prison is a rough place, and I spent several weeks there before being transferred to the Tucker Prison Farm, the home of "Old Sparky," the electric chair and death row. Never saw it. My punishment was enough for me. The prison farm experience resembles *Cool Hand Luke*, where the inmates sleep in open barracks and spend their days laying asphalt, cutting weeds and picking vegetables under the hot sun. The difference would be a walled prison, much like *The Shawshank Redemption*, which keeps its inmates secure behind metal and concrete. In Arkansas, the first months on a prison farm are spent on hoe squads, walking the bean and rice fields, chopping weeds with hoes while guys on horseback with guns yell things like "ska-bow" and "get them weeds, Convict!" It was miserable, exhausting and a mental drain like never before.

After six months of chopping weeds in the hot summer sun, I had an offer to attend a Vo-tech school in the prison that was teaching auto mechanics. It was a chance I didn't want to pass up, especially since I had another year to serve before parole would even be considered. After six months of schooling, I was made a trustee and assigned to the tractor barn to repair field tractors.

When planting of the rice began in the spring, I was assigned to a rice field with another inmate who had worked them before. As the levies were cut, we had to shore them up in our field, maintaining them throughout the year until harvest. Throughout my 18 months in the prison, I spent six of them waiting in the Pulaski County Jail for a slot in the system. I didn't get in too much trouble, opting to avoid it as much as possible. There were a few fights and threats from the guards that I might be fucking up, so I kept to myself most of the time, daydreaming about my release date.

I went before the parole board for the first time and got a six-month deferral, commonly known as a "re-write." It was nothing new, and I had another chance to impress them in a few months. The second time up, I made parole and was given a release date. I felt much relief.

Working the rice field as a trustee, I would be dropped off at the field early in the morning and picked up before sunset. With a pickup truck, the guards would load as many convicts as possible and drop them at designated fields. We would then make the rounds to each of the fields every day. We did it six days a week and had Sundays off. One Saturday, after I had made parole and was waiting on my release date, my rice field partner got picked up early, because he had a visitor. I was left to tend to the field alone. It wasn't the first time it had happened so I took the lazy Saturday walking the field, doing a small bit of patchwork and then swimming in the retaining pond where the water is held before it flows out to the field. In the hot afternoon summer days, it was a refreshing dip in cold water pumped directly out of the ground. For a short time, it didn't feel like prison.

As the afternoon slipped away and it began to get dark, I had gone over to my pickup spot... but the guard never came to get me. I sat for several hours until it was well after dark. That felt strange. I realized I hadn't been outside in the dark for about two years. That was when I figured they forgot about me. Maybe my parole had started early. Hell, maybe it was a test. If it was, I wasn't going to fail it.

I started to make the more than two-mile walk back to the main prison compound, strolling down the main road with no one to stop me from going anywhere else. About a half-mile out, one of the captains saw me. He was one of those that released the hounds after inmates who were caught running in the opposite direction. He was leaving the dog barn as he drove past me in the dark. He stopped and backed up. I just stood there looking at him.

"What the hell are you doing out here?" he asked. He was dumbfounded.

"I guess they forgot about me," I said politely. "I'm walking back. I'm hungry."

He couldn't help but laugh. As I climbed in, he radioed back to the prison.

"Has the last count been cleared?" he barked to the prison guard over the radio.

"Yes sir."

He looked at me and smiled.

"There's going to be some trouble tonight," he said to me as we drove back.

"Hell, boy, why didn't you just run away?"

"Shit, man. I just made parole. You ain't gonna run me away from here now."

He laughed again.

"Let's get you some food."

We arrived at the gate, and he went over and talked to another guard. Within a few minutes, the alarm sounded throughout the entire prison. I guess that made me a fugitive. Whatever. I just wanted some food. Everyone was locked down, and a new count began while the captain escorted me to the kitchen. Someone gave me a plate of the evening slop, and I filled up and went back to my room. On my release date, my mother came for me. It was a strange feeling to be out and on my own time again. And with my mother. After Marines and prison, I had no fear of her. I just wanted to stay away from her.

Within a few days of being released from prison, I had visited with my parole officer and found a job at an Oldsmobile dealership as a mechanic. Now, I enjoy working on cars, but it's no fun when you're under pressure to fix things just to make a paycheck. I also realized I couldn't get that gas and oil smell off my hands no matter how much I washed. Every night I was going to bed with that smell on my hands. I realized being a full-time mechanic wasn't going to be my destiny, and I quit less than a month later.

I picked up another job running a lathe machine on the night shift for Roll-Lift Corporation. Roll-Lift makes pallet jacks for the warehouse industry. I was cutting metal parts on the late shift, cutting and measuring and running up to five machines for eight hours in the middle of the night. I started at 11 p.m. and finished the next morning. It was money in my pocket, and at the time, that was what mattered.

I started dating some girls and not long after I had collected some funds to start buying drum parts for a kit. I met some guys, and we started jamming together. This was better than the Marines and better than jail. It may not have been my destiny, but making money and making music was what mattered to me.

I moved into a house with my brother down the street from one of the high schools in Little Rock. I started living a somewhat typical young Arkansan life, again, just trying to stay out of trouble. Most of the guys who played music didn't have trouble on their minds, instead putting their energy into music. It sounded like a good plan to me. After a few of us had played together, we were having enough fun that we started calling ourselves "The Arnold Layne Band" after the first single that Pink Floyd had released in 1967. The song was about a transvestite who stole women's clothes. I don't think there was a connection to our band, but it sounded cool. We mainly played British and European band songs like Black Sabbath, Led Zeppelin and AC/DC from the Dirty Deeds album.

We played parties around town and in pavilions at the river in Murray Park, a city park where hundreds of young people would gather on hot summer nights. It was great fun while it lasted. It was also a good way to meet chicks, but we weren't making any money. Just having fun.

One Friday night, I stopped at a bar on Asher Avenue in Little Rock looking for someone who wasn't there. It was here that I discovered Lightfoot. I already had a good buzz going, so I got a drink and sat in front of two guys doing an acoustic set in the corner, singing country and folk songs. Both playing guitar and singing. No beat. No driving beat. That's what I wanted to hear but was too lazy to find it at another bar.

After awhile, I started making comments and jokes that they needed a drummer. I was soft spoken at first, but as the beers kept coming, I became a little more aggressive. Finally during a break, Mack, one of the singers, had enough of me.

"Say dude. Are you a drummer?"

"Well, sure I am."

"I'll tell you what, pal, if you can drum, why don't you bring your drums here tomorrow night, and we'll have a drummer in our show. And if you can't play, we'll ask you to sit down, and you'll have to wait until we finish to get them."

I was drunk enough to take the challenge. I didn't make any more comments the rest of the night.

The next afternoon, I arrived, set my small drum kit up and played with the guys. They didn't ask me to leave, so I figured I aced the audition. Before the evening was over, all I heard was, "Do you know this? Do you know that?" Having grown up being forced to hear country music every day, the songs just seemed to be in my brain, and I was able to play most of them pretty well. Easy beats for two-stepping, waltzing, and Do-Si-Do kind of stuff. We were playing it all: The Flying Burrito Brothers, Merle Haggard, George Jones, Waylon Jennings and Willie Nelson, Mickey Gilley and Johnnie Lee and all the outlaw country being played on the radio. And "Wipeout." Why does everyone want to see the drummer play "Wipeout?"

After a couple of lineup changes, we named ourselves Lightfoot, and we settled in with Daryl, Mack, myself, a husband and wife that played bass and piano and another guitar player who also played fiddle. He had a collection of guitars including a Flying V, which seemed funny to me since we were mainly playing country. We had some fun playing pretty much every weekend. The crowds at The Palace Saloon started to increase, so the owner expanded the stage area, and more people came. A guy everyone called Dancing Bear shuffled along the dance floor all night long holding a mug of beer. He was a hit with the increasing crowds.

Usually once every weekend there would be a fight in the bar. It's just the way it always happened. A lot of the fights would be between women, and a few times if a fight broke out between two girls, the band would play some goofy jam and Mack would start calling the fight on the microphone like a boxing announcer. He was the comedian in the band and kept people laughing between the songs and sips of beer. My first wife and I were living our volatile relationship when one night a woman sitting at one of the tables close to the stage was looking at me the wrong way. That was all it took. My wife and this girl got into a shoving match and Mack cheered them on.

"The grand prize will be our drummer!" he announced.

The girl who had been staring escaped toward the exit door and just as she made her way out, my girl threw a long neck beer bottle like a rocket that smashed on the doorframe. The whole bar, almost a hundred of people, went silent as Tammy Sue ran out the door to catch her nemesis. Everyone in the band hit the door followed by about half the bar. Shit, this was going to be a good one, and like everybody else, I didn't want to miss it. The bouncer got to them before any real damage was done, but it was really fucking exciting there for a moment. An Arkansas Saturday night.

My parole was going well, with music and work seeming to occupy my time and keeping me from getting into any trouble. I worked several different jobs trying to find one to match my passion for music and my need to fill my pockets with dollar bills. I gave a shot at everything – welder's helper, finishing sheet rock, painting, and restaurant work. I worked for almost a year reading water meters for the Little Rock Water Company, walking on every street in the city. And then

I got a job driving.

It was a delivery truck for a chicken and meat distributor. The pay was good, and when I was first hired, I drove a small pick-up style delivery truck. After a couple of months I moved into a Ford 9000 tandem-axle bob truck that had a 10-speed transmission and topped 25,000 gross weights, the maximum allowed weight that particular vehicle can weigh when fully loaded. Driving throughout the state taught me how to work a clutch in a large diesel-powered vehicle and shift a 10-speed connected to a dual axle. I shifted that truck a million times a day.

It was a lot of hard, tiring work that wore me out most days, but I was never too tired to spend the night playing music. Who knew those two things would match up so well throughout the rest of my life?

EPILOGUE | WHEELS ON THE GROUND

Life has been described as a highway. I'm not really sure what that means. I do know for me that I've discovered it takes the highway to get to where life actually is. It's been the stops along those roads that added up to a life for me.

I've learned firsthand what great countries America and Canada are. My chosen career path has put me on the many roads that connect the towns and cities in North America. I've traveled all types of terrain, and I've met thousands of people along the way. I've discovered the common threads of human behavior and figured out many of the reasons for my own. What may be a small or momentary interaction to some have significant meaning to me and have contributed to who I am.

Life on the road, hopping from one place to another in short amounts of time, suits someone like me well. I'm a bit of a loner who doesn't like being that alone. I'm a bit of an individual who really enjoys working on a team.

At a young age, I ran from the many meanings of life, searching for a life only to realize that life IS about being a searcher.

After becoming an adult, I tried to avoid my parents. I spent a lot of effort shutting them out of my life. I didn't feel like either one of them had offered me much or that either of them had put me on a path of success. I went in search of it on my own. As a youngster and an adult, I didn't want their influences in my life.

My dad was a good man. Not being that close to him throughout my life and only seeing him occasionally, I saw how the world beat on him over the years. He never seemed to fight back. Many years passed between the few times I saw him. He kept trudging along. No matter the events surrounding him, he just went on. He didn't complain much when I saw him. He lived from paycheck to paycheck his entire life and never seemed to care much if he had financial security.

One day before he died, we talked about how much time we had actually spent together over the years. We narrowed it down to less than seven years. He was then in his 70s. Fifty years of my life and only seven years in my father's actual presence. What a loss I felt and still feel for that matter. He retired from the military after 25 years of dedicated service to our country. He then worked in the civilian world before retiring again. Four months after retiring from civilian work, he found out he had cancer. A year later, he died.

As I got older and my own family began to develop, the memories of my abusive upbringing began to subside, and I made efforts to communicate more with my mother. Michelle played an important part in that reconnection. Mom would come to family dinners, and she started participating in the love that our family shared. I believe she saw that it was possible to have disciplined and respectful children without forcing it upon them with abuse.

She never understood what I did in my profession or why I did it until she came to a concert while I was on a tour in the summer of 2003. When the tour came through my hometown, she was able to experience what I had escaped to. In a wheelchair, suffering from breast cancer and leukemia, she was able to see the respect by my co-workers and success I had found in my life. Sitting front row at that show, I think she felt the power of the love the entertainer I was traveling with at the time was putting out to the masses.

I saw her experience the love of the crowd that the entertainer was soaking up. I know she took in a little of it just as I do each time. Surrounded by people who were cheering and happy, I think she realized the positive, love-filled power that music, crowds and the touring industry had had on me.

Several months later she died. I was at home and able to say my goodbyes to her in the hospital before she passed. I learned an important lesson about forgiveness that day. While she didn't provide the most loving atmosphere in my life, in a twisted way, she showed me the important challenge of offering and encouraging a loving, nurturing and upbeat home for my own family, and by doing so, perhaps future generations have been changed.

I have made many good and bad choices in my life. Choosing to work on the road turned out to be one of the best decisions I've ever made. It lifted me out of the downward spiral I was headed toward had I never left Little Rock. Getting behind the wheel and learning how people live and interact from all walks of life and places saved me from a life of despair and destruction.

It affects me greatly when I think about the distance and separation that my job brings my children and me. But it also inspires me to make the time we spend together filled with quality. I try to make that time as special and meaningful as possible.

I enjoy home life, but I'm an adventurous soul who can't seem to sit still for any length of time. The constant drive behind the wheel is the only chance to be still for a moment and think. These days, I enjoy the simple pleasures of home while making a living on the road and enriching my life at the same time. I look forward to where the road takes me next.

One of my best friends and mentors said it best, "No one ever said the life of a rock and roll bus driver was going to be easy." It can, however, be very satisfying.

THE END

CONTRIBUTING WRITERS

Jillian McGehee of Little Rock, Arkansas, is a professional writer and editor with a Masters of Arts Degree in journalism. She has earned awards from the Associated Press and Arkansas Press Association.

Richard Duke is a writer and journalist who lives in Little Rock, Arkansas. He has been honored by the Associated Press and the Arkansas Press Association.

EDITOR

For 30 years a freelance writer, **Marcia Camp**'s stories, essays, and features have appeared in books, magazines, and literary journals. She is the author of *You Can't Leave Till you Do the Paperwork: Matters of Life and Death*, and *The Charity Letters of JoAnn Cayce.*

Lightning Source UK Ltd.
Milton Keynes UK
UKOW02f1343171015

260793UK00001B/17/P